Mabel Normand

Mabel Normand

The Life and Career of a Hollywood Madcap

TIMOTHY DEAN LEFLER

McFarland & Company, Inc., Publishers
Jefferson, North Carolina

Library of Congress Cataloguing-in-Publication Data

Names: Lefler, Timothy Dean, 1959– author.
Title: Mabel Normand : the life and career of a Hollywood madcap / Timothy Dean Lefler.
Description: Jefferson, North Carolina : McFarland & Company, Inc., Publishers, 2016 | Includes bibliographical references and index.
Identifiers: LCCN 2016006606| ISBN 9780786478675 (softcover : acid free paper) | ISBN 9781476623078 (ebook) ∞
Subjects: LCSH: Normand, Mabel, 1894–1930. | Motion picture actors and actresses—United States—Biography.
Classification: LCC PN2287.N57 L44 2016 | DDC 791.4302/8092—dc23
LC record available at http://lccn.loc.gov/2016006606

British Library cataloguing data are available

ISBN (print) 978-0-7864-7867-5
ISBN (ebook) 978-1-4766-2307-8

© 2016 Timothy Dean Lefler. All rights reserved

No part of this book may be reproduced or transmitted in any form or by any means, electronic or mechanical, including photocopying or recording, or by any information storage and retrieval system, without permission in writing from the publisher.

Front cover image: Mabel Normand, 1910s © Photofest

Printed in the United States of America

McFarland & Company, Inc., Publishers
 Box 611, Jefferson, North Carolina 28640
 www.mcfarlandpub.com

For Melissa and Brad
with all my love

Acknowledgments

I would like to thank the following individuals, institutions and sources for their invaluable assistance:

Thomas Lefler
Melissa Sossamon
Marilyn Slater
Marc Wanamaker
William Thomas Sherman
Tiffany Harris
Diana Molander
Rudy Cecera
David Pearson
Alanna Potter
Malnor Films
The Museum of Modern Art
PBS
Bison Archives
The Margaret Herrick Library
Special Collections staff, The Margaret Herrick Library

The Academy of Motion Picture Arts and Sciences
The Venice Historical Society
Picture Post
Getty Images
Hollywood Heritage Museum
Calvary Cemetery, Los Angeles
TheMabelNormand.com
Taylorology.com: A Continuing Exploration of the Life and Death of William Desmond Taylor
The Mabel Normand Home Page
Riddle Me This Productions
Cinecon

Table of Contents

Preface 1

Introduction 5

1 •	Hello Mabel	9
2 •	Over the Garden Wall	11
3 •	Staten Island Girl	14
4 •	Venus Model	17
5 •	The Griffith Touch	21
6 •	Hide and Seek	31
7 •	Keystone Mabel	36
8 •	The Fun Factory	42
9 •	Mabel at the Wheel	53
10 •	Tillie	58
11 •	Ice Cream for Breakfast	62
12 •	The Clock Strikes 12	69
13 •	New Woman	73
14 •	Mabel Inc.	79
15 •	Goldwyn Girl	89
16 •	*Mickey*	98
17 •	Mabelescent	103
18 •	Back to Mack	114
19 •	Gates of Babylon	120

20 • Different Names		126
21 • Her Story		131
22 • The Edge of Murder		135
23 • Fatal Tales		142
24 • Sail Away		150
25 • To Live Through Pain		155
26 • Final Frames		164
27 • A Tender Goodbye		173

Epilogue   178

Appendix A: Filmography   179

Appendix B: Last Will and Testament
of Mabel Normand-Cody   205

Appendix C: Transcript of Coroner's Inquest William Desmond
Taylor Murder Case, February 4, 1922   206

Appendix D: Transcript of Mabel Normand's Testimony
at Arraignment of Horace Greer, aka Joseph Kelly,
January 22, 1924, Los Angeles Courthouse   212

Chapter Notes   227

Bibliography   238

Index   241

As long as a girl goes up against the world and challenges its high places, there will always be Mabel Normand.
—T. Howard Kelly

Preface

  I decided to go see Mabel. After seven years of researching and writing about silent screen star Mabel Normand, I thought it only right that I pay my respects at her final resting place. It was a dark and cloudy afternoon and a light rain was just beginning as I got in my car. After about an hour's drive from my home, I turned my car through the main gate of Calvary Cemetery in Los Angeles. I rolled through the silent grounds, surrounded by green lawns and granite monuments to those who passed away long ago. The acreage was shrouded in a rainy mist that was both beautiful and eerie. I finally found the main mausoleum, a mammoth neo-classical structure. The main, square building sat atop two tiers of wide cement stairs. I parked my car at the curb and climbed the mausoleum stairs that were flanked on both sides by gigantic stone pillars. A carved angel sat on top of each pillar as silent sentinels to those who passed by. Above the imposing iron doors was a carved quotation from the Bible: "I am the resurrection and the life. He that believeth in me, though he be dead, shall live."

  I walked through the one open side of the double doors and was met by a flight of shiny beige marble stairs. The cavernous edifice was cold and dark. At the top of the stairs I arrived at the back of an immense Catholic church complete with pews, a long center aisle, a high ceiling and an ornate altar. This was my starting point. I unfolded the directions that I had printed from the Internet and held them in my left hand as I walked: "Stand at the back pew and turn left, make another quick left into a corridor, when you get to a flight of stairs turn right, go to the second row of tombs, look down, and count up two." And there she was:

Mabel Normand-Cody
1895–1930
"Rest in Peace."

As I contemplated the inscription I couldn't help wondering if Mabel was truly at rest. Five years ago I met a wonderful person named Marilyn Slater. Marilyn operates the largest website honoring the silent film star, and hosts the largest online club. She is truly the godmother of all things Mabel. We met at a beachside café in Venice, California, the location of many of Mabel's early comedies. Marilyn related her fascinating tales and I began scribbling on napkins and menus trying to keep up with her. And this book project had its beginning.

Marilyn's deep ties to the silent star began early. When she was a girl, her legal guardian was Mabel's nurse Julia Benson. After Mabel passed away, some of her belongings found their way into Julia's closet. Marilyn never forgot the time that she tried on Mabel's riding boots, only to have the boots start running on their own. Mabel's mischievous spirit was active from then on. She tripped Marilyn repeatedly during dance lessons and occasionally gave her playful pushes from behind. I wondered if Mabel had anything in mind for me.

I stood at Mabel's tomb and said a few quiet words to her. I was so focused on my thoughts that I didn't notice the hour or the departing light. Suddenly, I heard a booming KA-THUMP! echoing deeply all around me. I was puzzled for a moment. Then came the sickening realization that I was locked in. By now the mausoleum was dark and I found myself feeling my way along in the blackness of the tombs. Unable to read my directions I tried to retrace my steps backwards and remember the reverse sequence of turns. There were no sounds other than the clack of my shoes on the marble floors. The air was still and foreboding and I was getting more than a little nervous. Finally, with a couple of fortunate turns I found my way back to the Catholic church and gratefully headed down the stairs that would take me out. Just as I thought, the heavy main doors were barred tightly shut. After several more tries I knew it was hopeless. I sat down in the darkness on the bottom marble step and wondered what to do next. I wasn't worried about ghosts, but the lack of a rest room did concern me.

I remembered my cell phone and quickly dialed information to get the main number for the cemetery.

"Hi, this is Tim Lefler. I'm here at the main mausoleum and I guess someone locked the doors without checking. Can you send someone over here to unlock them?"

I was met with an unfriendly reply: "No. We are very specific. Our hours are posted at the gates. We don't unlock doors after hours."

"You mean I have to stay in here all night?" I asked.

There was a long, confused silence followed by a sputtering noise. "You mean you're *inside* trying to get *out?!*"

A few minutes later I heard the screech of brakes at the curb and someone hurrying up the stairs rattling a heavy ring of keys. I was released from my prison and headed for my car.

I was soon back on the freeway. After about 20 minutes I started to smile and then laughed out loud. I looked up at the stars through the moon roof of my car.

"Okay. Mabel, you got me."

Introduction

*She was vivid as summer lightning, beautiful as
dawn, and as natural as both.*—Jim Tully[1]

On the morning of August 29, 1911, a Staten Island teenager strode out to the edge of a diving board over a watery expanse. She flung herself into the air and into the sea of a thousand men's dreams. The film industry of the twentieth century had arrived. So had the black tights that clung to her voluptuous body. She exuded all that was scandalous, mischievous and free. The new industry was in search of itself. Now it had found its first metaphor.

Yet no one really understood why. It was 502 feet of film. The small movie crew that gathered that summer day in Huntington, Long Island, New York, hardly gave it a thought.[2] They were just filming an exuberant little girl at the beach doing what came naturally. And then the world took notice. With no language barriers to contain this brazen new art form, it unaccountably swept the globe. Curiosity grew up around her, but her employer, Biograph Studio, didn't identify its actors by name. This only fueled the world's fascination. The public demanded to know the name of "The Diving Girl." Her name was Mabel Normand.

She stood only five feet tall, with thick chestnut hair and large brown eyes. Despite her comic surroundings, her portrayals on screen were unique in their humanity, and could move from the manic to the wistful in a heartbeat. Like most successful clowns there was an undercurrent of sadness in her best work. She pretended to be what she wasn't, yet she couldn't hide who she was. The people of the world loved her. For a brief space of time, everything was hers.

Mabel Normand was an important movie star. Her endearing character "The Little Tomboy" took hold in the hearts of moviegoers years before

"The Little Tramp" found his focus. While other stars had their names above the title, Mabel's name was often *in* the title: *Mabel's Lovers, For the Love of Mabel, Mabel's Blunder, Hello Mabel* and many more.

Her brief lifetime was filled with innovation and achievement. She was among the very first women to write, direct and star in her own films. She was a producer and a studio head. She was the first comedienne to star in a feature film. She was the first sex symbol "bathing beauty." She blazed a trail across Hollywood that many would follow.

While the bouncing frivolity of her screen persona would captivate millions, few knew that the private Mabel had an introspective and serious nature. She was a student of the great thinkers of her own age and many others. She was a spiritual seeker. She celebrated her life and shared her love of books, art and music with all those around her. She showed amazing generosity to family and friends and, just as often, helped those she had only heard about. Affection for her overflowed into countless periodicals that referred to her as "Our Mabel."

"Our Mabel" was no saint. She was notorious for her temperamental antics and her rowdy excesses. Her personal life and her career were overwhelmed by tawdry rumors and sensational scandals. Not surprisingly, the yellow journalists of her age seized upon and embellished these tales, regardless of their truth. When Mabel is mentioned today, it is most often in connection with this maze of sordid stories. The scandals were very real. Mabel was associated with an infamous Hollywood murder. She was caught up in a shooting. She was blacklisted, extorted, called to testify, and legally and politically harassed for reasons that she could not control. Some falsely assumed that she was a murderess, a drug addict, a drunk, a philanderer and a major exponent of Jazz Age glitter and dirt. And, after her death, lazy journalists propelled the shadows of Mabel's legend, while ignoring the lights of Mabel's life.

Adding to the problem was Mabel's family and her closest friends. Long sickened by the pounding slander she had endured in the press, they were not eager to share their memories with reporters after she died. Ironically, the loyalty displayed by those who loved her left a void of information that the scandalmongers were only too eager to fill.

Further confounding the public's memory was the inaccessibility of her best work. With the arrival of sound, silent movies were relegated to another time and resigned to a season of neglect. All of Mabel's work was done for the silent screen, and in the decades that followed the silent era, few people were interested in viewing or preserving the antiquated art form that silent movies had become.

I believe that the time for a reassessment of her life and art is long overdue. I give you Mabel Normand, a star just out of reach. This is the story of the girl from Staten Island who ate ice cream for breakfast. Though never recorded, it's time for her voice to be heard.

1
Hello Mabel

Every man loved Mabel, given the opportunity.
—Adela Rogers St. Johns[1]

Mabel Normand was on a mission. German U-boats were openly engaged in unrestricted submarine warfare, and Kaiser Wilhelm II was making startling overtures to Mexico (even threatening to push America back to its pre–Mexican-American War borders). The United States had little choice. So on April 6, 1917, America declared war against the Central Powers. To help finance the war effort, Treasury Secretary William Gibbs McAdoo released the first run of war bonds since the Spanish American War. Issued in denominations of every amount, Liberty Bonds allowed citizens a tangible participation in the national conflict.

Almost overnight, a flurry of rallies, drives, parades, posters, slogans, songs and celebrity appeals to buy Liberty Bonds became conspicuous features of popular American culture.[2] Mabel was right in the thick of it. While she clearly loved her country, to her, the war was personal. Her brother Claude was in the 106th Machine Gun Battalion in France.[3] The preeminent celebrities of the moment, Charlie Chaplin and Mabel made short films supporting the Liberty Loan Drive. Charlie appeared in his self-financed *The Bond* and Mabel in the all-star vehicle *Stake Uncle Sam to Play Your Hand* (now presumed lost). Both films made use of Uncle Sam and the equally emblematic, though less remembered, Lady Liberty, as symbols of a patriotic America. Charlie's Tramp buys Liberty Bonds to provide rifles for the military, while Mabel's Tomboy buys Liberty Bonds to stake Uncle Sam in the biggest poker game ever played.[4] Mabel did all she could to help the war effort. Crazy things, too. Things that only Mabel Normand would do.

The Harlem Grand Theatre was filled to capacity. This was more than a bond rally, this was a homecoming. Mabel was the Staten Island girl who made good in the movies, and 20,000 New Yorkers were there to welcome her back. But where was she?

After sitting through the customary speeches and patriotic sing-alongs, the crowd was getting more than a little agitated. As committee chairman John Case again looked at his pocket watch, it became obvious that he needed to stall for time. From the wings, he sent out eight-year-old Clarice Boehm to sing a song. The crowd was polite, but this was not what they had come for. Suddenly a voice was heard backstage, "She's here!" As Clarice stepped off to perfunctory applause, Case strode triumphantly to center stage, and made the introduction: "Ladies and gentlemen, Miss Mabel Normand!" Wildly applauding, the crowd stood as one as Mabel, somewhat tentatively, appeared from the wings, waving to the crowd. Wolf whistles and all manner of whoops and shouting continued for well over a minute. The entrance was pure Mabel. She was beautifully dressed and terribly late.

She greeted Case with a hug. Mabel was secretly afraid of large crowds and would often embrace her host just to steady her nerves.[5] After some minutes of tumult, the audience was seated. Mabel held up a gloved hand to quiet them. Turning to the committee chairman, she announced, "Mr. Case, I pledge to buy a bond for $5000!" Thundering applause greeted her announcement. "And," she continued, "if it means anything at all, I will give a kiss to anyone who buys a bond of any amount."

A gasp hushed the crowd, as audience members exchanged wild-eyed looks of sheer astonishment, "Did she just say…?" One man immediately stood up. And then another. A few men began quick-stepping toward the stage, while others gave chase. Then the dam burst. Pandemonium erupted; elbows were thrown, money was dropped. Theater manager Arthur Hirsch and his assistants tried to restore order, but no one was listening. All over the theater, wives and girlfriends were deserted as their companions bolted toward Mabel Normand. Some women were amused, most were annoyed, all were alone.

Mabel kept her bargain. She was escorted down the steps of the stage and stood next to the donation table wearing a not-so-innocent smile. Predictably, most men arrived with big grins and wildly beating hearts, ready to give Mabel some extra appreciation. But Mabel could handle it. After each man bought a bond, she gently touched his chin with her thumb and forefinger, turned his face to one side and gave him a peck on the cheek.[6] She did it again, and again, for two hours. The event raised over $12,500 ($210,000 in today's money) for the Liberty Loan Campaign.[7] The number of marital squabbles she created was never counted. But the evening was an amazing success fueled by equal parts patriotism and testosterone.

2
Over the Garden Wall

As for poor Mabel Normand, she has made her peace with God.—Los Angeles Times[1]

On the cool evening of February 22, 1930, Father John Maron was summoned to the Pottenger Sanatorium in Monrovia, California. He came to administer the last rites of the Catholic Church to movie star Mabel Normand. Founded in 1903 by Dr. Francis M. Pottenger, Jr., the Pottenger Sanatorium was the product of his personal mission to find a cure for tuberculosis, the disease that had claimed his beloved wife in 1898.[2] Established at the foot of the Sierra Madre Mountains, the groundbreaking facility was justly famous for its studies and advancements in the treatment of tuberculosis and other respiratory diseases. With a focus on nutrition that was ahead of its time, Pottenger prescribed copious amounts of the high fat and easily digestible butter, cream and eggs to combat the wasting effects of tuberculosis. Supplements of adrenal cortex were added to the patients' meals to combat exhaustion; and—most surprisingly—blood transfusions were administered, long before either their safety or their efficacy had been firmly established.[3]

Father Maron was led through the lobby to a hallway that had been adorned, and then stacked, with floral arrangements from around the world. Most had cards still attached and unopened. More arrived every hour, and would soon fill the ward, and then the lobby. Father Maron gently crunched his way through the flowers to Mabel's hospital room. He found her door blocked by a Chinese changing screen. Mabel's friends, hoping to give her a feeling of home, had brought it from her Beverly Hills mansion. Father Maron stepped around the screen and tried not to gasp at the sight before him. Sunken into the billowed, white bedding was the sleeping, dark-haired beauty that had captivated the world for most of her life.

As Mabel opened her eyes, her chest heaving with each breath, Father Maron anointed her forehead with olive oil in the form of a cross. "Through this holy anointing, may the Lord, in his love and mercy, help you with the grace of the Holy Spirit." He then gently took Mabel's hands in his own and anointed them. "May the Lord who frees you from sin, save you and raise you up." Mabel looked at him with grateful eyes. Taking a gulp of breath, she silently mouthed, "Amen."[4]

The Pottenger Sanatorium had been Mabel's *de facto* home for months. She'd been in and out of hospitals for years, but nothing seemed to slow her steady decline. By September 1929, she finally consented to full-time care at Pottenger's. Still, Mabel pleaded to be sent home. But she was too sick to be moved. Friends were desperate to help.

Mabel was not without comfort. Her private nurse and devoted friend Julia Brew Benson became an effective resident at Pottenger's, staying in a room adjoining Mabel's. After emerging from a cloistered order of Franciscan Poor Clare Nuns, an order dedicated to contemplation and intercessory prayer, she became a registered nurse at St. Vincent's Hospital in Los Angeles. Having lost her husband John Benson to tuberculosis less than a year after their marriage, she knew the grinding demands of nursing those afflicted with TB. And she was determined not to lose Mabel.[5]

Fighting to remain conscious, Mabel clung to her lifelong habit of incessant reading. Included in her vast library were Freud's *Interpretation of Dreams*, Nietzsche's *Thus Spake Zarathustra*, Knut Hamsun's *The Growth of the Soil* and countless others.[6] Mabel's friends would remain equal parts impressed and puzzled by her endless search for knowledge. At her Beverly Hills home on Camden Avenue, she frequently took a book to the bathtub, read until the water got cold and then filled it up again.[7]

At her hospital bedside was a book entitled *The Answering Voice: One Hundred Love Lyrics by Women*. Some folded papers within the book were later found to contain Mabel's final written thoughts. She wrote of reading Nietzsche, and how it had depressed her. She wondered how long her "friends and flowers" would last. She noted that she disliked people who sent flowers and then considered their duty done. She wrote that she missed her dog and hoped that her dog missed her. Finally, "This thing is appalling!" And then, "Who cares?"[8]

Flowers from Mack Sennett arrived, and Julia debated over what to do with them. More than a decade before, Mack and Mabel had nearly destroyed each other in a heart-wrenching tug of war over position, possession and betrayal. Neither would have become stars without the other. And after their split, neither one would ever be the same. After some thought, Julia placed Mack's flowers on a shelf where Mabel could see them and guardedly told her about it. Mabel's face brightened. "He never forgot me," she said. Nor would he ever.

In early February 1930, Mabel's much-loved father unexpectedly died of pneumonia at the age of 59. Sensibly, Julia agreed with Mabel's sister Gladys that she need not be told. A black-rimmed card announcing the death arrived with a note for Julia. "Whatever happens, please don't allow Baby to see this—at least we can spare her this."[9] Mabel asked to see her Chow puppy that she had named "It Girl" after the actress Clara Bow. But doctors believed that the dog's fur would aggravate Mabel's breathing.[10]

After midnight, on February 23, 1930, Mabel was sinking rapidly. She was given some light nourishment by a nurse. The doctors knew that she didn't want to eat, but Mabel was always "a good soldier."[11] Several times she attempted to speak, but could not gather the breath. Her small chest heaved at irregular intervals. Julia stroked Mabel's brow and spoke to her reassuringly in hushed tones. Mabel asked Julia not to leave her alone, and Julia assured her that she would stay. At two o'clock in the morning, Julia lit a small candle by Mabel's bed. A few minutes before the end came, Mabel reached out, took Julia by the hand and asked her to pray. Leaning over, Julia whispered a prayer in her ear. Mabel smiled, closed her eyes as if she was going to sleep, and was gone. It was 2:35 a.m.[12] She was 37 years old. That night, Southern California radio stations ended their nightly programs by sending out a wish for Mabel's recovery. "And to you, Mabel Normand, out there in the hospital: Get well soon Mabel, and good night." It was one more expression of love that came far too late.[13]

3
Staten Island Girl

*Mabel was as skittery as a waterbug. And oh
my Lord, how pretty!*—Mack Sennett[1]

Through seven generations, with nominal variation, the Normand men plied the trade of carpentry as an almost obligatory part of the family lineage. But Claude Normand was a man of different dreams. He was a carpenter by trade but a musician at heart. Claude grew into a slim, darkly handsome, talented young man. He happily played piano in the orchestra pits of local vaudeville theaters. But the hard reality was that he was more likely to be building a stage than standing on one. His steady job was at the Sailors' Snug Harbor, a home established for retired seamen.[2] His inability to support his family by playing music caused him an inner unhappiness that seemed to weigh him down.

In 1885, Claude met and eloped with Mary J. Drury. Mary, a proper Irish-Catholic girl, had dark curls and remarkably long lashes that, in later years, made it hard for her to wear glasses.[3] Mary was a student of voice, and the couple's love of music gave them an immediate connection. Throughout their long lives together, music would never be absent from the Normand home. Together, Claude and "Minnie" (as she was known) would have four surviving children: Ralph (who died from tuberculosis at the age of 12), Claude Jr., Mabel and Gladys. Mabel Ethelreid Normand was born on November 9, 1892[4]; within the Normand family, she would always be known as "Baby."[5]

Mabel arrived in an upstairs bedroom of the home that her father had built at 91 Tysen Street in the New Brighton section of Staten Island. Born prematurely, she weighed only five pounds. Interestingly, she was born with a caul (a thin membrane) veiling her head, a phenomenon that occurs approximately once in every 80,000 births.[6] In Mabel's time, cauls or "veils," were seen as an omen that the baby was set apart for greatness. They were also believed to bring good luck. Claude and Minnie were able to sell the caul for a sizable sum, to augment with the family's limited income.[7]

Before the dawn of the twentieth century, transportation and factories changed America from a rural to an urban economy. In New York City, trolleys clanged on uncertain tracks. These soon gave way to elevated trains. Huge and sometimes luxurious train depots brought in large crowds. Ever newer and larger department stores were opened. By the 1890s, the new crowds created a need for police, water and sanitation services. Sprinkled upon this busy anthill was a desire for entertainment. The usual Vaudeville theaters sprang up. But this time there was something more. New York saw the arrival of the kinetoscope and then the nickelodeon. They gave a little girl with big brown eyes her first look at something called "the flickers." In 1894 a tiny movie house opened in Staten Island. Perhaps they exhibited Edison's *Record of a Sneeze*. More likely, it was *Carmencita*, a 39-second film of a young woman dancing and twirling in an ornate skirt.[8] In 1902, the first true movie theater, Tally's Electric Theatre in Los Angeles, opened. It was only a storefront but it did immediate and heavy business. Other movie theaters opened in Montreal and Pittsburgh. The luxurious Regent Theatre in New York City ushered in the era of the movie palaces. It was soon followed by the Mark Strand Theatre and the Al Ringling Theatre. Owners increased the ticket price to ten cents and the day of the tiny theater was over.

As an adult, when asked about her childhood, Mabel was often a cheerful and dedicated liar. Even among close friends, the first chapter of her life's story was noticeably vague. A deflective joke. A flippant reply. Endearing, but not revealing. Those who loved her came to expect and respect the limits of her creatively edited tales. Some saw a pain within her that was too raw to touch. Others saw a shame that often attends the very poor. A 1900 Census reported that Mabel at six years of age had not yet started school.[9]

What is unmistakable is that the wide beaches of Staten Island provided the young Mabel with a perfect playground and a perfect stage. She took to both immediately. She was described by childhood friends as "lovely" and "happy go lucky,"[10] her joyful personality masking a sensitivity that few could have imagined. Mabel would grow into a girl of many sides and abilities, her primary talent being an inner need to excel.

Always a good student, she attended Public School No. 17 in New Brighton; a large red-brick school building with its own clock tower. She finished her education by boarding at St. Mary's Convent School in North Westport, Massachusetts.[11] It is a measure of her parents' devotion that, at least once a month, they would find a way to buy her a ticket home on the

Fall River Line (a combination steamboat and railroad connection between Massachusetts and New York).[12] But at Mabel's own request she stayed in school during the summer months, so she could finish her schooling early.

Mabel was also a natural and accomplished athlete. Excelling as both a swimmer and a diver, she amassed a large collection of cups and medals, and mastered a repertoire of trick high dives that few could match. Never mindful of Victorian etiquette for girls, she routinely defeated boys and girls alike.[13]

Like her father, Mabel was an avid pianist, becoming an immediate and lifelong musician. While she would sometimes practice for six to seven hours at a time, she would come to feel that her family's poverty had prevented her from getting proper instruction. Her dream of becoming a musician was matched by a dream of becoming an artist. And, once her schooling was completed, she joined the Art Students League of New York as an economical way to get art instruction at night.[14]

From childhood on, she embraced a bequest from both of her parents, a deep-seated devotion to the Catholic Church. Throughout her life, in times of sorrow and need, she returned to the comfort of its teachings. As an adult, Mabel would laughingly recall a childhood blunder of dropping a quarter into the contribution box, rather than the nickel that she had intended. By her own account, while the man who held the box impatiently stood in place, she began digging through it "like a dog looking for the bone." In church or out, Mabel was still Mabel.[15]

4

Venus Model

I used to touch the paintings with my fingertips when they weren't looking.—Mabel[1]

Mabel hated standing still. Wearing an elegant evening gown embroidered with small pink rosebuds, she fixed a smile on her face and stared out the window at the passing clouds. Periodically she shifted her weight from one foot to the other. She allowed her mind to drift.[2] Without thinking, she anxiously began twisting the rosebuds off her gown, and dropping them to the floor. She was only 14 years old, but she knew enough to feel trapped.

Mabel's career as a fashion model began suddenly and without warning. In 1906, Mary Normand heard that the Butterick Company (the sewing pattern giant, still in business today) was hiring girls to work in the mailroom. Early one morning Mabel set out on the Staten Island Ferry with a few nickels in her pocket. Finding her way to their 16-story building on the corner of Spring and MacDougal Streets in downtown Manhattan, Mabel was hired on the spot. It was little more than child labor, and not what Mabel hoped for herself. But it was a chance for Mabel to help her parents, and she couldn't help but see it as an adventure.[3]

Soon her supervisor told her that she was too pretty to work in the mailroom and sent her to Carl Kleinschmidt in the art department. Kleinschmidt was responsible for the designs and illustrations in the Butterick-published *Delineator*, the leading women's fashion magazine at the time. He immediately put Mabel to work modeling the latest fashions for graphic artist and illustrator Hamilton King.[4] As Mabel remembered it, her first assignment was to model for an illustration advertising a new "soap shampoo." Mabel always cherished the excitement and gratification that she felt at bringing home the money to her mother after her first day of "posing."[5] At least for the present, Mabel abandoned her own dreams of music and art with disappointment, but without hesitation. If modeling would pay the bills, she would model. And, at 14 years of age, she became the main breadwinner for her family.

Working in the big city, Mabel's natural beauty drew attention. But she had no time for diversions. Young men were nothing more than opponents, and she genuinely felt sorry for the many who were so ardently trying to win her attention.[6]

As a type that lent itself to diversified costuming and advertising, she was soon en vogue with local artists. After she was hired by eccentric artist Penrhyn Stanslaw, he flew into a rage when she showed up wearing a rose-colored dress, pontificating at length about his hatred of that "atrocious hue." She never wore rose again.[7] With the tireless Henry Hutt, Mabel would finish the day by massaging his cramped legs until he could move them enough to walk away from his easel.[8]

Though she didn't realize it at the time, her professional ascent was swift and only gaining momentum. Mabel was soon engaged as a regular model by New York City's most prominent artists, Charles Dana Gibson and James Montgomery Flagg. Gibson produced sketches that commanded $1000 apiece and more. The Gibson Girls, his stylized pen-and-ink drawings of fashionable women, became iconic depictions of female beauty in the decades both immediately before and after the turn of the twentieth century. Typically appearing in a white cotton shirtwaist and a long flowing skirt, with thick wavy hair piled into a chignon on top of her head, the quintessential Gibson Girl seemed poised and self-assured, with a hint of mischief behind her studied reserve.[9]

Mabel, as portrayed by James Montgomery Flagg (Marilyn Slater/"Looking for Mabel").

Flagg, noted for his iconic "I Want You!" Uncle Sam recruiting poster, always identified Mabel as his favorite model of the era. Chuckling, he would describe her as being a delightful chatterbox and a superb mimic, and "darn cute" besides. He once told an (apocryphal?) story of her swimming across New York Harbor just to keep a posing date with him. It was difficult for the artists to talk about Mabel without some degree of hyperbole.[10]

Before she knew what was happening, Mabel was posing for Gibson in the morning and Flagg in the afternoon. As she remembered it, she received $3 a day—$1.50 in the morning and the same amount in the afternoon. The money (approximately $80 a day in today's money) was a Godsend for the Normand family.[11]

Occasionally she would skip her lunch break to pose for local commercial photographers who would sell their photographs to trade journals in New York City. Years later, she recited a list of the products that her image had helped advertise. It included cold cream, hairbrushes, shoes, stockings, combs, hair tonics, hair nets, veils, gloves, satchels, lingerie, umbrellas, necklaces, frocks, evening wraps, furs and bracelets.[12]

While being a model may have been many a girl's dream, it wasn't Mabel's. Being a good Roman Catholic girl, she knew what others thought of her profession. At the same time, being an object within someone else's vision made her feel strangely diminished. Her dream was to be on the other side of the easel—like the men she was posing for.

While Gibson had

Mabel endorsing "Ingram's Milkweed Cream" in *Photoplay* (Marc Wanamaker/Bison Archives).

always made it a policy not to use the same model more than twice, Mabel had something special, and he used her again and again. Over time, they developed a father-daughter relationship that both of them grew to cherish.[13] Perhaps sensing Mabel's inner conflict, Gibson allowed Mabel to view their work as collaborations. Between poses she would watch with true admiration as Gibson filled in the outlines of her face and body with soft crayons. And when the editor's messenger would come to pick up the completed illustrations, she felt like she wanted to cry.[14]

A true workaholic, Gibson would unlock his studio door each morning and walk directly to his easel to resume yesterday's work. Stopping to put on an artist's smock or even to remove his derby was a waste of valuable time. Gibson's studio was—to Mabel's ultimate frustration—positioned directly over Carnegie Hall. After fixing a pose, Mabel would listen for hours as the students on the floors below practiced their pianos, harps and violins and ran their vocal scales.[15] She longed to be among them.

Still, as the favorite model of New York's favorite artists, Mabel became the golden child of the New York fashion world, and her income increased proportionately. She was hardly more than an adolescent, with all the fears and uncertainties endemic to the age, and the pressure fell heavily upon her. For the next few years, Mabel spent her time modeling clothes that she couldn't afford and displaying products that she didn't use. She started to be recognized on the street. She made increasing amounts of money. She grew anxious, conflicted and unhappy. And, when she modeled, she couldn't stand still.

Of course, Gibson knew that she was pulling the rosebuds off her gown. She looked up to him as a great artist and a great man. And he provided her with the encouragement and the sympathy that she truly needed. She didn't want to disappoint him with emotions that she was only beginning to understand. With her gaze locked out the window, she didn't notice the artist walking toward her. Touching her on the arm, he startled her back to the moment. When their eyes met, Gibson smiled. He told her it was fine to tear off the rosebuds; he wasn't going to use that gown any more anyway. Struck by his kindness, young Mabel began to weep.[16]

5
The Griffith Touch

She was a frisky colt that knew no bridle.
—Linda Arvidson[1]

Thomas Edison established America's first movie studio in 1892. He produced America's first exhibited movie, a short film of Edison assistant Fred Ott sneezing with comical excess, and he owned most of the patents essential to motion picture production. By 1903, Edwin S. Porter, of Thomas Edison's motion picture company, produced *The Great Train Robbery*, the first movie to tell a story.[2] It was a fictional account of western outlaws stealing money from a passenger train, being pursued by a posse of lawmen, and ultimately getting killed, it was enormously popular. Not surprisingly, Edison's motion picture company soon found itself surrounded by a burgeoning community of imitators centered in Fort Lee, New Jersey.

Under threat of Edison's legal department, competing studios had to license their usage of Edison innovations under the Motion Picture Patents Company (also known as the Edison Trust) formed in 1908. Members of the Trust (American Pathe, American Star, Edison, Essanay, Kalem, Lubin, Selig and Vitagraph) functioned as a *de facto* monopoly within the film industry.[3]

The notable exception was the American Mutoscope and Biograph Company, founded by Edison defector William Kennedy Dickson.[4] To avoid the Edison patents, Dickson devised both a wide-format film (68mm rather than Edison's 35mm) and a camera design that used a friction feeding method rather than the Edison sprocket system.[5] While free from the legal threat faced by other independents, the studio ultimately succeeded not thanks to a technical sidestepping of the Edison Trust, but because of one man, D.W. Griffith.

A son of the Confederacy, Kentucky-born David Llewelyn Wark Griffith was an aspiring playwright when he came to New York City in 1907.[6] Unsuccessful as a playwright, he kept himself afloat financially by appearing as an extra on the New York stage. Within the year, he was working for Edison, appearing in one-reelers (approximately 15 minutes in length) such as *Rescued from the Eagle's Nest* (1907), *Caught by Wireless* (1908), *At the French Ball* (1908) and *Her First Adventure* (1908).[7]

In 1908 Griffith was offered an acting job at the American Mutoscope and Biograph Company. There an event, almost cinematic in its improbability, changed his life and career. Biograph's main director, Wallace McCutcheon, had become incapacitated by illness, and Griffith offered his own services. Exceeding all expectations, his first directorial effort, *The Adventures of Dollie* (1908) ushered in a new era of filmmaking.[8]

While brilliant, Griffith had the annoying habit of innovating film technique and then telling the world all about it himself. He pioneered the use of the close-up, the long shot, the flashback and parallel editing. Griffith proclaimed, quite correctly, that he had revolutionized the modern motion picture drama. Indeed, by 1910, Griffith *was* Biograph.

Griffith ran his sets with iron discipline, a fact he demonstrated on the set of *The Adventures of Dollie*. The film was shot on the beach at Long Island Sound and in the cast was Griffith's old friend Charlie Islee. Friend or not, Charlie quit the set when he discovered that the crew drank all the beer that was promised for the cast. He wiped off his makeup and headed up the beach. But Griffith raced up behind him and caught him by the back of his collar, ordering him back to work. The actor refused. Griffith threw a devastating right hook and knocked the actor down. When Charlie got up to his knees, he delivered another right hook, knocking him out. "Okay everybody," he said brightly, "back to work!"[9]

That same year, the United States Census listed Mabel Normand as a "poser."[10] But the restless Mabel was growing increasingly unhappy. Modeling had become a necessity and a confinement. As it happened, Mabel's friend and fellow model Alice Joyce was making extra money posing for lantern slides—glass images projected onto movie screens between films. Lantern slides were usually used for advertising. At Alice's urging, Mabel tagged along the next time she was hired for a sitting. Immediately offered a job, Mabel recalled that for her first sitting, she stood under an artificial peach tree and looked longingly at her betrothed as he left for the big city to make his fortune. It was easy money for the popular model and, for the first time, she saw shadows of the life that was to come.[11]

It wasn't long before an excited Alice met Mabel with the news that she had been cast in Kalem's film, *The Deacon's Daughter*. Having once auditioned for, and been rejected by, Biograph Studios—by D.W. Griffith himself—Alice was thrilled with this second chance.[12] Mabel was delighted with her friend's good fortune and was even more excited when Alice invited her to come to the studio with her for the day's shooting. Grabbing Alice by the hand, the ebullient 15-year-old Mabel ran straight to the local drug store and telephoned her mother to ask permission to visit the movie set.

Mabel was confused by the process but intensely interested in everything going on around her. She was introduced to Frank Lanning, a model famous for his "Indian types." He urged Mabel to go see Griffith to ask for work as an extra.[13] After some delay, Mabel gathered her courage and "took the great plunge."[14] Primed by Lanning, and undoubtedly recognizing the famous poser, Griffith hired her on the spot for five dollars a day.

Before she knew it, Mabel was tiptoeing onto a Griffith movie set dressed as a medieval page. She was embarrassed to the point of tears by her silk-clad legs. The harsh lights, the loud banging and the gaggle of cables, cameras and shouting scared her. Mabel, by her own description, stood on one foot "like a pelican" peeking out from behind a post. It was the first take of her first film, and all she wanted to do was go home. Adding to her discomfort was her chore of carrying the extending train of a glamorous noblewoman. The "noblewoman" was legendary beauty Florence Lawrence, widely regarded as the first American movie star.[15] Later, recounting her feelings of inadequacy, Mabel described Lawrence as wearing a beautiful ball gown, with long golden hair almost sweeping the floor.

When four o'clock came, the company was told that they were going to work late. They would get paid $2.50 extra if they worked until nine o'clock, and $2.50 more if they worked after that. Knowing full well what her mother's reaction would be, Mabel also knew that her income had become essential to the family coffers. Conflicted, she decided to stay late and hoped for the best. Finishing the shoot at 11 that night, Mabel did not get home to Staten Island until two o'clock in the morning. Mary, hysterical from fear, confronted her at the door, rushed her into the house, and in no uncertain terms ended her movie career on the spot.[16] Without even bothering to quit, Mabel went back to work for Gibson and Flagg and forgot about the acting career that she wasn't even sure she wanted.

Three months later, at the 42nd Street subway station, she was spotted by a trio of Griffith partisans, actor Henry B. Walthall (soon to be famous for his role as "The Little Colonel" in 1915's *Birth of a Nation*), director Del Henderson (future comedy foil for the Three Stooges, W. C. Fields, Laurel and Hardy *et al.*) and the man who was soon to change her life, self-proclaimed Griffith protégé Mack Sennett.[17]

The son of Irish-Catholic immigrants, Mikall Sinnott was born on the family farm in Quebec, Canada, on January 17, 1880. While he was still in his teens, his parents John and Catherine left the farm in the care of family and moved with Mack to the U.S., first to East Berlin, Connecticut, and then to Northampton, Massachusetts.[18] It was in Northampton that "Mack" (as he was always known) saw his first vaudeville show and announced to his overbearing, and now horrified, mother that he had decided to go into show business. Catherine forbade him from doing so, but Mack would not be dissuaded.

Panic-stricken, Catherine somehow pestered the mayor of Northampton (and future president of the United States) Calvin Coolidge to sit down with Mack and try to talk him out of his career choice.[19] Extraordinarily close to his mother, Mack would spend his life seeking her approval and her support. Yet for possibly the only time in his life, he was willing to go ahead without it. He had something to prove.

He adopted the surname Sennett (to avoid a name that sounded like "snot") and on legal documents wrote his first name as "Macklyn."[20] He moved to New York City, where he grew to 6'2", with a ruddy complexion, a hefty build and tousled brownish-gray hair. As Mabel remembered it, he looked like a "flatfoot store detective."[21] In New York he served an undistinguished apprenticeship as a chorus boy, comedian and would-be opera singer. Failing to make his mark on the legitimate stage, he belatedly, and somewhat grudgingly, turned his attention to the "flickers" and soon found his way to 11 East 14th Street, Brooklyn, the home of Biograph Studios.

Surprising even himself, Mack fell in love with the process of making movies. Always at Griffith's elbow, matching him stride for stride, he became a true disciple of both Griffith and his ability with a motion picture camera. He built sets, shifted scenery, toted cameras and absorbed as much moviemaking technique as possible.[22] In contrast to Griffith's Southern manners, Mack was aggressive and embarrassingly ambitious. Soon he was dreaming of a studio of his own.

By the time the Griffith trio spotted Mabel at the 42nd Street subway station, Mack was a full-fledged director. She remembered the three men from the day that she had "page-fright" (as she called it) at Biograph. She remembered Sennett, in particular, as the "stocky, red-faced Irishman" who had spent the day starring at her. It is quite possible that their "accidental" meeting was no accident at all.

Confronting the petite beauty, the three men informed her that an entire day's shooting had been wasted because of her thoughtless disappearance. She had cost the studio a large sum of money and besides, it was dangerous for any actress to anger the prestigious Mr. Griffith. Laughing at them, she asked the trio if they would buy her a malted milk shake with an egg in it. Demonstrating the impossibility of anyone (particularly men) to stay angry with Mabel, they bought her a milk shake and conspired with her on how to get her back into Griffith's good graces. Mabel told them that her mother had quashed her career as an actress. They implored her to ask her mother's permission, just one more time, to return to work as an actress.[23]

Mabel had no real sense of her own success or her own importance. By 1910, she would have been an asset to any motion picture company. She did not have a household name but she *did* have a household face, one that had been featured on advertisements, sheet music, catalogues, magazine covers and illustrations of every variety. The truth was that Griffith *wanted* her for his movies, and Mack Sennett wanted her for himself.

Mabel Normand, 1913 Keystone publicity portrait by June Estep (Marc Wanamaker/ Bison Archives).

With her mother's reluctant consent, Mabel returned to Biograph and began working continually and successfully in a large variety of roles. Owing, in part, to her time as a model, she was capable of expressiveness unique for an actress of her comparative youth. She possessed an intuitive ability to throw herself into a role with abandon. Mack would later describe her as being "pure emotion."[24]

She also gave free rein to the Mabel-esque exuberance that, a few years hence, would define her screen persona. For *The Squaw's Love*, Mabel suggested a risky backwards dive off a cliff. Griffith agreed but he was so nervous that he shot it with three different cameras (a cinematic first) so she would only have to do it once.[25] Mabel came up smiling and begged to do it again.

While it was true that Mabel's high-wattage performances were lighting up the screen, in Griffith's opinion they were also taking over his films. Adding to his growing distaste was Mabel's refusal to venerate the famous director in the manner to which he had become accustomed. Once, when

Griffith was directing actress Lillian Walker (a successful character actress commonly known as "Dimples") in a scene of high drama, Lillian burst into hysterical laughter. Turning around, Griffith saw Mabel dressed as a clown. With a white face, a black nose and red lips, Mabel burst into a spontaneous dance routine for the diretor.[26] Lillian was in hysterics. Griffith was not amused.

In order to ensure Mabel's continuing presence, Sennett—who was now shadowing Mabel like a lovesick puppy—filled Griffith's ears with exuberant opinions of her acting ability. Even Linda Arvidson, D.W.'s wife, believed in Mabel's talent and begged him to keep her around. They were opinions that Griffith no longer wanted to hear.

There was a new girl on the Griffith lot, Mary Pickford. Born Gladys Smith on April 8, 1892, she was put on stage at age seven by her dominant and desperate mother. The family was near starvation and the pay was $8 a week. Unlike her siblings Lottie and Jack, young Gladys immediately caught on. Audiences adored her wide blue eyes and golden curls that gave her an angelic appearance. But "success" was a grinding existence of endless train trips between shoddy theaters. The experience of countless performances far from home hardened Mary and turned her into a professional. She became a sharp negotiator who was determined to provide for her mother and family. On a troupe stopover in New York, she resolved to see Broadway's greatest impresario David Belasco. She sat in his outer office for days only to be turned away. One morning she would wait no longer. She began screaming at the top of her lungs that she *would* see Belasco in his office.

The meeting was golden for both of them. Gladys Smith became Mary Pickford, and David Belasco had a starlet who gained momentum with each performance. Mary knew her worth, but in the summer of 1911, when the theaters went dark, she found that her fame couldn't pay the bills. Her mother Charlotte ordered Mary to report to the "movies" to get

D. W. Griffith put Mabel into films, but as time went on he found her antics pretty hard to take (Marc Wanamaker/ Bison Archives).

temporary employment. It was this 16-year-old professional actress who presented herself to D.W. Griffith, expecting immediate employment and careful courtesy. But Griffith would not allow himself to be impressed by any newcomer. And Mary, soon to be known as "The Biograph Blonde," was not going to be deferential to anyone. She proclaimed herself to be a Belasco-trained veteran. Griffith just sneered that she was "too little" and "too fat," and then hired her for $5 a day. But the camera loved her. Her tiny parts were soon expanded, provided, Mary explained, that her pay be increased as well.[27]

Griffith and Pickford's dance of dominance exhausted both of them. Each claimed the professional high ground and each disparaged the other's importance. But eventually, with three films a week to complete, D.W. found it easier to let Mary do it her way and get the movies in the can. The battle was over. Griffith had vision, but Pickford had destiny. Her subtle, naturalistic style was screen dynamite and produced an intimacy with her audience that led her to become America's first real superstar.

Biograph's other performers, while of secondary importance, were at least treated as equals. The company of actors helped each other in any way they could. In *Her Awakening*, Mabel played the lead while in *The Making of a Man*, she was little more than an extra.

In January of 1910, Griffith, Sennett and a company of Biograph regulars made history by traveling to Los Angeles to shoot films in that milder climate.[28] Mary was invited, Mabel was not. Left without a job, and surely disappointed, she was an established actress and Griffith veteran and immediately found work at Vitagraph Studio in the Flatbush section of Brooklyn.

Vitagraph was the realm of John Bunny, a stage actor and film comedian with a rotund figure and a bulbous nose. He was the first of the "fat" comedians, and America's first comedic movie star.[29] Making $1000 a week, he was said to be "the man that made more money than the President." While loved by the public, Bunny was considered by his colleagues to be rude, obnoxious and all but impossible to deal with. When a scene was ready to be shot, Bunny would frequently be found with his feet up, snoozing in an easy chair. With no one willing to rouse the volatile actor, it fell to an amused Mabel to climb onto his lap, thank him for all that he had taught her, and ask him if he would mind doing the next scene.[30]

Mabel made at least two films with Bunny, *Troublesome Secretaries* and *The Subduing of Mrs. Nag*, both 1911. Only *Troublesome Secretaries* survives. Playing the role of Betty, Mabel's youthful energies were presented to good effect. She even took a deft turn at the piano. Soon given her own series,

Mabel starred in *The Indiscretions of Betty, Betty Becomes a Maid*, and *How Betty Won the School*. Some critics found Betty a little too free with her hugging and kissing, and complained that Mabel's acting was lacking in both taste and refinement. But the films were successful, and that was all that mattered.

Successful or not, her stay at Vitagraph was short-lived. Fed up with the elevated trains that were incessantly rattling her makeup mirror as it rumbled past her dressing room window, she expressed her frustration by exposing her backside to passengers as a train roared by. Amid heated complaints from the railroad, Vitagraph decided to reprimand the young actress. But Mabel went on the attack: "What do those dirty dogs want to look in my dressing room window for anyway?" she demanded. Mabel was fired, but totally unrepentant.[31]

Liking what he found in California, Griffith shot films in various Los Angeles area locations, most notably a Latino melodrama called *In Old California*, the first film ever to be shot in a town called Hollywood. Upon returning east, he brought a glowing report about the wide variety of natural settings he found in the vicinity of Hollywood. Eager to escape both the bad weather and the long arm of Edison's legal team, a film colony migration to Hollywood soon began.

By now, Griffith had made Mack his second director and put him in charge of an autonomous comedy unit within the Biograph organization. It was almost an afterthought. Griffith didn't know about comedy, and he didn't want to know about it. If Mack wanted the job, he could have it.

Now that Mack was successful, his mother—who had moved back to the family farm in Danville, Quebec (after John Sinnott died)—was able to overcome her misgivings about show business and visit Mack in New York. Sometimes staying for weeks at a time, she made it her business to know every detail of her son's life.

Knowing that Mack's return to New York would guarantee her a steady paycheck, Mabel reported to Biograph as soon as they arrived back. Mack seized the chance to make Mabel his star both on screen and off, and her creative influence was felt immediately. Mack's willingness to accept Mabel as a collaborator in such a male-dominated business was not evidence of his broad-mindedness. Their first collaboration, *The Diving Girl*, was certainly Mabel's idea. Yet it is difficult to know if Mack thought it would be a good idea for a film, or if he simply wanted to see Mabel in a bathing suit.

Biograph actresses Blanche Sweet and Constance Talmadge observed the birth of the Mack and Mabel romance firsthand. Blanche, with a background not unlike Mabel's, lifted her family out of poverty with her smart, quick-witted portrayals in films such as 1913's *Judith of Bethulia* (Griffith's first full-length feature).[32] Constance, with a story not unlike Mack's, spent her screen career trying to live up to the demands of a domineering mother.[33] Both women adored Mabel, and would remain loyal to her, but neither had the slightest regard for Mack. Blanche described him as insecure, immature and unable to commit to one woman. Constance said he was utterly incapable of providing Mabel with any kind of security, and was the worst thing that could happen to her.[34] They believed, with some justification, that Sennett was a mama's boy, forever seeking his mother's approval. Neither Blanche nor Constance considered Mack, in the classic sense of the term, "husband material." Sitting up with Mabel night after night, they counseled her about her choice of boyfriends. They tried dozens of times before giving up, with a sad, and somewhat disgusted, resignation.

While it's clear that Mack gave Mabel a ring before he went to California with Biograph, his motivation is not clear. He may have done it to make sure that Mabel would still be around when he returned. But Mack thought the ring showed his good intentions. "It was a cheap ring. It cost two dollars and a half, but it had a lot of shine to it. I had to save up to buy it, and Mabel knew that."[35] Mack said he gave it to her "one evening on the ferry, on the way home to Staten Island. Mabel was staring at the dark water which had wide splashes of moonlight in it." Mack held out the ring and waited. Mabel was unexpectedly quiet. "I don't know about you, Mack Sennett," she finally said. "I don't know whether you are a man to fall in love with or not, and I haven't said that I *have* fallen for you!"[36]

Blanche doubted whether Mack ever told his mother about the ring or the fact that he and Mabel were "engaged" (especially since it was a relationship that he concealed from her). Adding to the confusion was Mabel's initial willingness to go along with the charade. Sometimes Mama Sinnott would come in one door and Mabel would go out the other. Mabel didn't wear the ring, but she didn't return it either.

As difficult as it was for people to understand, Mabel loved Mack. Some later claimed he was the only man that she ever loved. Mabel took pride in her humble origins and once expressed a general dislike for "ritzy people." In fact, she had more in common with Mikall Sinnott than anyone could have imagined. They were both Irish-Catholic, with French-Canadian family roots. They both loved riding horses, they both read the *Police Gazette*, they were both enthusiastic drinkers, and they were partners in a dream.

In a strange way, they complemented each other. Mack was indecisive, and never quite sure what he felt about anything until he lost it. Mabel was resolute and expressed her emotions directly at all times. Mack was tight-fisted with money while Mabel was wildly generous. Mack wanted security. Mabel wanted fun. Mack was liked. Mabel was loved.

In some ways, Mabel was the older of the two. She was childlike, but not childish. She wanted marriage, but didn't need it, and she would never lack for love. Yet, despite everything, when she was asked what kind of man she preferred, she proudly declared, "a brutal Irishman who chews tobacco, and lets the world know it."[37]

6
Hide and Seek

It's hard to kiss a girl that won't sit still.
—Mack Sennett[1]

    D.W. Griffith's move to California was a major undertaking, but he was certain that the risk would pay off. It was 1912, and the Griffith train west carried Mabel Normand, Mack Sennett, Mary Pickford, Ford Sterling, Blanche Sweet and Fred Mace directly into the pages of Hollywood history. The journey also gave Mabel time to teach 16-year-old Blanche how to smoke and do card tricks.[2]
    Initially, the troupe did not find itself welcomed in Hollywood. Feeling that a movie studio was a blight on their rural community of orange groves and cattle and sheep ranches, the locals derisively called the actors "movies." Griffith's uprooted New Yorkers first stayed at various hotels but soon began a search for more permanent homes. Despite newspaper rental ads that featured the phrase "no movies," Mabel found a home at the Baltic Apartments at 1127 South Orange Drive in Los Angeles.[3] Mack boarded at the Los Angeles Athletic Club and, as soon as he could scrape together enough money, sent for his mother. He rented for her a small house a few blocks from the studio, and it became a second home for him; he spent most nights there himself.
    Mack was never able to put another woman ahead of his mother—and that was the way she wanted it. When Mack took his mother to the set, it didn't take long for her to notice Mack and Mabel's eye contact and to understand what it meant. When Mabel introduced herself, the matronly woman pounced: "I know you have designs on my son. I could tell by the way you looked at him. I sent my son to America to make something of himself, not to be involved with some actress!"[4] Mabel bit her tongue.
    Mabel and Mack shot three films together during their first month in

Mack Sennett's Biograph comedy unit stops near Albuquerque, New Mexico, on its way back to New York after filming in Los Angeles, June 1912. Back row, from left: Fred Mace, Eddie Dillon, an unidentified man, William J. Butler, Mack Sennett, Mabel Normand, two unidentified men, and Alfred Paget. Center: Grace Henderson. Front row, from left: Dell Henderson, Charles West, and an unidentified man (Marc Wanamaker/Bison Archives).

California: *A Spanish Dilemma, Hot Stuff* and *The Engagement Ring*. The latter was written by Mabel, which perhaps suggested a frame of mind. In early 1912, Mabel was unexpectedly cast with Mary Pickford in the Griffith-directed drama *The Mender of Nets*. As the title character, Mary spends her days sitting on the beach, mending the nets of sailors. When a young sailor sees her, he deserts Mabel and seeks her affections. Mary has compassion for the heartbroken Mabel. When Mabel's brother angrily seeks revenge on the sailor, Mary intervenes, urging the sailor to return to Mabel. Mary then returns to her life on the beach.

Biograph began to release the real names of their players. One review identified Mabel as "the popular 'Betty' of Vitagraph stock."[5] The women performed well together. It was Mabel's most successful collaboration with Griffith, and her last.

Though Mack's acting ability was nothing short of terrible, he frequently performed with Mabel in her comedies. His expressiveness ranged from a silly grin to a wide grimace and back again. And his consciousness of the camera makes his performances almost unbearable to watch. Mabel was not afraid of the camera. She delighted in taking the audience into her confidence and allowing them to share in her hijinks. In *What the Doctor Ordered*, shot in the snow-covered San Bernardino Mountains, a candid moment is captured when Mabel breaks character and begins shoving snow into Jack Pickford's face. In *Tomboy Bessie*, Mabel rides a bicycle toward the camera and waves at the viewer as she goes past, "breaking the fourth wall." She waved at the camera because she wanted to. And that was the Mabel that her fans loved.

In many ways, the 13-minute *Tomboy Bessie* was her most emblematic performance to date. In the title role, Mabel plays the little sister of Cissie, a girl Mack desperately wants to marry. Mack asks Cissie's father for her hand in marriage, and the old man declares that if Mack can entertain little Bessie, Cissie will be his. Bessie becomes his tormentor: She forces him to give horseback rides, uses him for a slingshot target and even arouses the wrath of a farmer by releasing his chickens and making Mack take the blame. The film presents Mabel at her most enthusiastic. She runs, jumps, bounces and laughs her way through it as if she were doing a hundred-yard sprint. It would become the standard against which all of her "Little Tomboy" performances would be measured. As one theater owner put it, that kind of performance was why there was standing room only on "Mabel Normand night."[6]

Mabel's Biograph comedies often centered on Mabel's ability to attract men and the comic potential of human relationships. Protective fathers, scheming fiancés, jilted boyfriends and jealous husbands revolve around Mabel's careless flirtations. In *Helen's Marriage*, when Mabel's father objects to her fiancé, she tricks the old man into watching a movie-scene wedding that turns out to be real. In *A Spanish Dilemma*, she indulges the competition for her hand by two suitors before agreeing to marry a third. In *The Tourist*, a sightseeing Mabel attracts the attention of an Indian chief. Enraged, the women of the village go on the warpath and chase Mabel back to her train.

Mack's direction was basic. At the fade-in, Mabel is almost always in the foreground on the left. She then begins flitting about, embodying the conflict of the story. Her energy is truly captivating. In *Tomboy Bessie* and *What the Doctor Ordered* she literally bounces up and down throughout the film. She most often appears as the only woman in a world populated with men. When other women do appear, they are plain and transitory. Mabel is the only pretty female in most all of her early films with Mack. Perhaps this was Mack's tribute to the girl he loved. He saw the gift Mabel had and was even envious of it.

Because of Mack's training, or perhaps despite it, Mabel became the more innovative of the two. Mabel's ideas—never welcomed by Griffith—

Mabel was an aviation enthusiast and was likely the first woman filmed in flight. She is seen here with Joseph Bocquel, one of five pilots Mabel knew who perished in a crash (Marilyn Slater/"Looking for Mabel").

became money in the bank to Mack. As Sennett later recalled, "Mabel alone was good for a few dozen new suggestions on every picture."[7] Many involved putting herself in harm's way. Whether riding a galloping horse, speeding in a racecar or going aloft in a hot air balloon, Mabel loved the stunts, even ones that could turn deadly. "With all risk comes a certain fascination," she explained.[8]

A case in point, *A Dash Through the Clouds* tells the story of Chubby, a chewing gum salesman in love with Mabel. Despite Chubby's overtures, Mabel's heart belongs to a daredevil pilot, played by Philip Parmalee, one of the finest aviators in America at the time.[9] The conflict reaches its peak when Chubby offends a group of Mexicans, and Mabel and Parmalee must come to his rescue from the air.

Although riding as a passenger in an airplane was rare at the time, Mabel did not consider it particularly risky or particularly unusual. Having flown with barnstorming pilot Horace Kearney on several occasions, she was already an experienced and enthusiastic flyer. She dreamed of becoming a pilot herself. The film provided the most extensive footage known of the Wright Model B. *A Dash Through the Clouds* is considered an important historical record. And, without realizing it, Mabel's appearance in the film made history as well. Her plane is seen in long shots at heights of up to 1000 feet, likely making Mabel the first woman to be filmed in flight. Yet her first flight on film came close to being her last. The Wright Model B's gasoline engine cut out in midair. Evading disaster, Parmalee made a rough landing on uneven ground, somehow keeping Mabel, himself and the aircraft all in one piece. While the narrow escape left everyone unnerved, Mabel was exhilarated by the experience and insisted on doing take after take.

Within one year of the film's release, both Parmalee and Kearney were dead. Parmalee was killed on June 1, 1912, while flying at a Yakima, Washington, air show. Hit by violent air turbulence, he lost control of the aircraft and crashed. He was killed instantly. In his pocket was an unopened letter from his father expressing relief that he was "finally going to quit."[10] Kearney died when his hydro-aeroplane "Snookums" crashed into the ocean. His remains were found atop a life preserver wrapped in kelp.[11]

Mabel was certainly saddened, but this turn of events also left her frustrated and angry. "Now nobody'll take me! They're all afraid! But if I have to run one of those machines myself, I intend to be up in an aeroplane!"[12]

7

Keystone Mabel

She'd start giggling and couldn't stop.
She was a wonderful giggler.—Fred Mace[1]

With the financial backing of Adam Kessel, Jr., and Charles O. Baumann, Keystone (a name Mack borrowed from the Pennsylvania railroad) was founded by Mack Sennett, Ford Sterling, Fred Mace and Mabel in April of 1912.[2] While Sennett described his backers as two bookies who received a film company to satisfy a debt, the truth was less colorful. Kessel and Baumann had run the Empire Film Exchange (a supplier of films for nickelodeons) on 14th Street in New York City before forming the New York Motion Picture Company on April 14, 1909. The various brand names operating under the New York Motion Picture Company umbrella were Domino, Kay-Bee, Bronco and Bison. Domino and Kay-Bee produced comedies and dramas, while Bronco and Bison produced westerns exclusively.

Bison Studio was founded in 1911 by producer-director Thomas Ince, a specialist in assembly-line westerns. He built his studio at 1719 Alessandro Street in the Edendale section of Los Angeles (now encompassing Echo Park, Los Feliz and Silver Lake). By 1912 Ince had outgrown his Edendale studio and relocated to a 460-acre parcel of land in the Santa Monica hills, immediately dubbed "Inceville." The Edendale studio, abandoned by Bison, was described by Mace as a bunch of dilapidated wooden buildings. But to Mack it was the site of his dreams, and it became the home of Keystone Studio.

Sennett was now a bona fide studio head, and he reveled in it. Keystone's rustic two-and-a-half acres came to include a writer's studio, a blacksmith shop, a scenery warehouse, a diving tank, a main stage, a fleet of studio cars, a communal dressing room for cast members and some conveniently placed hitching posts for the horses that Mabel and Mack borrowed from

Together Mabel and Mack changed film history, and each other's lives (Marc Wanamaker/Bison Archives).

the ranch next door.³ For himself, Mack built an office atop a 30-foot tower in one corner of the lot. It boasted leather furniture, a brass spittoon and a deep, rectangular bathtub.⁴ Enthroned in his tub, he would conduct business in style, basting his skin, chewing his plug and fretting over Mabel. His tower office was functional for all three jobs. "Where else can you put a bathroom," he wrote, "and still keep an eye on Mabel Normand?"[5] Mabel mocked him, calling him Napoleon because it made him happy and then "Nappy" because it made him angry.[6]

It was an exciting time for Mabel. Signed for more money than she ever thought possible—$125 a week—it was a chance for her to provide her family in Staten Island with the comforts and niceties of life that money could provide. It gave her a chance to buy herself a library and to pay for the painting and music lessons that she had always craved. It also seemed to bring her a step closer to a future with Mack Sennett.[7]

But, whether following the money, following her heart, or simply carried along by the momentum of events, Mabel's signature on the Keystone contract of June 1912 was the point of no return. For the rest of her life, Mabel Normand was a star.

Keystone's first film release, premiering on September 23, 1912, was a "split-reel" (two short films on one reel) comedy, *Cohen Collects a Debt* and *The Water Nymph*.[8] In *Cohen*, a film that is truly embarrassing to watch, Ford Sterling shamelessly burlesques a Jewish money-lender and secondhand clothing dealer. In *The Water Nymph*, Mabel stars in a re-working of

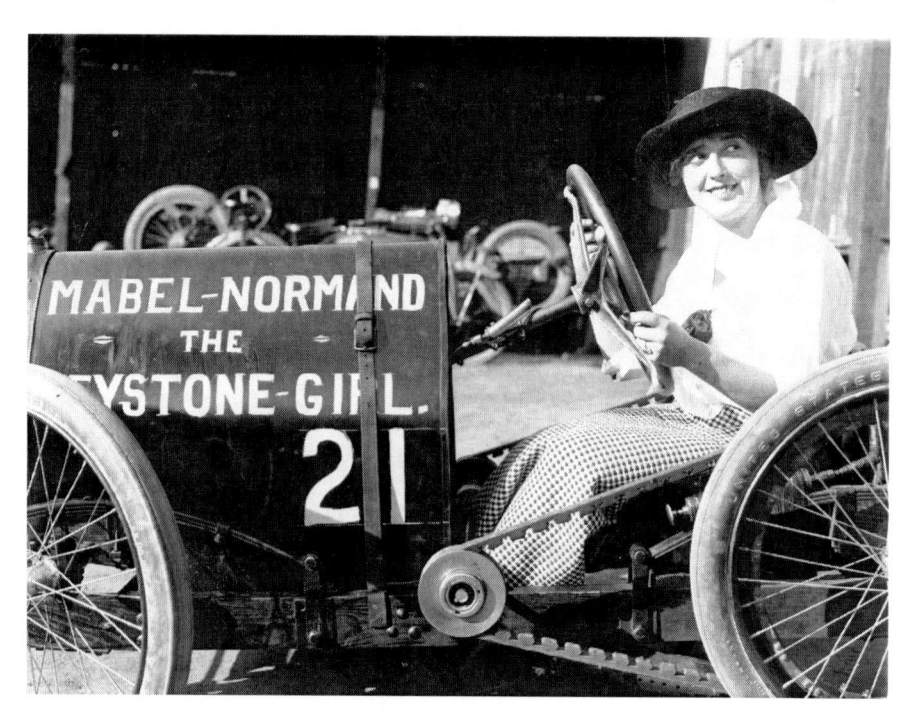

Keystone Mabel (Marilyn Slater collection).

7. Keystone Mabel   39

Looking out of the women's dressing rooms at Keystone, Mabel is fourth from left. (Marc Wanamaker/Bison Archives).

The Diving Girl, the Biograph film she and Mack did in 1910. While there is a thread of a plot that goes nowhere, it was the spectacular (for that time) sight of Mabel's very womanly figure in black tights that immediately put Keystone on the map. "The Girl in Black Tights," as she became known, did a series of trick dives that lifted the film just above the line of acceptability, and the money rolled in. The great director King Vidor was a small town Texas boy when he went to see the film. "Mabel was my dream girl!" he recalled. "I remember how those black tights covered her body!"[9] Mack had made a solid hit.

To cash in on *The Water Nymph*'s success, the Sennett Bathing Beauties were born. The group ultimately featured such future screen stars as Mae Busch, Gloria Swanson and Carole Lombard. Appearing in movies and making personal appearances

The bathing beauty (Marilyn Slater/"Looking for Mabel").

around the country, they became a financial bonanza for the studio. Would-be actresses soon flocked to the Keystone Studio. And, without Mabel knowing it, Mack began "auditioning" new bathing beauties in his tower office.

In New York, Kessel and Baumann found their own way to cash in on Mabel. As she recalled years later, "There'd be a Mabel Normand Amusement Company and a Mabel Normand this and a Mabel Normand that. All of the companies were organized without my knowledge. They would raise money on these interminable companies, put them into three or four pictures then let the company die and raise more money."[10]

To meet the continuing need for product, Mack's film crews would shoot something potentially usable, walk to another site and shoot something else. Most often a film project found itself as it went along, and story conferences came down to someone talking in Mack's ear while they were walking to the next location. Almost any idea was acceptable. If a parade, an auto race or even a natural disaster was happening nearby, a film crew shot of it for use in a future project. And if someone thought of a story idea, actors were thrown in front of a camera to act it out. If the footage was good, Sennett kept it in the film. If the footage was bad, he also kept it in the film. And—as reported by the *Moving Picture World*—Mack, Ford, Fred and Mabel began turning out split-reel comedies "at a merry rate."[11]

Mack's timing was perfect. By 1912, motion picture theaters were springing up overnight, and customers flocked to them. Comedies, dramas, newsreels, even raw footage—it all made money. There were dozens of wildcat film companies like Keystone. They went up like rocket flares and burned out just as quickly. But Sennett's wild brand of comedy (a combination of sex, slapstick and outrageous ethnic stereotypes of early vaudeville) made it easy to distinguish the Keystones from the competition, and it gave them an instant fan base. Soon the little studio on Alessandro Street became the breakout success of the West Coast film skirmish.

Artistry was never Mack's goal. Neither was originality. And, in this, he succeeded admirably. The idea of following a single comedic protagonist through a maze of circumstances began with French comedy star Max Linder. Max portrayed a high-society dandy with an easy smile and a twinkle in his eye, forever getting into quandaries due to his pursuit of women and good times. In his most famous film, *Seven Years' Bad Luck*, he pioneered the mirror illusion routine of another actor pretending to be his reflection. Despite the sight gags—a hallmark of French cinema—it was Max's personality that sold the story. Mabel and Mack took this lesson to heart. Whatever the merits of the writing, the directing or the performances, it was Mabel's persona that was at the forefront.[12]

Mabel thought that Mack's newfound success would lead to a marriage commitment. But the rise of Keystone only seemed to uncover a hidden panic within him, and Mack began spending every waking hour at the studio. He wrote some of the stories, lent a hand with the scenery, answered the phone, served as part-time gate man and then went back to the studio at night to cut film.[13] His initiative may have been laudable, but his frenetic pace was reminiscent of his films. Somewhere within him, he felt that if he turned his back, it would all be taken away.

Mabel became disappointed and frustrated with Mack's behavior. She was tired of being left alone at night, and grew weary of his hovering mother. She even heard whispers of his infidelities, and wondered if he had any intention of marrying her at all. Not surprisingly, the two began to quarrel.

Over time, an unexpected ally came to Mabel's defense. Mrs. Sinnott began to have sympathy for Mabel, and her attitude toward her would-be daughter-in-law softened. She probably realized that Mabel was her only hope of getting her son married and providing her with grandchildren. She soon began losing patience with her professional bachelor of a son. When she asked Mack, for the hundredth time, "When are you going to marry Mabel?" Mack would respond dismissively, "I don't know. We're just good friends. Anyway, I'm too busy."[14]

8

The Fun Factory

> *Mabel belongs to the new generation where the watchword is: do anything, dare anything, and get away with everything!*—Gertrude Price[1]

With hundreds of palm trees blowing in the warm wind, downtown Los Angeles in 1912 was the trendy place to be. The Vernon Country Club, opened by boxing promoter Baron Long, was located just outside the city limits, evading local liquor laws. It provided both the Keystone out-of-towners and the novice movie industry at large with a place to play after work. With money to spend, time to kill and energy to burn, this new crop of Hollywood youth would pack the Vernon every night.[2]

Mabel would regularly ask Mack to accompany her to the Vernon and he, just as regularly, turned her down. Mack was not attracted to the night life. In fact, in those days, apart from his career, there wasn't much that he *was* attracted to.

Journalist Adela Rogers St. Johns of the *Los Angeles Herald-Examiner* and *Photoplay* magazine was Mabel's closest friend at this time. Many nights the two women would sit on pillows in Mabel's living room and talk for hours.[3] Mabel revealed an introspective side to herself that few got to know, confiding to Adela that she was still a virgin and that she loved Sennett.[4] She talked about the Catholic Church and the hours she would spend there, seeking wisdom and praying for answers.

However, just as often, Mabel would set aside her lofty ideals and take Adela with her to the Vernon.[5] Its manager Bill Jones was charged with barring underage girls. But no one could withstand Mabel's charm, and soon she and Adela could be found at the bar. Mabel most often drank whiskey with apricot brandy, claiming it warmed her up when she was cold.[6] The young women, unescorted, provoked the ire of every woman present. Once

Looking lovely in an early publicity still (Marc Wanamaker/Bison Archives).

a women hit Adela on the side of the face with her purse, full and jangling, with silver dollars. Neither of them cared. With dance partners eagerly offering their services, Mabel and Adela would dance the night away doing the Turkey Trot, the Grizzly Bear, the Black Bottom and others.[7]

Sometimes Mabel and Adela stayed out all night, with Mabel reporting to the Edendale lot directly from the bar. Other times they crashed at Mabel's apartment. Adela recalled, "I'd drop off to sleep in my chair, or on the floor. I never saw Mabel asleep. If I woke up, she was flitting about like a firefly."[8] According to Mack, he once sent a car to pick her up in the morning; after the car honked its horn, Mabel called down from her window that she was "leaving in her own car!" Whereupon the car drove away and Mabel went back to bed.[9]

Mabel didn't regard her actions as insubordinate. In fact, she considered it just compensation for what she had to put up with from her so-called "boyfriend" Sennett. By now, the line between Mabel and Mack's professional and personal lives had all but disappeared. In Mabel's mind, that not only gave her a certain amount of freedom, it also gave her license. And she took it. Mabel could be wildly irresponsible. When she wasn't coming in late, she was staying away entirely.

Mabel began to explore her world. She smoked, drank and used makeup at a time when, to some, such things placed a woman just above the level of a prostitute. She supported the Socialist Party. And in early 1913 she embarked on a tour of Los Angeles nickelodeons in what was billed as a "Socialist Propaganda Campaign."[10] She spoke out on behalf of Women's Suffrage, publicly announcing, "When Women's Suffrage invades California, I shall run for mayor of Los Angeles on the Suffrage ticket!"[11] Soon Mabel became convinced that she could write and direct films at least as well as Mack Sennett, and probably better.

Despite Mabel's impulsive and heedless ways, there was something indefinably lovable about her. A reporter who knew of her errant ways wrote, "It is this strain of the *genuine* that is dominant in the personality of Mabel Normand. You believe in her without reservation."[12] As one studio workman explained it, "If anyone has trouble with Mabel Normand, he is to blame for it. I cannot imagine anyone finding fault with her."[13] But, increasingly, Mabel's nightly excursions left Mack angry and jealous. When she arrived at the studio in the morning, Mack demanded an hour-by-hour accounting of her whereabouts the previous night. Sometimes she laughed, sometimes she just walked away.

When bantamweight boxer Frankie Nolan arrived at Keystone one morning to star with Mabel in *Wished On Mabel*, Mabel did much more than coach him on screen technique. As she remembered, "I just doted on him!" Frankie and Mabel formed a close friendship. He began explaining his sport to her and she fell in love with boxing. She continued her habit of reading *The Police Gazette*, a publication that named the champion in each weight class. Though Mack must have been furious, he knew enough to steer clear of the professional fighter.[14]

8. The Fun Factory 45

Shown here with a Keystone production manager, Mabel rarely showed up on time and used her charm to get away with as much as she could (Marc Wanamaker/ Bison Archives).

Mabel was still young enough to arrive at work without showing residual effects from the night before. And despite her wild streak remained an extraordinarily hard worker. Between 1912 and 19 appeared in 77 Keystone short comedies. She demonstrated an er for stunt work that Mack was only too willing to exploit, somer extreme. A brief listing of Mabel's on screen stunts include:

Diving off a cliff into a river—*The Squaw's Love*
Riding in an airplane—*A Dash Through the Clouds*
Diving off a pier—*The Diving Girl, The Water Nymph*
Riding a galloping horse—*Cohen Saves the Flag*
Lying in front of an oncoming locomotive—*Barney Oldfield's Race for a Life*
Engaging in a brick-throwing fight—*A Muddy Romance, Mabel at the Wheel*
Being dragged by a rope through the mud—*A Muddy Romance*
Going up alone in a hot air balloon—*Mabel's New Hero*
Riding tandem on a motorcycle—*Mabel at the Wheel*
Driving a race car—*Mabel at the Wheel*
Hanging by her hands from a high tree limb—*Fatty and Mabel's Simple Life*

Mabel was an enthusiastic boxing fan. She is seen here on the Keystone lot with heavyweight boxing champion Jack Dempsey (left) and Winifred Sheehan, vice president and general manager of Fox Studios.

Diving off a bridge—*The Little Teacher*
Being battered by ocean waves—*My Valet*
Clinging atop a drifting house—*Fatty and Mabel Adrift*[15]

    Inevitably, accidents would happen, and injuries became an ongoing part of her Keystone career. In December 1913, *Photoplay* reported that Mabel went up in a balloon anchored off Venice Beach. When Sennett couldn't get the balloon down, the terrified actress was forced to shimmy down the rope, knees tightly clinched, ankles together, hand over hand, until she reached the sand.[16] On another shoot, she was positioned on a rock formation jutting out from the surf. As the waves repeatedly pounded Mabel against the rocks, Mack kept the cameras rolling until he got the shot he wanted. When the crew swam out to retrieve her, she was unconscious and badly bruised.[17] Commenting on her injuries, Mack snidely told the press, "There is a wonderful future in the movies for a girl with beauty and brains, who is willing to discard all sentimental nonsense and work like a slave." Forty-five years later, he still regretted saying it.[18]

Mabel's natural film acting style set her apart from the grimaces of her co-stars in this still from an early Keystone film with Ford Sterling (center) and Mack Sennett (Marc Wanamaker/Bison Archives).

In one notable offering from this period, *The Speed Kings*, Mabel's father (Ford Sterling) has a race car driver picked out as her future husband. She has her eye on another driver. On race day, Dad sabotages her boyfriend's car to be sure that his choice wins the race. Win or lose, Mabel stays loyal to her true love, much to Dad's frustration. The film is fascinating because it is almost a solo effort. Apart from the excitement of the car race and some slapstick between Sterling and Roscoe Arbuckle, the film is all Mabel. Her exuberance moves the plot, motivates the action and celebrates the climax.

Another compelling entry is *Mabel's Dramatic Career*, a surreal *tour de force*. Housemaid Mabel is heartbroken when her fiancé (Mack) leaves her for another woman. Her luck changes when she is discovered by a movie studio and made a "star." In an ironic twist, Mack finds himself in a theater, sees Mabel on the screen and is overcome with regret for having left her. Then a new plot begins when an actor on the screen begins threatening audience member Mack. This sets him in angry pursuit of the fictional character in the movie.

Shown here with racecar driver Barney Oldfield, Mabel usually preferred being behind the wheel (Marc Wanamaker/Bison Archives).

More conventional, *A Muddy Romance* tells the story of a couple eager to marry while trying to escape the pursuit of a jealous rival. A true Mabel moment occurs when she is roughly dragged through an open window. Supposedly in distress, Mabel laughs as she is being pulled to "safety."

Mabel, now a seasoned professional, wanted her turn at the helm. It is impossible to believe that Mack anointed Mabel to be one of *the* first female directors. It is easy to believe that he tired of her complaints and told her to go do it herself. Easier still is the belief that Mabel wanted to direct a film with no interference and did it whether Mack liked it or not. She directed, or co-directed, at least seven films: *Won in a Closet, Mabel at the Wheel, Caught in a Cabaret, Mabel's Busy Day, Her Friend the Bandit* (not known to exist), *Mabel's Blunder* and *Mabel and Fatty Viewing the World's Fair at San Francisco*.

Mabel was dismissive of her directorial efforts. She told director Robert Florey in 1922, "It would be pretense to say that the comedy chases were directed by a director truly exercising his *métier*. The director, as we know him today, was then virtually non-existent. The films which I directed or appeared in were made without any directorial technique or photographic artistry. Our pictures were a group effort, and our comedy evolved out of suggestions made by everyone in the cast and crew...."[19]

Won in a Closet (released in Europe as *Won in a Cupboard*, to avoid the connotation of a water closet) was Mabel's first effort as a director. Though the plot of mistaken identity is somewhat disorganized, Mabel knew what she could do best, and close-ups of her wistful expressions give the film an artistic quality that elevated it above the slapstick.

Mabel showed her fluency in Griffith film language with *Mabel's Blunder*, which she also wrote. She portrays a secretary engaged to the boss' son. The boss is fond of Mabel too. When a new woman arrives in the office to meet with her fiancé, a jealous Mabel disguises herself as a male chauffeur. She drives the couple to a party to spy on them. Meanwhile, back at the office, the real chauffeur is forced to put on Mabel's clothes and wear a veil over his face to avoid being discovered. He is spirited away by the boss, who believes him to be Mabel. The mistaken identity falls apart in usual style and the mystery woman is revealed to be the young man's sister.

The short features effective close-ups, fine comic pacing and a tight script. Her pantomime skills were so polished that only three title cards were needed in the 13-minute film. Considered the first cross-dressing movie, the film was added to the National Film Registry by the Library of Congress in December 2009 for being culturally, aesthetically and historically significant.

Mabel's rising popularity was enhanced by the appearance of a new co-star, Roscoe "Fatty" Arbuckle. Born on March 24, 1887, "Fatty" was one of nine children born to William and Mollie Arbuckle. He was 13 pounds at birth, and Roscoe's slim father was left to forever doubt his paternity. In a bizarre effort to disavow the boy he named him "Roscoe Conkling" after a stalwart Republican politician whom he particularly hated.

When Roscoe was 12, his mother died, leaving him in the hands of his abusive—and now, alcoholic—father. Soon abandoned, Roscoe was broke and alone. For eating money, he took a job cleaning hotel rooms. To lift his spirits, he sang to himself as he cleaned, eventually using his singing voice to carve out a meager living in small-time vaudeville.[20]

By 1908, Roscoe was receiving $50 a week performing as a singer-comedian in a summer stock presentation of *The Wheel of Fortune*. It was performed at the Byde-A-Wyle Theatre at the Long Beach Pike (an ocean-front amusement center featuring arcades, theaters, roller coasters, restaurants, shopping and the like); the cast included a young dancer named Minta Durfee, whom Arbuckle would soon marry. In a wedding that only a thespian could love, Roscoe and Minta were married on stage by Long Beach's mayor, Charles H. Windham, on the evening of August 5, 1908. Tickets sold for 25 cents, 50 cents and 75 cents.[21]

As Mabel would tell it, in early 1913, Roscoe walked through the gates of the Keystone Studio just in time to witness an argument between herself and Mack. Standing at the head of the staircase that led into Mack's tower office, the squabbling pair were interrupted by a voice calling out from below, "They call me Fatty! I'm the fat man in the Long Beach Stock Company, but I want to get into the movies. Watch!" Whereupon he did a backflip, landing at the foot of the staircase. Sennett hired him at once for $50 a week."[22]

While Roscoe had appeared in a handful of films for Selig Polyscope in 1909, he was basically a vaudevillian having a go at the flickers between bookings. Mack saw the potential to build some gags around his appearance, but Mabel saw something more and invested time and training into his pantomime skills. Wisely, Roscoe took to his coaching from Mabel well and, beginning with 1913's *The Waiter's Picnic*, he and Mabel became frequent co-stars.

In their "Mabel and Fatty" series they most often appeared as an engaged or newlywed couple. The shorts were charming and romantic, a style of comedy heretofore unseen at Keystone. Onscreen, Mabel was a flirtatious but feisty wife, Fatty a devoted but weak-willed husband. When he gave in to temptation, he became the victim of his own shenanigans.

8. The Fun Factory   51

The Mabel and Fatty series moved away from broad sight gags and placed the emphasis on affection and real situations (Marc Wanamaker/Bison Archives).

In *Fatty and Mabel's Married Life*, a monkey escapes from his organ-grinding owner and climbs into the couple's home. Mistaking both the monkey and his pursuing owner for burglars, Mabel calls the police, initiating a chase and wild confusion.

That Little Band of Gold begins with Mabel and Fatty getting married.

Soon Fatty is out on the town, flirting with another woman and laughing at a henpecked Ford Sterling. Getting his revenge, Ford calls Mabel to let her know of her husband's behavior. Confronting Fatty, Mabel takes him to divorce court. After leaving the courthouse she decides to forgive him, and they joyfully head back inside to get remarried.

Wished on Mabel presents Fatty and Mabel at their most flirtatious. After a chance meeting at the park, they abandon Mabel's chaperone-mother for a playful game of hide and seek. When Mother's watch is stolen, the game leads to the thief being apprehended.

In *Fatty and Mabel's Simple Life*, perhaps their best film, Mabel is at her most beautiful, and is clearly delighted to be surrounded by farm animals. Milking a cow, she playfully squirts milk at Fatty as he flirts to get her attention. When a neighbor offers to pay off her father's mortgage *if* Mabel will marry his son, Mabel balks and tries to elope with Fatty. A wild chase ensues, during which Fatty and Mabel get a minister to quickly pronounce them husband and wife. While the plot is simple and reminiscent of a dozen other films, the material is constantly elevated by Mabel and Roscoe's high spirits and genuine affection for each other. The film concludes with both stars looking into the camera and giving a charming "farewell" to their fans.

Their comedies became easy money for Mack Sennett. The toned-down slapstick was a move that registered with Mabel. She was tired of knocking her brains out in Keystone comedies and she began to resent doing an endless string of what she called "flour-barrel, custard pie, cheap-jack comedies."[23] And now she was too big a star to ignore.

9
Mabel at the Wheel

*Charlie is prompt to acknowledge the
strength he found in my arms.*—Mabel[1]

This was outright mutiny. Charlie "The Little Englisher" Chaplin was refusing to follow the directions of a woman.[2] On the set, Mabel explained to Charlie that his character would hose down the racetrack with water, so that the villain's car would slide away. Charlie wanted to stand on the hose, look into the nozzle, then nonchalantly move his foot, taking the full blast of the water in his face. Mabel wouldn't budge. Neither would Chaplin. Literally. He sat down on the curb and refused to move.

Exasperated, Mabel announced that they were going back to the studio. But the crew wasn't finished with Chaplin. They had built up Keystone Studio with their bare hands and they adored Mabel. No English music hall dandy, who had only been employed there for two weeks, was going to tell Mabel what he would and would not do. They rose as one to form a tight semi-circle around a still-seated Charlie. "Let me slug him!" a crew member barked. "No!" shouted Mabel. Leaping between them, she saved Charlie's insolent skin.

Back at the studio, Chaplin sat dejectedly in the men's communal dressing room waiting for the ax to fall. Right on cue, a red-faced Mack Sennett burst in. "Contract or no contract, you'll do as you're told or get out!" With $1500 saved, Charlie was already making plans to go back to England. He didn't like working in the movies anyway.[3] He couldn't keep pace, he didn't understand what to do, and shooting sequences out of order made him crazy. Ironically, the only one willing to help him was Mabel Normand, the director he wouldn't heed.[4]

Charles Spencer Chaplin was born on April 16, 1889, into an impoverished London family of English music hall entertainers. His father Charles

Sr., suspecting that the boy was not his, gave the child his name and promptly abandoned the family. His mother Hannah, suffering from a syphilis-induced psychosis, was committed to a lunatic asylum when Charlie was 14, leaving Charlie and his older brother Syd consigned to a life of orphanages and workhouses before they gravitated to the theater.[5] At 19 Charlie landed a spot with Fred Karno's comedy troupe and was soon touring America. He found his niche playing a drunk in a production they called *A Night in an English Music Hall*. Mack and Mabel caught his performance in New York and offered him a chance at Keystone.[6] Though Charlie didn't know it, Mack was scrambling. His main comedian Ford Sterling was leaving. And, while Mack didn't see star potential in Charlie, he did see talent and a new addition to his stable of comedians. But after two weeks, Charlie committed the sin of offending Mabel Normand.

At the last minute, Mack's hand was stayed by a call he got from New York asking for more Chaplin films. In fact, they wanted to know how soon to expect more Chaplin films. Having Chaplin under exclusive contract suddenly seemed like a good idea after all. However, he still had the directing situation to contend with. After the blow-up with Mabel, no other director on the lot would work with Chaplin. Mabel said she would direct him if he would listen to her. Charlie said he would listen to her if she would listen to him. Mack couldn't afford to alienate either one of them. He threw up his hands and declared them to be co-directors, and hoped the whole situation would go away.

It did. Both Charlie and Mabel cared about their work and, over time, a warmth developed between them. She said, "We reciprocated. I would direct Charlie in his scenes, and he would direct me in mine. We worked together in developing the comedy action, taking a basic idea and constantly adding new gags. Each day Charlie would come to the set brimming with new ideas, which he would act out for me. I would add my suggestions, and soon we were ready for a take. Some of our films took only a few hours to make, others occupied us for as much as several days."[7] Charlie became a regular visitor to Mabel's dressing room, to get coaching on film pantomime. He soon began coming around more often than was necessary. Like so many men before him, he was completely smitten with Mabel.

At first, Mabel was oblivious to his intentions. She was simply helping a friend: "I'm proud to say that he held my hand while he found his way through the swamp of learning the game."[8] But Chaplin wanted to do more than hold her hand. He described her "full lips that curled delicately at the corners of her mouth, expressing humor and all sorts of indulgence."[9] "Mabel at the time, was pretty and charming," he said. "Everyone loved her."[10]

9. *Mabel at the Wheel* 55

Chaplin once explained his growing relationship with Mabel: "When you work under intense circumstances sometimes there is a casual flirtation that leads to a perfectly natural little romance. If it is a stock company romance, it usually ends when the show closes. But on a movie set, things are different. You go from film to film on the same lot sometimes opposite the same leading man or lady. And everyone knows what is happening."[11]

Mabel and Charlie fit well together. Their similar heights and body shapes made it easy for them to play off each other, unlike the diminutive Chester Conklin and the towering Mack Swain. Over the course of their co-starring roles, Charlie's character changes from an unmotivated nuisance to something resembling his iconic tramp character.

Together, Mabel and Charlie appeared in a series of films together (all 1914): *Mabel's Strange Predicament*, *Mabel at the Wheel*, *Caught in a Cabaret*, *The Fatal Mallet*, *Her Friend the Bandit*, *Mabel's Busy Day*, *The Masquerader* (Mabel only appears in a cameo role near the beginning of the film), *A Gentleman of Nerve*, *His Trysting Place* and *Tillie's Punctured Romance*.

Mabel's Busy Day may be the most violent film that Mabel appeared

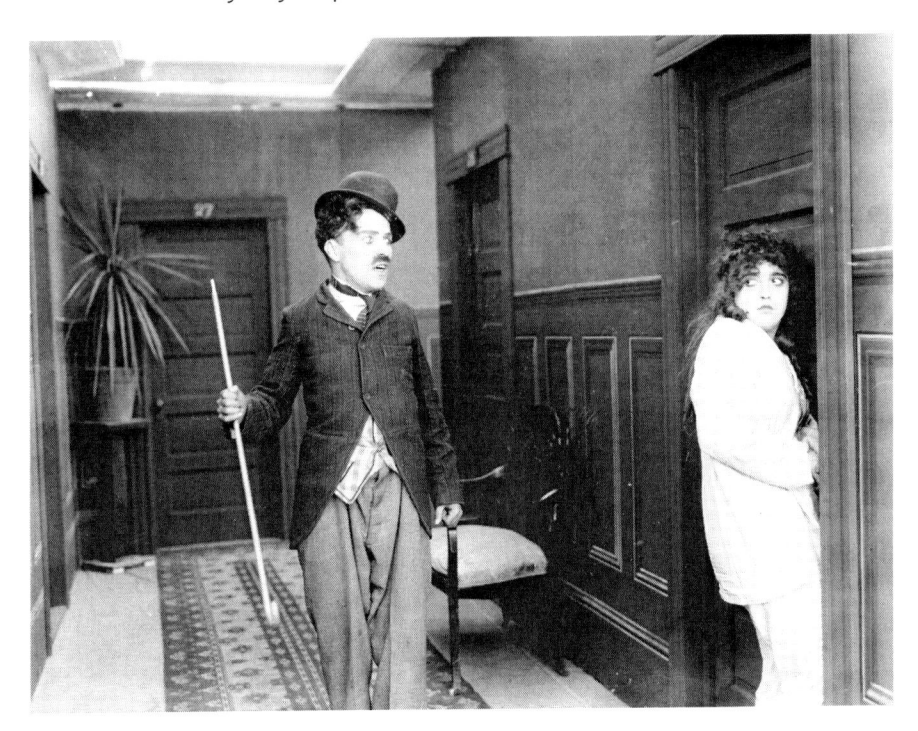

Despite his pleas Mabel did not allow her friendship with Chaplin to turn romantic (Marc Wanamaker/Bison Archives).

in. It seems almost impromptu. Wild comedy abounds as the cast slaps, kicks and hits one another in unmotivated action unusual for a Mabel Normand directorial effort. Without his Tramp persona, Charlie plays a troublemaker whose only purpose is to interfere with those around him. When hot dog vendor Mabel is distracted, Charlie steals her hot dog box and gives them away to the crowd. Mabel alerts the police and sets off a Sennett-worthy melee.

The Fatal Mallet shows a completely different Mabel. She is unusually pretty and flirtatious. Her wandering attention motivates the action as three men and a boy vie for her affection. Charlie, Sennett, Mack Swain and even Mabel take turns throwing bricks at each other. When Charlie discovers a mallet in a barn, he uses it to dispatch a rival. But while Charlie and Swain battle over Mabel's attention at the water's edge, Sennett makes his move and escorts Mabel away.

Caught in a Cabaret (a film that Mabel wrote and directed) features

Mabel and Chaplin on the set of *Caught in a Cabaret*, 1914. He initially resented being directed by the young actress, but she soon became his greatest ally (Marc Wanamaker/Bison Archives).

more situational comedy than most other Keystone entries, plus an unusual number of title cards. Charlie plays a waiter. When he pretends to be a Greek ambassador, he is invited by Mabel to a swank garden party where he angers her jealous boyfriend.

Inevitably, Charlie decided to pursue Mabel. One evening, at a studio party, when Mack was called away from the table, Charlie whispered to Mabel that he was very attracted to her. Mabel whispered back that she was attracted to him as well, but that things had to remain professional. Still thinking he had a chance, he waited months for the right moment. Finally, at a San Francisco charity function where Mabel looked "radiantly beautiful," he made his move. As he placed her coat over her shoulders, he kissed her. Mabel kissed him back. Charlie leaned in again. "No, Charlie," Mabel whispered. "I'm not your type, neither are you mine."[12]

Decades later, Chaplin wrote what he really thought of Sennett's films. "I thought they were a crude mélange of rough and tumble. However, a pretty, dark-eyed girl named Mabel Normand, who was quite charming, weaved in and out, and justified the studio's existence."[13] There were millions of people around the world who felt the same way.

10

Tillie

She had courage and that is a quality I admire above all others. —Marie Dressler[1]

Sennett was fascinated with the idea of producing the first feature-length comedy. It was a big gamble, and he had to make big promises. Kessel and Baumann weren't thrilled with Sennett's idea, and would only agree to the project if Mack could get an established star—outside of Keystone—in an established property. Mack finally settled on filming Marie Dressler in her hit Broadway show *Tillie's Nightmare*. As a musical, it did not readily translate to the silent screen, so Sennett called his version *Tillie's Punctured Romance*.

When Mack presented the idea, Kessel and Baumann acquiesced, and a budget of $50,000 was cautiously approved. The other Keystone players weren't thrilled with the idea of an outsider coming in and being handed a starring role. Mack knew he needed Charlie and Mabel in the movie, and assured them again and again that their roles were just as important as Dressler's.

Marie was an unlikely star, but a star she was. Standing 5'7" and weighing 250 pounds, she was, by her own description, "plain." Yet it was these characteristics that made her so popular. Audiences loved this actress absent of glamour, but full of homespun humor.[2] Unfortunately for Mack, Dressler knew exactly what she was worth, and intense negotiations began. Marie finally signed a contract for 12 weeks at $2500 a week. Mabel was livid about Marie's salary, especially since Marie, the new "movie star," had never appeared in a movie. Mabel demanded $2500 a week for herself. A weary Sennett told her she was contracted at $1500 a week and that's where she would remain, whether she liked it or not.

The powderkeg exploded when Mabel reported to work on the first

Mabel loved animals despite several mishaps with them on set (Marilyn Slater/ "Looking for Mabel").

day of shooting. Her coveted Dressing Room #1 had been invaded. She ordered the strange, heavyset actress out of her dressing room. But Broadway's Marie Dressler sat in her newly acquired splendor, refusing to budge. Mack was in his office with his head in his hands. He had been waiting all morning for the eruption he knew would come. Mabel was predictably late, which gave Keystone stagehands the task of removing Mabel's belongings and replacing them with Marie Dressler's. Mack should have told Mabel sooner. But he finally decided that one big explosion was better than many over several days.

Mack sheepishly told Mabel that Marie's contract entitled her to Dressing Room #1—Mabel's dressing room. History doesn't record the four-letter tirade that Mabel let loose in Mack's face. But, whatever she said, Mack immediately decided to begin construction on a second star dressing room.[3]

Mabel wasn't finished with Marie Dressler. Except for snide comments that would circulate back and forth, the two women stopped speaking to each other. When Mabel brought her maid to the studio, Marie brought two. When Marie brought in a Pomeranian puppy, Mabel did as well. Mabel's studio friends had to assure her that *her* Pomeranian was cuter than Marie's Pomeranian.[4]

Finally Mabel stood up in the studio cafeteria and challenged Marie to an auto race. Mabel was an expert (and reckless) driver and was sure that Marie would back down. But Marie stood up and barked back that she accepted the challenge. Word got out, and soon the bookies were in business. Bets were taken at both Mabel's Keystone and on Marie's Broadway.[5] The race was set at Ascot Park in Santa Monica.[6] Mabel was in her Stutz Bear Cat, Marie in her Fiat. But rain caused a postponement and that gave Mack time to emphatically call the whole thing off, warning the combatants that they had no right to kill each other in the middle of his shoot.

The movie's plot begins with Charlie trying to win wealthy Tillie's (Dressler) heart. They elope, but Charlie soon joins forces with ex-girlfriend Mabel to steal her money. They get Tillie drunk and take her pocketbook. When Charlie later reads in the paper that Tillie has inherited three million dollars from a dead uncle, he leaves Mabel and pursues Tillie again. Charlie persuades Tillie to move into the uncle's mansion with Mabel working undercover as a maid. They throw a riotous party. The uncle turns up alive and well and has them all arrested.

As a coda to the shoot, Marie believed that her husband-manager "Sunny Jim" Dalton had negotiated a verbal contract with Keystone that gave her a percentage of the film's profits. When Kessel and Baumann said no such agreement ever existed, Marie sued.[7] She demanded $122,000 and was so uncompromising that when the judge awarded her $50,000, she refused to collect the money and sued again.

A huge success, *Tillie's Punctured Romance* confirmed Mack's conviction that audiences would sit through a feature-length comedy. But it wasn't the kind of success that either Mabel or Marie had counted on. While they watched each other, Charlie walked away with the picture. Critics raved about his performance and declared him to be the true star of the film. He instantly demanded a raise and instantly received it. A lesson was learned. Mabel and Marie saw each other again a few months later. When their eyes met, Marie grinned and let out an exaggerated sigh. After a pause, Mabel erupted into a loud giggle. The two women declared a truce and spoke well of each other for the rest of their lives.

11

Ice Cream for Breakfast

*She'd have ice cream for breakfast,
while reading Freud.*—Mack Sennett[1]

Before the movies, relatively few individuals—mostly monarchs and military heroes—were internationally known. Now Hollywood movie stars became a new kind of royalty. They possessed wealth and influence, without the obligations of position. As one actress remembered it, "Many of us became queens overnight, but Mabel became a goddess."[2] She was inundated with mail, most requesting money, romance or a chance in the movies.[3]

Adding to the pressure, Mabel and Mack's emotional death grip on each other's souls continued. They frequently brought out the worst in each other. The more Mack worked late, the more Mabel felt ignored. She acted out to get his attention, causing him to retreat even further into his work. During work hours on the Keystone lot, Mabel was always the emotional barometer. When she was feeling happy and well, she kept spirits up with friendly banter and random pranks. But the bad days took everyone down. At the sound of slamming doors, screaming from Mack's office or objects hitting the wall, co-workers made themselves scarce. One more explosion from Mabel would lead to one more half-hearted proposal from Mack, and the cycle would begin again. The climate at the Keystone Studio was controlled by the emotions of a 20-year-old girl and her overgrown adolescent of a boyfriend.

It was all too much for Mabel. She looked around for friends, or at least allies. Charlie was gone now. At the end of Chaplin's one-year contract with Sennett, he followed Mack's own adage ("Start with Sennett, get rich somewhere else"[4]) by signing with the Essanay Film Manufacturing Company in December 1914. With the promise of creative control and a weekly salary of $1250, plus a $10,000 signing bonus, the decision was relatively easy. With Chaplin's departure, the Mabel and Fatty collaborations took on even greater importance to Keystone. Fortunately, the public couldn't get enough of them. Both actors now wanted greater autonomy from Sennett, who agreed to anything to keep the money rolling in and to keep Mabel quiet.

Over time, Mabel formed a close friendship with Roscoe and his actress-wife Minta Durfee and became a regular visitor to their Venice beachfront home. As they would talk into the early hours of the morning, her visits became overnight stays and then weekend stays. Roscoe and Minta were sympathetic listeners, particularly Roscoe, who never overcame the anguish and shame of his own childhood. While quick to offer his support, the truth was that Roscoe couldn't help Mabel, any more than he could help himself. While silently offended by both her profanity and her drunken excesses, Roscoe and Minta genuinely loved Mabel and became her round-the-clock psychologists, crisis counselors and witnesses to the Mack and Mabel disaster-in-waiting.[5]

The legend of Mabel Normand swimming with the dolphins was a famous Hollywood tale. Yet, in her old age, Minta was emphatic that, in the spring of 1915, it happened in front of her Venice beach home. For Mabel, a visit with the Arbuckles was not complete without a brisk morning swim in the crashing waves. It became both a much-needed release from her growing anxiety and a happy reconnection to the childhood she had spent in the choppy waters off Staten Island.

With Minta watching from the sand, Mabel's swim was interrupted by a pod of dolphins, jumping, nudging her and bidding her to play. While spotting dolphins was not unheard of in Venice, it was Mabel's acceptance of their invitation to play that would forever astound Minta. "There was something going on, you couldn't make up your mind just exactly what it was, but I could see her arm over something. It was a dolphin! And, instead of being frightened like anybody would—because none of us knew anything about dolphins in those days—she just put her arm over a dolphin's neck, and they swam right along with her!"[6]

Roscoe and Minta's counseling was welcome and it may have had an effect. Mabel no longer wanted to talk about marriage, and she disliked being asked about it. But marriage proposals came at her by the hundreds. They were shouted at her in public and mailed to her in private. As the *Los Angeles Times* told its readers, "Mabel has a whole bag of engagement rings."[7] Suitors crossed oceans to meet her. She was pursued by both Edward, the Prince of Wales, and Prince Ibrahim of Egypt—a man Mabel referred to as her "hindoo prince." Prince Ibrahim offered to give up both his throne and his religion, if she would marry him. Mabel quickly declined.[8]

Mabel with Prince Ibrahim of Egypt who offered to give up his throne and religion for her (Marc Wanamaker/Bison Archives).

Appearances with an escort (after Mack would refuse to accompany her) would invariably lead to marriage rumors. After it was reported that Mabel had married Bert Levey—a successful manager of West Coast vaudeville houses—and would be giving up her career to stay at home, she had to call reporters to state, with some annoyance, that she and Bert were only casual acquaintances.[9] One man, knowing that he could never have her, tried to drown himself in a toilet bowl.[10]

One day, the elegant Dutch actor and man-about-town, Lou Tellegen, decided that he had to meet Mabel. Or, more to the point, that Mabel had to meet him. He was certain that, unlike the others, his charm would open doors. Impeccably dressed and groomed, he found his way to Mabel's dressing room. He gently tapped on her door and called out, "Are you in there, my lovely creature?"

"Yes indeedy."

"May a devoted slave come in?"

"Not at the moment, dearie," Mabel sang out, "I'm on the chamber pot!"[11]

Mack was jealous of other men and frustrated by her refusal to listen to his orders. To get her cooperation, he sometimes resorted to trying to get her drunk. At Pop Levy's Café at Fourth and Spring Street, Mack insisted they drink many Horse Necks, a concoction of bourbon, ginger ale and lemon peel. He sat and lectured her on both morality and proper decorum, though he was deficient in both categories himself.[12]

Mabel and Mack now argued openly on the set. One memorable fight occurred on the set of *The Little Teacher*. Witnesses remember Mabel screaming at Mack that she was sick of his mother and that she wasn't going to wait any longer.[13] The cast and crew became adept at predicting both an argument's outcome, and a probable timetable for when they could get back to work. Almost as a matter of course, Mabel continued to demand more money. Mainly to keep her placated, Mack raised her salary again and again.

Mabel became one of the highest-paid women in America. She didn't know what to do with her riches.[14] With more money than she had ever imagined possible, she began to indulge her every whim and soon became larger than life. She began racing a cycle car at Ascot Park.[15] She bought a 60-foot yacht for the sole purpose of taking her friends to Catalina Island.[16] She took flying lessons from aviator Walter Brookin.[17] Then there were the art lessons, the piano lessons, the French lessons and a neverending stream of books. In one of the happiest moments of her life, Mabel bought her parents a large Staten Island home.

It was as if she were racing against time. Writer James R. Quick noted, "That was the keynote of her life—her avid eagerness for all that life held. It was as though she realized in some dim way that she had not long to live."[18]

Mabel contracted tuberculosis. In the early twentieth century, the disease was killing approximately 110,000 Americans every year, and was synonymous with death.[19] When her susceptibility to colds, her persistent cough and her frequent bouts of fatigue could no longer be attributed to hard living, she sought medical attention. The devastating diagnosis became a closely guarded secret from all but her family and closest friends. Mack took the news in stride, although it was hard to tell if he was being strong or just emotionally detached. Mabel was profoundly impacted by the news. She quickly employed the escape and denial techniques and the deep spirituality with which she approached all difficult situations.

While Mabel embraced her wealth, and the freedom that it gave her, her pursuit of peace and happiness led her on a search for something deeper. She regularly read philosophy, poetry and the Bible. And at six a.m. every Sunday she attended mass at the Church of the Good Shepherd in Beverly

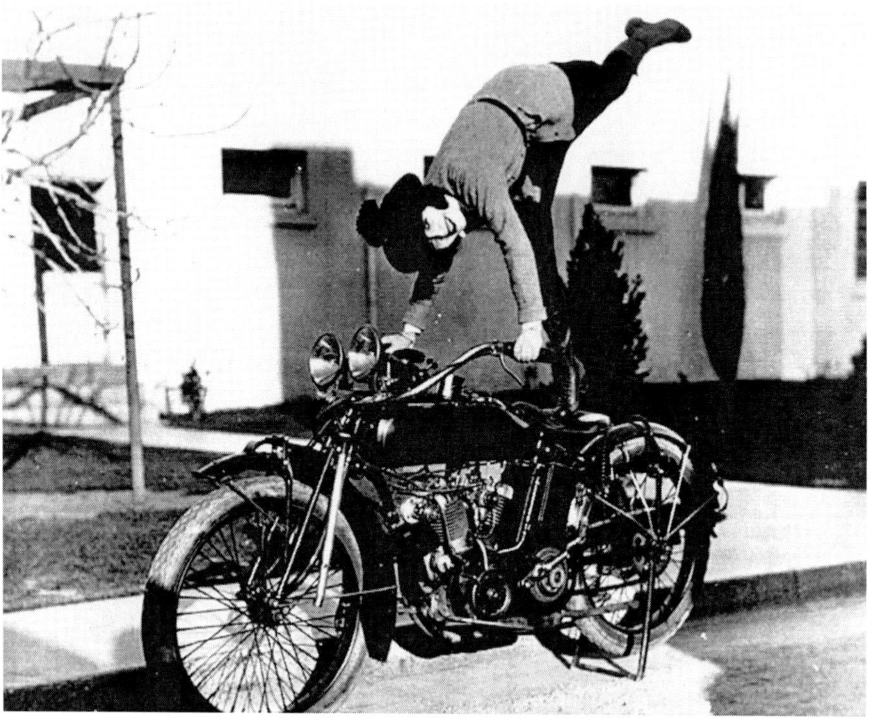

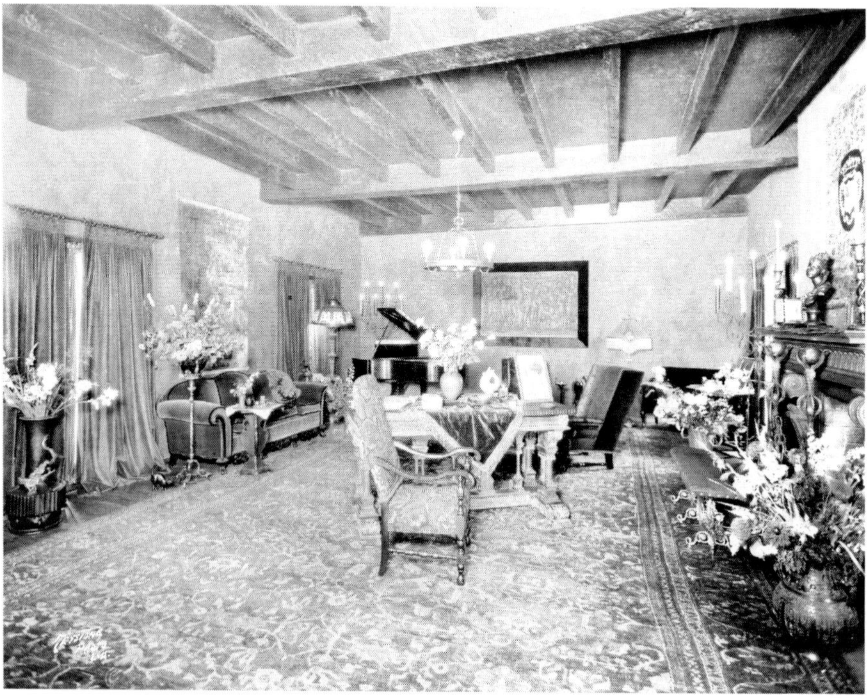

Hills and grew close to her priest, Father Chiappa. He appreciated her open heart, and the two of them enjoyed many discussions about spiritual truths.[20] Mabel's confessions were achingly blunt, and unsparing of herself, and she would whole-heartedly do her penance. As Mabel once said, "I am a Catholic, but don't hold that against the church."[21]

Then trouble arrived from far away. On June 28, 1914, the Archduke Franz Ferdinand of Austria, heir to the throne of Austria-Hungary, was assassinated by Gavrilo Princip, a Yugoslav nationalist seeking unification of Bosnia-Herzegovina and Serbia.[22] Declaring war on Serbia, Austria-Hungary invoked its pre-war alliances that had been developing for more than a decade. The Central Powers loosely aligned the Austrian-Hungarian Empire with Germany, the Ottoman Empire and Bulgaria. Serbia also invoked its alliances. Known as the Allies, the Serbian alliance was led by the Triple Entente of the United Kingdom, France and the Russian Empire.[23] World War I, known at the time as "The Great War," had begun. President Woodrow Wilson tried to keep the U.S. on a path of strict neutrality.

With the outbreak of war, the foreign markets for Mack's films narrowed. He characteristically responded by pushing himself even harder. His increasing need to get films in the can ultimately, and perhaps inevitably, backfired. It led to *Oh! Mabel Behave!*, probably the worst Keystone film ever produced. In this singular instance, the practice of shooting footage until a plot emerged completely failed. No plot emerged. And, despite the title, Mabel appeared in only eight of the film's 35 minutes. Ford Sterling takes up most of the film mugging outrageously in a series of sequences that have no connection to each other or to anything else in the film. One critic said it was hard to tell if the Mabel footage was meant to pad a Ford Sterling comedy or if the Ford Sterling footage was meant to pad a Mabel Normand film. Even Sennett considered the film un-releasable. He withheld it for years before quietly dumping it on the market in 1922.[24]

Help arrived from Harry Aitken. In 1911, Aitken had begun a string of production and distribution companies. By 1914 this led to the formation of an apparatus devoted exclusively to the distribution of feature films. This specialization made Harry a natural fit for D.W. Griffith to produce and market his feature-length film *Birth of a Nation*.[25] Encouraged by the huge returns, on July 30, 1915, Aitken, along with Adam Kessel and Charles O. Baumann, formed the Triangle Film Corporation to release the films of Griffith, Sennett and Thomas Ince.[26]

Opposite top: Mabel couldn't resist anything fast (Marilyn Slater/"Looking for Mabel"). *Bottom:* Mabel's living room on Camden Drive in Beverly Hills. The baby grand piano was a favorite possession (Marc Wanamaker/Bison Archives).

The agreement required Sennett to produce a staggering number of films that would turn his studio into a virtual sweatshop. Mabel's talents and vitalities were taxed as never before. As Minta Durfee described it, "Mack built everything around her. He would have worked her to death if he could, 24 hours a day, seven days a week!"[27] There were days when she would work through breakfast, lunch and dinner. She began to get chronic headaches. Minta noted a marked deterioration.

Mabel continued to feel as if her life were going nowhere. The ambitious nature that drove her as a child had morphed into a kind of dissatisfied agitation. She was no longer willing to wait for her dreams to come true. Mabel would write, "Well, the years slid along. And Nappy and I battled more and more. I wanted better pictures, and I was becoming financially independent. Also, I was getting tired of grinding out short comedies. Other stars, in other companies, were featured in pretentious films, and were paid far more than I was."[28]

But the problem was not just the pictures that she was making. Mabel's other dream was for a home, a husband and children. To get them, she would have to change a man who wouldn't change. It was an impossible situation. Future movie star Gloria Swanson—with whom Mack was having an affair at the time—summed it up: "You can't change men. Men are what they are, 'men.'"[29]

One evening, after relentless prodding from Mabel, Mack took her to a party at the Vernon. There Mack said something in anger, and Mabel pulled away and angrily trotted off. Sulking in a chair by the wall, Mack sat up when he saw Mabel spinning around the dance floor with former model, and newly minted leading man, Jack Mulhall. At song's end, someone announced that Mabel and Jack had won the trophy as the evening's best dancers. Jack graciously accepted the cup and handed it to a delighted Mabel, who held it up it to great applause. Red-faced, Mack stood up, slammed his fist against the wall and advanced on the happy couple. Roughly pushing Mabel aside, he knocked Mulhall flat with a crushing right hand. Mabel rushed to grab Mack's right arm but slipped and landed flat, and her trophy flew across the dance floor.[30] It was vintage Mabel and Mack.

12

The Clock Strikes 12

My pillow's always wet in the morning.
I guess I cry in my sleep. —Mabel[1]

In 1915, Mabel and Mack were finally getting married. In Mrs. Sinnott's opinion, Mack's relationship with Mabel had gone on long enough, and she all but ordered her son to get married. She was amazed, and possibly grateful, that someone in Mabel's position would continue to wait for her son.

But it was Mabel's stardom that kept her bound to Mack Sennett. Mabel was no fool. She knew that the men who trailed behind her didn't know her. But Mack did. He cared about her before she was rich and famous. His love was the only kind that was real to her, and it was time to make it official. As if in covenant, Mrs. Sinnott gave her future daughter-in-law an ivory crucifix, something that Mabel would always cherish.

Mack grew resigned to his fate and, perhaps, was even happy about it. It was hard to tell with Mack. In June 1915, he finally proposed, officially, and this time it came with a $50,000 emerald engagement ring.[2] As Mack remembered it, Mabel just dropped it into her purse and continued to wear the cheap ring from years ago.[3]

Most of Mabel's co-workers were pleased with the engagement, and probably relieved. Now, they hoped, all the madness would stop and Mabel and Mack would become a real Hollywood power couple. Yet one player was not happy: Charlie Murray, an established character actor, years older than the others on the lot. He had listened to Mabel's endless tales about Mack and emphatically told her not to marry him because he would always be dominated by his mother. Murray allowed himself the hope that, perhaps, this time would be different.[4]

The storm clouds began to gather almost at once. Mack insisted on a quick elopement but Mabel wanted it all: the dress, the flowers, a Catholic ceremony and a long honeymoon. Predictably, Mack said he was too busy. Just as predictably, Mabel said he wasn't. She wanted to be a priority in Mack's life. Mack finally agreed, but Mabel knew better than to allow a long engagement. So the wedding date was set for July 4, 1915, two weeks hence.[5]

Mrs. Sinnott traveled to Staten Island to meet with Mrs. Normand and the Normand family. Realizing the folly of trying to pull together a full wedding in just two weeks, Mabel agreed to bump the wedding to September and was soon happily counting the days. But conflicts continued to arise. Mack wanted Mabel to become a full-time wife and a mother.[6] Mabel flatly told him that she had no intention of giving up her career.[7] These opposing expectations should have ended their marriage plans. Yet Mabel had waited so long. She may have thought that she could change Mack once they were married. He may have thought the same thing about her, and he knew his mother's mind was made up.

As the big day approached, Mack became a nervous wreck, gripped by the feeling he was making a mistake. On July 19, 1915, he struck a pedestrian while driving up the coast. To make things worse, he failed to appear in court to answer the charges. He sent his lawyer, who explained to the judge that, as a busy man who earned over $100,000 a year, Sennett could not be expected to show up in court. A profoundly unimpressed judge told Mack's attorney, "I better see Mr. $100,000 in front of me on Friday morning." Apparently Mack appeared, and the matter was resolved.[8]

Mack and Mabel once again began fighting on the set, and Mabel began to sense a pulling-away. She wondered if a half-hearted proposal was better than none at all. While everyone at Keystone was impressed with the enormous ring that Mack had given her, Mabel began to wear it less and less often. When Mack wasn't around, she put on the $2 ferry boat ring. She told anyone who asked that the tiny ring, from years before, had more honesty and love behind it.[9] As the wedding day approached, Mabel was nervous but optimistic.

Family and friends began arriving from Staten Island at what should have been an exciting time for the bride and groom to share. But, Mack was nowhere in sight. Not surprised, Mrs. Sinnott privately assured Mabel that one last fling before the wedding was nothing to be concerned about. While she had put up with Mack's infidelities for years, Mabel was suddenly in no mood to turn her head. Over the phone, an actress friend of Mabel's told her of a hotel room where she could find Mack and advised her to get over there straight away.[10] Mabel was out the door.

The story of the final break-up of Mabel Normand and Mack Sennett is spread across a dozen Hollywood memoirs and a dozen more interviews and legends. The details vary, but they all agree that on the eve of their wedding, she caught him in bed with actress Mae Busch, a close friend of Mabel's. Mabel had known her in her New York modeling days. Mae was once stranded on the West Coast when the road company musical she was in went bust; Mabel took her into her apartment on Seventh and Figueroa and provided her with food and support. She even got Mae a job with Sennett. The versions in print have been sanitized, but not the oral history left by Minta Durfee for an autobiography that was never finished.

An anxious Mabel received a phone call. Mack was holed up with some girl in a room at the Hillview Hotel and Apartments at 6531 Hollywood Boulevard.[11] Mabel was soon knocking loudly at the door. Believing that it was room service, Mack opened the door wearing only his boxer shorts. When he saw Mabel, he turned white and began howling of his undying love for her. Mabel saw a woman in lingerie crouching behind a divan and began screaming at her. As Mack continued to stumble over words, Mabel pushed him aside to confront the woman. But it was Mabel that was about to be confronted. It was Mae Busch. With the ferocity of misdirected emotion, the two women began screaming at each other, with Mabel on the advance. Backing up and feeling trapped, Mae picked up a heavy glass vase, threw it wildly and hit Mabel directly on her forehead.

Mabel dropped to her knees. Mack frantically grabbed a white hotel towel and held it to Mabel's head to stop the bleeding.[12] In a confused frenzy, she pushed him away and staggered to the elevator, holding the towel tightly to her head.

Making it to the curb in front of the hotel, unable to see, she somehow managed to flag down a cab and crawled inside. Sprawled out on the backseat, she asked to be driven to Venice Beach. Roscoe and Minta would help her. The cab driver carried Mabel to the Arbuckles' front door, where a shocked Roscoe and Minta directed him to the couch inside.[13] Arbuckle paid double the fare in the hope of keeping it quiet.

Mabel's hair and face were matted with blood. Only one eye was visible from under the blood-soaked towel she was compressing onto her forehead. Mabel was only half-responsive to Minta's questions and kept muttering, "Oh, no, no, no...." When Roscoe wanted to take her to a hospital, she violently refused. Not willing to upset her, Roscoe called a studio doctor he knew, a specialist in being discreet. The doctor took one look at Mabel's red pillow and said that if they wanted to keep her alive she would have to go to a hospital. By now, Mabel was too weak to object.

Registered at the hospital under an assumed name, she almost immediately fell into a coma.[14] Mabel lay for days between life and death, and she was sinking. Her physician, Dr. O.M. Justice, was compelled to speak to the press:

> Miss Normand has been unconscious for several days and has not responded to the efforts of science to restore her to normal condition. No rally is expected today as the information was given out. Miss Normand's illness is attributed to an accident in the studio of the Keystone Company, of which she is a leading lady, a little more than a week ago. It is stated that the beautiful star fell, sustaining injuries to her head. Since the fall Miss Normand has suffered concussion of the brain and not once since the accident has she uttered a coherent word.[15]

The next day, undoubtedly at Mack's direction, Keystone publicity put out a story that Mabel had been injured while doing a wedding scene with Fatty Arbuckle. According to the story, as Fatty and Mabel emerged from the church, Mabel was hit in the head by a pair of old shoes.[16] Within days the story was changed to Mabel falling down at the studio.[17]

After one week, Mabel had stabilized, but was not making the kind of improvements that her doctors hoped. It was decided that she needed surgery to drain some of the blood from her head, a risky procedure. Minta remembered the morning of Mabel's surgery, when she had to report for work at Keystone. Everyone was standing around—the actors, the extras, the cameraman, the crew—and the whole place was quiet. Nobody was setting up for work. Finally Mack came in and yelled, "What's going on here? Is this a workday or not?"[18]

The surgery was marginally successful and Mabel slowly began to recover. When she was finally able to go home, it was with a private nurse, and she remained secluded for months. During this time, Roscoe and Minta were loving and faithful visitors. Mack was not. In fact, there'd been no word from Mack at all, no card, no flowers, not even a phone call. On the lot, Mack told everyone to mind their own business. But Charlie Murray loved Mabel like a daughter. He grabbed Mack by the shirt collar and looked him right in the eye. "If that little girl dies, you son of a bitch, you better not set foot around here." It was a remarkable statement, coming from employee to employer.[19] On September 25, Mabel's secretary Betty Johnstone announced to the press that, despite reports to the contrary, Mabel was not dead.

13

New Woman

*She wasn't going to give him, or his mother,
the satisfaction of dying.*—Minta Durfee[1]

Mabel sat down by the roaring fireplace, and opened her heavy jewelry box. Some of the pieces inside were from Mack Sennett, some from other men. It didn't matter. Scooping out handfuls of jewelry, she arranged them in a line on the brick hearth. Picking up a hammer with two hands, she began smashing them to bits.[2] And with each crack of the hammer, she somehow felt better.

Mabel was on her own now, and that was the way she liked it. Her medical recovery gave her plenty of time to reflect. She was over Mack Sennett once and for all. But it wasn't just Mack. After Mabel's head injury, she was a changed person. Never again would she trust others to validate her life or career. She began reading her contracts and demanding better ones. She undoubtedly suffered a frontal lobe injury when the vase struck her. Frontal lobe damage affects the ability to self-correct and distinguish between good and bad choices. One fateful evening, she made a bad choice.[3]

Mabel was dining with friends at the swanky Café Nat Goodwin on the privately owned Bristol pier in Santa Monica. Among the group that night was Adela Rogers St. Johns and Wallace Reid. Suddenly Mabel muttered something like, "This is doing no one any good." She excused herself from the table,[4] walked to the end of the pier and stared out at the black waves. She was unable to find a reason to go on. Adela rose from the table and went to look for her friend. She caught sight of Mabel standing at the end of the pier—and then silently drop into the darkness. Adela's screams alerted her friends, and within a short time Mabel was safely on the shore. "It would have been better if you'd let me go," cried Mabel, "I just don't belong in this world."[5] Clearly it was a cry for help. Mabel was a champion diver and swimmer, having won a swimming competition in the Pacific Ocean as recently as September 10. She obviously had some more healing to do.

After an extensive rest, Mabel's interest in life returned. She told all who would listen that she felt able to go back to work. It would be a challenge more mental than physical. The morning arrived when she was ready to report to the studio. As the studio limousine neared Edendale, her nerves began to fail her. "I can't do it—I can't," she said and ordered the chauffeur to turn the car around. Then she began to accuse herself. "You've got to do it," she repeated. "You've *got* to do it." And the chauffeur was directed back. Three times she headed back home and, just as many times, got mad at herself for bowing to fear.[6] Finally she arrived at the Keystone gates. She charged straight into her dressing room and locked the door. It was a hard-won victory.

Tentatively, and almost heroically, Mabel resumed her shooting schedule. But, everything had changed. Sennett's Fun Factory was blanketed in disquiet. Production slowed to a crawl and, worse, no one felt funny. Mercifully for all concerned, Mack avoided Mabel's sets whenever possible. When he did have to make an appearance, he did little more than watch and nod. When she spotted him, Mabel halted production and sat down. She refused to perform while *he* was watching.

But Mack was determined to win her back. And, with the dogged determination with which he once pursued his career, he now pursued Mabel. He wrote out long letters to her, pouring out his heart. His letters were returned unopened. He began a daily campaign of sending her flowers, but the flowers were also sent back.[7] At Mack's behest, Mrs. Sinnott visited Mabel and gave her several items that had been blessed by the Pope. While Mabel expressed her appreciation, she said that it didn't change anything.[8] Mack even asked his mother to give him her diamond ring. When she agreed, he carried it in his pocket, in a tiny chamois bag, waiting for the perfect moment. But when he dropped it in Mabel's lap, she refused to open it. He arrived at Mabel's home at all hours, asking for forgiveness. Once he boldly embraced her. But Mabel didn't respond at all. Without meeting his gaze, she sighed, "I'm so tired. Please stay away."[9]

Everyone at Keystone felt caught in the middle. It soon became obvious that the situation was untenable and Mabel and Mack could not be on the same lot together. The Triangle Film Corporation had studio space in Fort Lee, New Jersey, and it was agreed that Mabel could work from there. Thrilled to be going home, she was put on a train with Roscoe and Minta, who were charged with taking care of her. They did it as a favor to Mack. Minta

Triangle/Keystone crew preparing to leave Los Angeles just after Christmas to work at Fort Lee, New Jersey. On the train are, left to right, Roscoe (Fatty) Arbuckle, Minta Durfee (Mrs. Arbuckle), Ferris Hartman, Al St. John, Mabel Normand, Mack Sennett, and Joe Bordeaux. Standing below train car are, left to right, Charley Murray, Ford Sterling and Fred Mace, 1915 (Marilyn Slater/"Looking for Mabel").

recalled that for all Mack's professed loved, he still regarded Mabel as a legally contracted player and he wanted movies.

Her coughing was now getting noticeable worse, and Mabel began carrying around a bottle of strong cough syrup that she called her "goop." She sometimes coughed up blood and mucus and said, "Oh, I better take my

Edwin Carewe directs with Mabel on the set at Samuel Goldwyn Studios in Fort Lee, New Jersey, 1915 (Marc Wanamaker/Bison Archives).

goop. I feel like I'm having a little hemorrhage."[10] She was thinner perhaps, but healthy, and she continued to do exactly as she pleased.

Having already shot the exteriors in Los Angeles Harbor for their latest (and ultimately their best remembered) collaboration *Fatty and Mabel Adrift*, Roscoe, Minta, Mabel and Arbuckle's cousin (and screen second banana) Al St. John went to work in the east. *Fatty and Mabel Adrift*, released on January 9, 1916, stars Mabel and Fatty as newlyweds in their first home, a beachfront cottage given to them as a wedding present by Mabel's parents. During their first night together, as Fatty, Mabel and their dog Teddy sleep, a violent storm develops. Seeing his chance for revenge, St. John, once a rival for Mabel's hand, hires accomplices to help him push the cottage from its moorings, and the house drifts out to sea. Waking up in their floating (and sinking) cottage, Fatty frantically attaches a note to Teddy's collar and sends him swimming to shore for help. A classic Keystone rescue ensues.

Perhaps as a result of Mack's geographical distance from the project, Roscoe directed this movie with a sensitivity rarely seen at Sennett. It was

13. New Woman 77

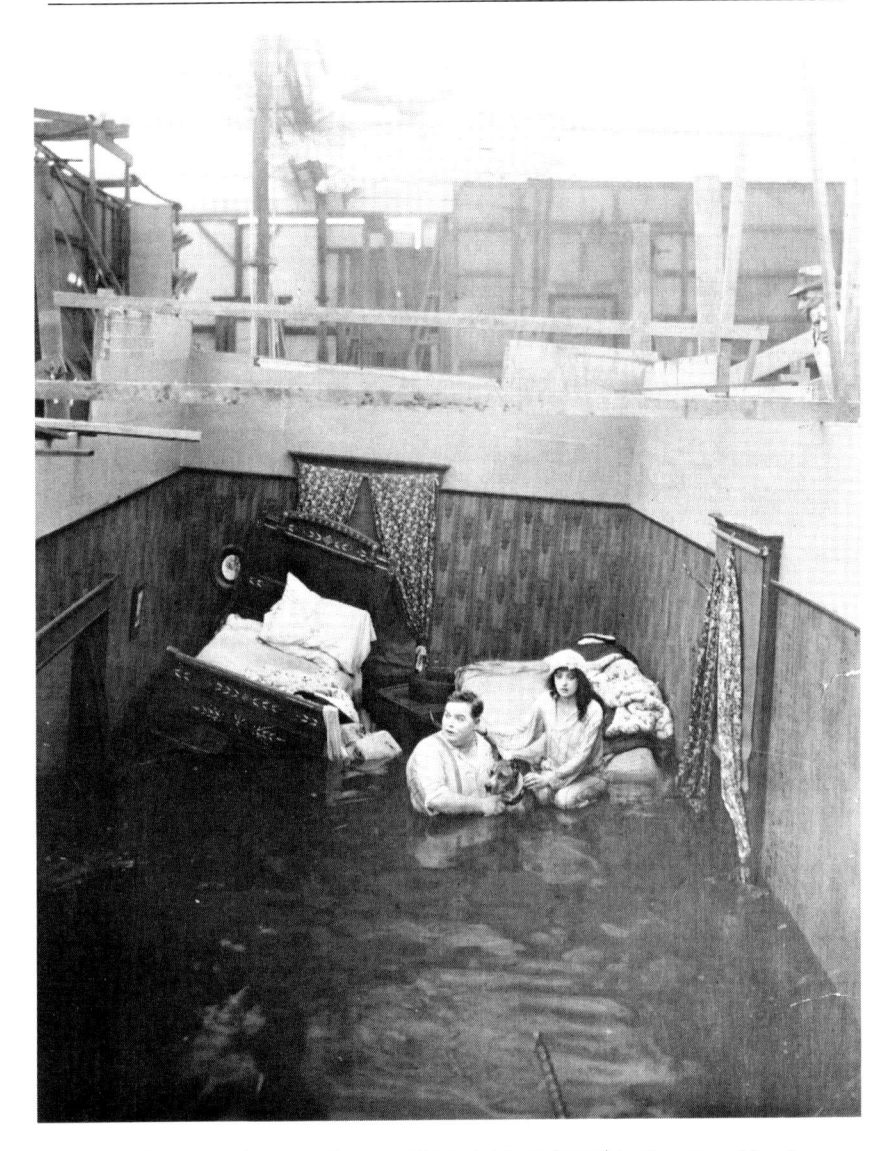

Mabel and Roscoe shooting *Fatty and Mabel Adrift* (1916) in Fort Lee, New Jersey (Marilyn Slater/"Looking for Mabel").

famously epitomized by the "phantom kiss." In the film, Fatty—checking on his sleeping bride—casts a shadow over Mabel that appears to kiss her goodnight. If slapstick was an art form, then this was surely its highest expression.

Fatty and Mabel shot two more films together in Fort Lee: *He Did and*

He Didn't and *The Bright Lights*. Both were successful, and both were directed by Roscoe. Their collaboration might have continued were it not for their individual successes. In 1917, Roscoe left Sennett to form his own studio, the Comique Film Corporation. With complete creative control and a salary of $1000 a day, Roscoe became one of *the* highest paid movie stars. His star was on the rise, and there was no end in sight.[11]

For Mack Sennett, it was a different story. His campaign to win Mabel back failed. He had to regain the upper hand, no matter how strong Mabel was. He could be ruthless in his business dealings. And he needed Mabel back, both emotionally and financially. Suddenly, he knew just how to do it.

14

Mabel Inc.

Knowing Mack was on the run, I had my way.
—Mabel[1]

One after another, the workmen arrived at 1206 Bates Avenue in Edendale. Heavy trunks arrived containing elegant, carefully folded gowns. Three men lugged in a large Oriental rug. Another arrived with a golden birdcage, complete with a canary. Then the cushions arrived, followed by the bathroom fixtures, the wicker furniture and a peanut roaster. And, of course, books—boxes and boxes of them. Meanwhile, several crews were busily doing the landscaping, planting flower gardens and installing hanging vines on Mabel's balcony. Time was of the essence. Mack was frantic over the cost but he couldn't afford to object. He gave Mabel her own studio and the freedom to decorate it. No one, not even Mabel, knew when the deliveries would stop. She might think of something else she wanted, and then something else after that. Mack wanted a reconciliation. But Mabel wanted a reckoning.

In Hollywood, news travels fast. Especially the greatest news of all: A bankable movie star was unhappy. Sam Goldwyn had been coveting Mabel from afar for quite a while, both as an actress and as a woman. He quietly put out feelers. His discreet contacts may or may not have reached Mabel. But they instantly reached the other studio heads. Sam's interest started the whole town salivating at the thought of having her under contract. It was rumored that Sam was going to offer Mabel her own company.

Some thought that Mack's broken heart would preclude him from the bidding war. But Mack's heart wasn't broken that badly, except at the thought of losing millions of dollars. By now, Mack had given up trying to ingratiate himself to Mabel on a personal level and instead began focusing on her career. He gave her everything that she asked for: feature pictures, better scripts, less slapstick, believable characters and more money. More than that, she would have her own studio.² That last part sealed the deal.

Mack found four tracts in the Hyperion Tract in the Sunset Boulevard Terrace section of Los Angeles. The contract was a one-year lease enacted on September 4, 1917, for $300 a month. There was an option to extend the lease one extra year at $400 a month.³

The Mabel Normand Feature Film Company was a large, triangular, white-stucco building that boasted a large mezzanine, cozy dressing rooms, a spacious stage and plush surroundings. Mabel's second floor dressing room was lavish. She had her own shower and tub, a sitting area, a large, comfortable bed and two French doors that led outside to a wide balcony.

A sweetheart deal, her contract stipulated that she make no more than eight pictures a year. It recognized her right to play dramatic roles. It gave her the option to borrow scenery and props from Keystone Studio. It granted her access to Sennett's advertising and public relations apparatus. It allowed her to use Keystone directors, actors, crew and personnel. The best part was that she was in no way creatively accountable to Sennett.⁴ Mabel was the first female studio head in history, and she gloried in it.

But while Mabel had her creative independence, the company was completely underwritten by Keystone. This potentially awkward situation didn't

Mabel gloried in having her own studio, but it was not to last (Marc Wanamaker/Bison Archives).

bother Mabel in the least. And while her motives for grabbing all she could from Mack Sennett were less than noble, she did have a vision. As she explained it, "My ambition is to make my studio, in its own small way, a model plant. Efficiency comes first, of course, but I don't see why a studio should be a huge, unlovely barn of a place, just because it is built of wood. So I planned for comfort and beauty, as well as efficiency."[5] When Keystone players were summoned to the new studio, they were more than happy to leave Mack's lumber yard of a studio and head over to Mabel's warm and inviting domain. And they delighted in their little boss.

As a new studio head she immediately developed a notorious relationship with reporters. She was late, uncooperative and generally impossible to deal with. The irresponsibility that Mack had been covering up for years, now became common knowledge. The interviews she did give amounted to a recitation of the same trivia she'd been giving the press for years: she carried a small ivory elephant for luck, she liked black lace stockings, she liked the color violet, she liked dime banks, and her favorite days were dark and windy enough to blow trees over. One interviewer complained that, during the four hours allotted for his interview, she only sat still for about eight minutes. And much of what she did say was unprintable. He said that Mabel reminded him of "a dancing mouse; whirling all the time, but without purpose."[6]

The few journalists that could put up with her, and somehow appreciate her incorrigible ways, were usually rewarded with good copy and, sometimes, with friendship. One reporter that she took to her heart, *Photoplay*'s Herb Howe, grew to love Mabel and, over time, grew to understand and even protect her. He knew that Mabel hated interviews. She was much more interested in hearing a life story than in telling one.

At first, Herb was just another writer for Mabel to keep waiting. But, unlike the others, he had both the patience to wait for her, and the willingness to accept her for who she was. When Mabel and Herb went out to lunch, she ordered nine martinis and a baked Alaska. Herb didn't print a word of it.[7] Mabel took notice. They developed a teasing rapport that blossomed into friendship. Herb, a heavily cloaked gay man in Hollywood, discovered that the peripatetic movie star had a deeply empathetic nature. "She had an intuition about people," he said, "even a clairvoyance. If Mabel could sense it, that was all that she needed to know."[8]

She began sending him books to read and they even attended Mass together. Soon Herb was one of Mabel's select group of 24-hour-a-day lifelines and protectors.[9]

One memorable night, they sat for hours in the back booth of a dimly lit Hollywood restaurant and Mabel told him her life story. Her *real* life story. It was a tale that he would never repeat. Then she invited him into her home. And, in a moment of profound vulnerability, she took out one of her diaries. Without speaking, she handed it to Herb. He wanted to say something, but he was too moved to speak. He slowly began thumbing through the pages. And as he read through the night, the tears came. He read poems of sadness and poems of joy. He read about Mack. He read about her failings and her fears. As Herb described it, he read "the beauty of her inner self, and the things that would never be revealed."[10] Mabel never made him promise to keep secret the things he read that night. She didn't have to. He truly loved her.

As with many of her closest friends, Herb developed an intense loyalty to Mabel. And, there were many things throughout Mabel's life that—for better or worse—were never repeated or reported. But, despite her vivacious manner, there was nothing particularly salacious about her private life. Mabel was raised in a strict Roman Catholic home and, as a young woman, was expected to maintain her chastity. In fact, somewhere under Mabel's reckless manner was a Puritan morality that would never leave her. As Adela Rogers St. Johns would describe her, "She was unusually pure."[11] Writer Harry Carr once remembered seeing Mabel dining at the Alexandria Hotel. When a famous actress, recently named in a divorce action, came over to her table to say hello, Mabel went on the attack. "Don't talk to me! I may not be a Sunday school character but I've never broken up a home! I leave married men alone!"[12]

When she first became ill, she considered herself to be pledged to Mack, at least as pledged as he would allow. Now unattached, Mabel may have found it uncomfortable to bring tuberculosis into a relationship. Often interfering with a woman's monthly cycle, tuberculosis can render a women effectively barren, and this may have entered into her thinking as well.[13] She may have concluded that, without the possibility of children, a husband was not worth the effort. Either way, Mabel's romantic life was set aside, at least for now. Her relationship with Mack was over, and she was in no hurry to find a new one.

Mack was sure that with all his concessions, he'd finally made amends. He called Mabel. "Is it all right? It's all right between you and me?" "I didn't say that," she replied. "Let's discuss the picture."[14] The picture would change Hollywood history. And it was a Mabel Normand production.

For the first time, Mabel began to realize that her life could be a short one, and she became fatalistic in her thinking, "I just live from day to day," she told a reporter. "What's the use of making plans to go places or marry people?"[15] By now, her excessive drinking was well documented, and rumors of cocaine use (as prescribed by her doctor for the treatment of tuberculosis) were accepted as fact. The Harrison Narcotics Tax Act of 1914 was a first response to the growing problem of cocaine addiction in America. Technically designed to tax and regulate the importation, distribution and production of opiates and coca products, the courts interpreted it as a distribution policy that was confined to a physician's consent.[16]

When filming on *Mickey*, originally called *Mountain Bred*, commenced in August, there were immediate problems with director James Young. Mabel found him impossible to work with, and fired him after a month. He was replaced by J. Farrell MacDonald—who lasted barely a week.[17] In fact, the only director that Mabel wanted was the only one that Mack disapproved of. His name was F. Richard Jones. Jones was only 22 years old, slender, with thinning hair, dark eyes and a mustache. He started his career in the Keystone film lab before working his way up to writer and sometime director. He wasn't respected or well-known but he had two things that Mack didn't have: compassion and understanding. Mabel needed both in good measure. Predictably, when Mack declared Jones unsuitable, Mabel announced that he was her favorite director and hired him on the spot.[18]

Never romantically involved, the two became devoted friends, and were often seen walking hand in hand. Jones was willing to work around Mabel's bouts of illness, and he wanted, or at least asked for, her input on everything. As Blanche Sweet recalled, he "granted her the license of a fairy princess."[19] He also had a unique approach to directing: "I try to draw out the individual personalities of the players. And, for this reason I never act out any of the play for them."[20] Mabel loved the creative freedom, and for the rest of her life, Jones would remain her most frequent director. As Mabel remembered the *Mickey* shoot, "Dick and I threw away all the earlier scripts, and started with enough to fill just one sheet of paper; making it up as we went along."[21]

With the authority to pick her own cast, Mabel chose George Nichols to play her father and Minnie Devereaux to play his Indian housekeeper. Wheeler Oakman was chosen as the handsome love interest. Minta Durfee played her scheming cousin, and Lew Cody appeared as a conniving rogue.

Cody was born Louis Joseph Cote in Waterville, Maine, on February 22, 1885. He was a medical student at McGill Medical College in Montreal until an early success in the school's annual play steered him toward the stage. He left for New York where he studied drama and began appearing in local productions. While touring the West Coast in a road company, he was spotted by Thomas Ince, who put him in the movies. He found his niche playing slick villains and desolate souls.[22] In person, he was an extroverted raconteur and well-known partier. A handsome six-footer with black-gray hair, a debonair mustache and a twinkle in his eyes, he was called "The Butterfly Man" for his colorful wardrobe. A Staten Island boy himself, Lew would forever claim that he remembered Mabel as a child scampering along the beaches near her home. On the *Mickey* set, Mabel and Lew made each other laugh and discovered a shared love of great books. They formed an immediate friendship. Even so, the cast and crew didn't see the relationship going anywhere. As one crew member put it, "They seemed too good as friends to fall in love."[23]

Once started, the *Mickey* shoot was repeatedly suspended. Sometimes it was due to bad weather. Other times it was Mabel's injuries; she was bitten by a dog and by a squirrel. But most often it was by Mabel's activism on behalf of America's burgeoning peace movement. The war in Europe had been raging since 1914, and Mabel was determined to keep America out of it. On October 30, 1916, she was invited to the Panama-California Exposition in San Diego. The exposition—open from March 9, 1915, until January 1, 1917—was meant to celebrate the opening of the Panama Canal and promote San Diego as the United States' southernmost port of call for ships traveling west via the Canal.[24]

Mabel agreed to appear but used the event to organize and lead a march for peace around the grounds of the exposition. What made Mabel's vision unique is that the march was primarily designed to attract children. Mabel believed that children could and should be educated about the destructive powers of war. At the march's conclusion, Mabel and the children dug a "grave" in Montezuma Gardens, burying a rifle, a sword and a pistol. On top of the plot they planted an olive tree as a symbol of peace. Mabel and other speakers urged the young marchers to never forget the awful cost of human warfare and to stand for universal peace as they grew into adulthood.[25]

Gathering momentum, Mabel was invited to organize another march, now referred to as a "Peace Army," at the Arizona State Fair on November 14. The day of her march was designated as Mabel Normand Peace Day. Joined by Arizona Governor George Hunt and two veterans of the American Civil War, Mabel again buried the "weapons of war" and planted another olive tree. Her remarks on that day were preserved. They were, in part:

Dear boys and girls, parents, and educators of Arizona:
I am very proud and happy because I have been asked to tell you about our Peace Army Plan, and what you can do to help it along. There are many acres in Arizona which, not long ago, were barren and desolate. There are many acres in Europe which, little more than two years ago, were productive and beautiful. While Arizonans have been making productive and beautiful the barren lands of Arizona, Europeans have been making barren and desolate the productive lands in Europe.

Mabel greets a young fan on the set of *Mickey* (Marilyn Slater/"Looking for Mabel").

> During this dreadful war, millions of boys and girls have lost their fathers and their homes. I do not believe that this war would have come if the grown people of Europe had been taught, when they were boys and girls, that God has put us here to conquer the earth, and not to conquer men; to create, and not to destroy beautiful and useful things; to love each other, and not to hate each other; to save human life, and not to slay human life.[26]

In *Mickey*, Mabel was turning in the best performance of her career, and she knew it. She plays the title character, an orphan being raised in the rustic backwoods by Joe Meadows, her dead father's mining partner. Herbert Thornhill, a wealthy young mine owner from New York, meets tomboy Mickey, first in her town, and then at her cabin, while surveying his own mine holdings. But his real introduction to Mickey comes that afternoon while peering through a theodolite focused on a rocky bluff. There he spots an unclothed Mickey doing an unaffected dance of joy, before high-diving into a clear mountain lake. (Mabel did the scene nude or with a very convincing body stocking. She performs it without a hint of embarrassment.) Herbert resolves to have Mickey for his own.

Joe wants to provide Mickey with some feminine role models and writes to Mickey's only relative, a snooty Mrs. Drake living in Long Island to ask if she would consider taking Mickey in. Believing Mickey to be the heir to a valuable mine, Mrs. Drake eagerly agrees, and Joe drops Mickey off to live at the Drake estate. When Mrs. Drake finds out that Mickey's mine is worthless, she puts her to work as an unpaid servant. In the meantime, Herbert returns to Mickey's cabin to proclaim his love for her. But he finds her gone, and he returns to New York alone.

Elsie, Mrs. Drake's spoiled daughter, has been pursuing Herbert herself and finally gets him to propose. When Herbert arrives at a party given by Mrs. Drake, he is shocked to find Mickey there. They quickly renew their friendship, and he later tells his best friend and business partner Tom that he regrets his proposal to Elsie.

Mickey's mine strikes it rich while, at the same time, Tom informs Herbert that *his* mine has gone bust. Naturally, when Elsie learns of Herbert's poverty, she breaks their engagement. Relieved, Herbert gets a tip on a "sure thing" at the horse track and bets the last of his money in a plan to restore his wealth and marry Mickey. When Mickey learns that the race has been fixed against him, she dons the rider's silks herself and tries to win the race. She is thrown at the last minute and loses the contest. Regardless, Herbert and Mickey marry. They are cheered by the news that Tom had invented the story of the mine's failure in order to help his friend get out of his engagement to Elsie. Leaving for their honeymoon, the couple wave from the back observation car of their train, as a forlorn Elsie and Mrs. Drake look on.

In April 1917, after eight months of starts and stops, *Mickey* was in the can, but the problems kept coming. Claiming that Mack owed him $16,000 from a previous project, F. Richard Jones kidnapped the final two reels of the film, placed them in an Arizona safe deposit box and demanded his money. Mack threatened to send a couple of detectives to find Jones and reclaim the film, but that was a bluff and Jones knew it. To keep Mabel happy, Sennett had to keep Jones happy. Jones got his money, and Mack got his film.[27]

Convinced that *Mickey* would be a huge hit, Mack began a lavish advertising campaign:

> Coming!! She is coming! The lass you'll never forget
> Say it's a masterpiece,
> Interweaving humor and pathos,
> Love, and adventure
> She is Cinderella with a kick!
> She is doing thrilling acrobatics
> She is all girl, All mischief, All lovable
> M-I-C-K-E-Y
> Starring Mabel Normand
> The girl of one million modes and expressions[28]

The finished film was an artistic success, but Mabel's attention was already somewhere else. On April 2, 1917, President Woodrow Wilson asked a joint session of Congress for a declaration of war against the Central Powers in Europe. With America's entry into the Great War, young men were sent to France to fight in the trenches, Mabel's brother Claude among them. Mabel saw no conflict with her previous ardent pacifism and wholeheartedly supported the military. Her donations of cigarettes became so consistent that she put in an order with a tobacconist to send regular parcels overseas. She made endless appeals to sell Liberty Bonds and responded to every soldier's letter that she could. She was known for her love of chocolate cake and even tried to send chocolate upon request. On October 22, Mabel made a whirlwind speaking tour of eight New York City theaters on behalf of the Liberty Loan Drive. And for the rest of the War, in private gestures, and on public platforms, Mabel extended her compassion and proclaimed her patriotism at every opportunity.

Meanwhile, Triangle was coming apart. The weight of excessive costs, accumulated debts and overlapping rights and obligations spelled its demise, at least in its current form.[29] Desperate to remain financially viable, Mack was forced to sign over both his share of *Mickey*'s potential profits, and his rights to the name Keystone, to free himself from Triangle. But Sennett's departure would only complicate things for the troubled company. *Mickey*'s release date would be held up indefinitely. When Kessel and Baumann finally saw it, they hated it. They saw no room in the marketplace for a feature film starring a single comedienne. Mary Pickford's first project for 1916, *Hulda from Holland*, was a flop, her follow-up *Less Than the Dust* a complete disaster.[30]

Besides, war fever was sweeping the nation. Patriotic films like *Pearl of the Army* and *The Sinking of the Submarine* were the movies of the moment. The film executives who actually saw *Mickey* viewed it as a quaint oddity. Mabel, deeply hurt by the rejection of *Mickey*, blamed Mack for not promoting it. But Mack was not to blame. He travelled to New York and arranged special screenings for everyone in town. Nobody would touch it. Then his New York agent Arthur Graham sent him word that Mabel was about to sign with Sam Goldwyn. Mack went into a panic and sent Arthur a telegram to give to Mabel, urging her to wait. But when Graham cornered her with Mack's telegram, all hell broke loose.

Graham's colleague replied by telegram:

Client absolutely unmanageable and unalterable she refused absolutely to have anything to do with me or yourself in connection with any business proposition. Moreover, she is determined to go through with the contract the terms of which Graham has telegraphed you under all circumstances and without any further delay. There is no way that Graham can show her your telegram as suggested because of his pledge not to communicate with you nor anyone else in connection with her business affairs.[31]

Mabel signed with Goldwyn. *Mickey* was put high on a shelf and forgotten. The Mabel Normand Feature Film Company was no more. But all was not lost. As Adela Rogers St. Johns put it, "Where Mabel was concerned, I believed in miracles."[32] And a miracle is exactly what happened.

Sam Goldwyn convinced Mabel to sign with him (Marc Wanamaker/Bison Archives).

15

Goldwyn Girl

> *When Sam learned that Mabel was free, he became*
> *a stark-raving, crazed, insane, lunatic, madman!*
> —Blanche Sweet[1]
>
> *I was a very valuable young lady.*
> —Mabel[2]

Samuel Goldwyn was born Shmuel Gelbfitz in Warsaw, Poland. He always evidenced a determined desire to succeed. As a teen, he crossed his homeland on foot and found his way to Birmingham, England, where he took the name Samuel Goldfish. In 1898 he immigrated to Nova Scotia, Canada, and then traveled south to New York. Landing a job at the Albano Glove Company, he quickly became their most gifted salesman.

In 1913, after seeing his first motion picture, Sam was inspired. With his brother-in-law Jesse Lasky he helped form the Jesse L. Lasky Feature Play Company in New York City.[3] They obtained the rights to the successful stage play *The Squaw Man* and set out for the West Coast. It became the first feature-length film shot in Hollywood. After a merger with Famous Players, they became Famous Players–Lasky and found even greater success. Bald, bespectacled, pushy and often rude, Sam proved impossible to get along with, and was forced out of the company on September 14, 1916.[4]

Determined to stay in the movie business, he set his sights on an actress recently voted the "world's favorite movie star," Mabel Normand. When rumors began of a possible break with Sennett, Sam arrived at Mabel's proverbial doorstep with lots of offers and lots of promises. Mabel's initial unwillingness to pay him any mind seemed to fuel his pursuit.

Resolved to win both her heart and her signature on a contract, he sent her $11,000 diamond earrings from Cartier's.[5] He promised to limit her output to no more than four pictures a year and guaranteed her light comedy and dramatic roles. And he promised that filming would exclusively be in Fort Lee or New York. Mabel signed with Goldwyn. All that was left was to wire Mack. She said, in part:

> Start work Sept. 1. Company said I didn't look well. Must rest and go away. So I won't be able to peep at you ever again. Wanted you to know I signed although you never wire.
> M
> July 24, 1917
> 2:10 am[6]

Sam told Mabel to take a Florida vacation. Mabel's idea of resting turned out to be water skiing around Long Island. Her neighbor, future columnist Hedda Hopper, recalled, "In the spring and summer of 1917, Mabel Normand hid out in Great Neck, Long Island. She rode a surfboard attached to a high-powered boat around Long Island Sound."[7] Mabel wore a long sweater as she skied past, leaving Hopper to wonder if she was wearing anything underneath.

With Mabel's signed contract in hand, Sam confidently approached brothers Edgar and Archibald Selwyn. As part of the merger with the brothers'

Goldwyn (left), Mabel and Chaplin (Marc Wanamaker/Bison Archives).

All Star Feature Films Corporation, the names Selwyn and Goldfish were combined, and Goldwyn Pictures was born. To expand the perception of his power, Sam legally changed his name to Goldwyn, a name he would use for the rest of his life.

In a matter of days, Goldwyn had called reporters to make it official. "Everything that this big new organization can do for a star of Miss Normand's magnitude will be done at once," he gushed.[8] Mack was crushed. Mabel had left her own studio to become a paid employee of Sam Goldwyn. Sitting on a locker room bench in his beloved Los Angeles Athletic Club, a sweaty towel hung over his shoulders, Mack held his head in his hands. How had it all come to this? All that was left to do was for Mack to make one more midnight phone call.

"Come home," Mack pleaded.

"Why?"

"I need you!"

"You *had* me." Mabel hung up.[9]

Unable to ignore Sam's generosity and his many kindnesses, Mabel became his half-hearted companion at a few Hollywood gatherings, always making sure that there was no time for a private rendezvous afterward. It was a forced and, at times, a cruel relationship that never should have begun at all. Among her friends, Mabel would perform devilish impersonations of Sam, and once announced that she had gone to St. Patrick's Cathedral to pray that he would get a nose job. But Sam continued to believe that she had feelings for him.[10]

Mabel recognized that Sam would grant her anything, and she was ready and willing to take full advantage of the situation. But even Sam realized that Mabel's "rest" was lasting for months. Goldwyn's biggest star had yet to set foot on a Goldwyn lot, and she was collecting $2500 a week. The studio politely asked her to report for work. Mabel ignored them. When more forceful entreaties arrived, their star became evasive, even off-handedly remarking that she might choose to work for someone else. Sam saw himself as a master negotiator. But with Mabel Normand, he was completely out of his league. Finally, in an action that would set the tone for their entire relationship, Sam sought an injunction against her, preventing her from working anywhere else:

> Miss Normand entered into a contract on September 16, 1916, with Samuel Goldwyn. She was engaged to star in motion pictures under his management for two years at a weekly salary of $2500. Under this contract she was to act exclusively for Mr. Goldwyn. Miss Normand was scheduled to begin working for Goldwyn in its studio May 1 and arrived in New York soon after that date, manifesting

an immediate intention of not entering upon contract. Her response to notification as the date beginning work proved to be evasive. Goldwyn came into possession of information that Miss Normand planned to work elsewhere and for other individuals.

It is alleged in the Goldwyn complaint that Miss Normand, in violating her contract in this or any other similar matter, will inflict upon Goldwyn a monetary loss of $500,000, and that investments already have been made by the company in costly literary materials fitted to the personality of his particular star and not at all suited to the personality and capacities of any other star because of Miss Normand's specialized type of work on the screen.[11]

Mabel finally showed up on the set for her first Goldwyn film, *Dodging a Million*. But as Sam soon learned, getting her on the set and getting her to act were two entirely different things. Searches on the lot for Mabel became commonplace. The crew once found her behind some scenery rolling her own Bull Durham cigarettes. Another time, Sam located Mabel in her dressing room, out of makeup and costume, calmly writing letters. When he asked her for an explanation she said, "I'm sorry. But I just can't be funny so early in the morning."[12] Her excuses for being late in the morning became legendary. She once claimed to have stopped to pick up a group of soldiers in her limousine to keep them from being AWOL at Camp Merritt. "There's a war on!" Mabel explained. "I only did my patriotic duty. Whose side are you on anyway?"[13]

Mack soon heard the gossip and couldn't help but be amused. When he encountered Sam at a Hollywood function, he couldn't resist twisting the knife: "Say, Sam, she's a pretty expensive luxury, isn't she?" When Sam sternly insisted that all was well, Mack just snick-

Mabel in *Dodging a Million* (1918), her first Goldwyn film (Marilyn Slater/"Looking for Mabel").

ered and walked away.[14] Sam couldn't bear to reprimand Mabel himself, so he turned the matter over to studio vice-president Abe Lehr. A middle-aged man with deepset eyes and thinning hair, Lehr was in charge of the day-to-day operations at the studio. He sat and talked to Mabel for hours, explaining how vital it was that she be on set and on time. He begged her to sleep at night and stop her carousing. She promised to do better. And sometimes she would keep her promise for several hours, or even an entire day. But being Mabel Normand's babysitter was completely exasperating. Their objectives were conflicting and irreconcilable. For Abe, dealing with Mabel was business. For Mabel, dealing with Abe was sport. She deliberately misspelled his name: Mr. Lerr, Mr. Leer, etc.[15] One morning she brought him cookies. Another morning she hit him on the chin.

Lehr had spies all over town that would report where Mabel was the night before. He even put private detectives on her trail. But Mabel soon realized she was being followed.[16] She finally discovered a way to get completely away from Abe and from everyone else: She went camping. In the back of one of her luxury automobiles she kept a tent, an Army cot, an oil stove and dishes.[17] Then she sent him an inscribed photo:

> To Abe, my favorite:
> Roses are red, violets are blue,
> When I'm late, I think of you.
>   Love and Kisses,
>   Mabel[18]

When Abe's constant nagging became too much for her, she snuck into his office, sprayed his coat with cheap perfume and smeared lipstick on it. Then she had a friend call Mrs. Lehr and tell her that Abe had been spotted coming out of a popular Manhattan whorehouse. It took Abe weeks to get his marriage back.[19]

Finally Sam had no choice but to deal with her himself. He sent studio janitor Herbert Terrell to Mabel's dressing room to fetch her. Mabel immediately sent Herb back to fetch *him*. Growing angry, Sam called the front gate and announced that Mabel could not leave the lot until she came to see him. When Mabel heard about it, she called her chauffeur and said that she was leaving the lot at once. Terrell was dispatched again to Mabel's dressing room to bring her to Sam. The huffy star sat with her arms crossed and refused to budge from her chair. Terrell, seeing his own quitting time held up indefinitely, picked Mabel up, chair and all, carried her across the lot, and deposited her in front of Sam, Mabel's grim expression never changing.[20]

But Goldwyn was powerless and Mabel knew it. He had an ever-growing stable of stars that included John Barrymore, Jack Pickford, Will

Rogers, Tom Moore, Pauline Frederick, Mae Marsh and Lou Tellegen. But Mabel's pictures cost less and made more money than anyone else's.[21]

Dodging a Million revealed the glamorous vision that Sam had in mind for her. For her role as a saleswoman in an upscale Fifth Avenue dress shop, Sam hired the best fashion designers to provide Mabel with a stunning array of costumes. Released on January 28, 1918, the film proved to be an immediate hit. Despite a promise to allow Mabel time to rest between pictures, Sam announced to the press that a new Mabel Normand film would be released as soon as possible.

Coming out only three months later, *The Floor Below* was a rushed production, and it showed. As a comedy-suspense, the film deserves credit for taking Mabel in a new direction. As Patsy O'Rourke, a newspaper copy girl, Mabel angers her co-workers with her endless pranks. When she's on the verge of being fired, her editor gives her one more chance: find the perpetrators of a string of local robberies. By movie's end, she has solved the mystery, kept her job and been proposed to by the man of her dreams. While critics found little to recommend the film other than Mabel's charm, that was good enough for her fans, and the film was a success.

Mabel's third film for Goldwyn, *Joan of Plattsburg*, was one of her most interesting. As the title character, Mabel is an orphan girl, living in an asylum during World War I. While reading a book on Joan of Arc, she accidentally overhears German spies plot to capture an important invention from the nearby Plattsburg Army training camp. Believing it to be the voice of God, she warns the camp and, after a series of misadventures, helps capture the spies. The shoot was largely uneventful until a goose bit Mabel on her backside. Whacking the goose unconscious, she dragged it by the neck into Abe Lehr's office. "There's your damn, man-eating goose!" she screamed. "If he bites me on the ass again, I'll wring his damn neck!"[22]

At the film's release, Mabel learned that her fans included the First Family. When Mabel arrived at a special screening for charity, she was stunned to see First Lady Edith Wilson sitting in a private box. After the film was screened, Mrs. Wilson sent for Mabel. When the star arrived, Mrs. Wilson extended her hands and exclaimed, "I have always loved you in motion pictures. You have whiled away many a dull hour for me, and I now love the real Mabel Normand even more."[23] Hoarse from nervousness, Mabel could only manage a few words of thanks. She proudly expressed her thanks and acknowledged that she had much to live up to. But in private, Mabel's reaction was quite different. She was furious. She refused the hotel room she was provided with and demanded a suite with a parlor, bedroom and bath. She insisted that she needed the upgraded amenities because Mae

Marsh received them when she was in town. Mabel got what she wanted and went to sleep.²⁴

Mabel continued to spend her money lavishly. She adorned herself in the finest apparel that money could buy. She wore custom gowns by her favorite dress designer, Madame Frances. On one New York trip she spent $16,000 on clothes in one day.²⁵ And she was always receiving jewelry as gifts, particularly from suitors or would-be suitors. At one point her jewelry was valued at $250,000.²⁶ Yet Mabel got just as much pleasure from the peanut roaster in her dressing room.

It is perhaps not surprising that with vast amounts of money rolling in, and vast amounts of money rolling out, Mabel's financial life was spinning completely out of control. Mabel's generosity was undisciplined, unwavering and oftentimes random. It extended to people that she met in the course of her day. She once tipped a chef $100 for a piece of apple pie.²⁷ As Sam Goldwyn observed, "Gifts came from her as unprovoked as manna!"²⁸ When she

Mabel spent lavishly on the finest fashions of the day (Marc Wanamaker/Bison Archives).

Mabel gave her accountant fits with her extraordinary generosity to friends and to virtual strangers. Her checkbook was always handy (Marc Wanamaker/Bison Archives).

learned of a young girl, suffering from tuberculosis, she immediately went to the child's bedside and played with her for hours. When she left, she put a folded-up paper into the girl's hand. The girl's parents discovered it to be a check for $1000.[29] She thoughtfully kept journals listing the birthdays and anniversaries of those close to her, and of those she may have met only once.

In truth, Mabel had more money than she knew what to do with. While Sam was contractually obligated to pay for half of Mabel's wardrobe, he soon wondered why he had never received a bill. Mabel explained that she didn't feel right charging him anything.[30] To his credit, Sam convinced her to let him and Lehr invest half of her pay in bonds and California real estate.[31] When Lehr traced a studio surplus to 11 of Mabel's uncashed checks, for four thousand dollars each, he confronted her. "You work me so hard I can't get to the bank," she claimed. "I'll fix it up next week, you old pumpkin head."[32]

In her next picture *The Venus Model*, Mabel portrayed a bathing suit model posing in a storefront window. The store owner's son is in love with Mabel and breaks off his engagement with a young woman to be with her. The spurned fiancée sues him for breach of promise. Mabel saves the day by getting his former fiancée a job in the same window. When the former fiancée attracts the attention of a desirable man, she drops her legal action and Mabel gets her man. One writer saw the film as an opportunity for Mabel to wear an "extraordinary bathing dress."[33]

In her fifth film for Goldwyn, *Back to the Woods*, Mabel is a wealthy heiress who travels out west to meet a real man. As fate would have it, the man she meets is an eastern novelist, pretending to be from the backwoods to get material for his next book. After false heroics and misunderstandings on both sides, the couple cast off their pretenses and fall in love.

While Mabel was working for Sam, Mack was working for Mabel. At least, that's how he explained it. But first he needed to break free from Triangle. He moaned for months about how valuable the Keystone label was and how he was loath to part with it. Then he sold all rights to the brand and re-organized as Mack Sennett Comedies Corporation, with a deal to distribute films through Paramount.

He was still determined to get *Mickey* seen and released. No longer a Triangle insider, Mack used the only means available to him to hasten the film's release: publicity. He began *The Mack Sennett Weekly* as an industry publication. It featured a photo of Mabel on the cover of *every* issue.[34] It heaped lavish praise on *Mickey*, assuring readers that it was the movie of the decade. His unflagging efforts to publicize the film, and Triangle's ongoing refusal to release it, produced an unintended impression in the minds of the public. *Mickey* was seen as a special event, worthy of an unprecedented advertising campaign before its release. At a time when the interval between a movie's completion and a movie's release could be as little as two months, Mack's protracted publicity campaign aroused intense curiosity. *Mickey* must be something special.

Then a manager of a tiny theater in Bayside, Long Island, found himself out of product. He drove to Baumann and Kessel's film exchange to get another movie. When he arrived he found nothing. The manager insisted that he couldn't leave empty-handed. Well, there was one film back in storage, he was told. It was a Mabel Normand movie called *Mickey*, but it wasn't any good. Exploding with relief, the manager quietly said that he would be glad to take the film. That was the moment the Earth moved. Hollywood would never be the same.

16
Mickey

Mickey is the greatest picture ever seen!
—*The Journal & Republican*[1]

Mickey has everything imaginable!
—*Movie Picture World*[2]

Next to the President, there is no better character than Mickey!—*The Tattler*[3]

By three o'clock, Sunday afternoon, August 11, 1918, the throngs of customers stood two deep in a line that stretched for three blocks. In self-defense, the theater ran the film again and again throughout the night. But the throngs were still coming, and the police had to be called to maintain order.[4] *Mickey* had been released.

The Mishler Theatre in Altoona, Pennsylvania, showed a $3000 profit in the first three days. The Merrill Theatre in Milwaukee reported earnings of $5400 in a single week.[5] The movie industry was stunned. A feature-length comedy starring a single comedienne? Never been done. A trouble-making tomboy instead of a damsel in distress? It won't work. Completely unprepared, Triangle ground out print after print of *Mickey*, and still could not keep up with the demand. It effortlessly surpassed the box office returns of Griffith's *Birth of a Nation*, a feat that no one had thought possible.

Mickey had something for everyone. Children loved the funny animals. Men, as always, loved every inch of Mabel. But, for women, it struck an especially deep chord. This was a new kind of Cinderella. The moviemakers had it wrong. By 1918, women were tired of being portrayed as helpless virgins, exotic vamps and mindless jazz babies. There was a war on. They could not reconcile the feel-good, flag-waving films of the moment with the devastating landscape of orphans, and boys coming home without arms or legs. The world was a hard place. They gloried in this spunky, All-American girl

16. Mickey 99

Initially written off as a disaster, when *Mickey* was released it became a box office juggernaut and took Mabel's career to new heights (Marc Wanamaker/Bison Archives).

who overcomes all and sails away with the handsome guy. Never had a movie gotten it so right.

Critical response for *Mickey* was almost breathless. *Movie Picture World* wrote, "*Mickey* is a digest of the science of producing motion pictures. It has everything imaginable that might be conceived by the most inventive producer past or present!"[6] *The Tattler* exclaimed, "For a sweeping, country-wide popularity among old and young, rich and poor, in city and country, nothing in years has equaled *Mickey*! No creation in drama, fiction, screen, or song has caught the public fancy and been taken to the public heart as *Mickey* has. She will go down in popular history!"[7] Oddly enough, for a good Catholic girl like Mabel, her only critics came from her own church: "We find in it a place where Mabel Normand appears entirely nude. It will do untold harm to the souls of Catholic people and especially to the souls of our children."[8]

Mack remembered, "I felt like a justified wizard! I reminded everybody within earshot that Mabel Normand was the greatest comedienne in the world. There were days when I warmed up so much enthusiasm about Mabel in *Mickey* that I completely forgot that she was not under contract to me, either to make pictures or to get married!"[9]

Mack called Goldwyn Studios, and demanded to be connected to Mabel's dressing room. "I've got news!" he shouted. "*Mickey* is a real hit. A smash! You don't know how hard I've worked to get that picture shown!"

There was a pause. "Good for you, Nappy," Mabel said quietly, "I'm awfully glad for your sake."

"Mabel, listen, please. Don't hang up. Don't you see? That is the kind of picture for you. We've got it. You and me. I know what to do now, how to treat you, what kind of stories to give you!"

"I'm due on the set," Mabel said. She ended the call.[10]

The real impact of *Mickey* was not known until it completed its run. The airwaves were appropriated for the exclusive use of the military, and thousands of American families made going to the theater to see *Mickey* again a weekly treat. In a scene repeated across America, they arrived at their neighborhood theaters, then left disappointed and angry. For exhibitors, it was a disaster. It was the height of the flu epidemic of 1918, and any type of public gathering was sparsely attended. Roller rinks, amusement parks, restaurants, vaudeville houses and even churches reported a sharp downturn in attendance. America was not flocking to see movies. They were flocking to see *Mickey*. Theater owners begged Triangle to send them prints of the film.

Hollywood was blindsided by this unprecedented reaction to a movie. Triangle had no choice but to release *Mickey* again. It was shown throughout 1919, withdrawn from release, released again in 1920 and then again in 1921. *Mickey* completed an astounding four-year run in 1922. In an era when movie tickets were 15 cents, the film generated 18 million dollars (an estimated income value of 12 billion dollars today).[11] Never again would Hollywood ignore the power of repeat business.

Photoplay, August 1918 (Marilyn Slater/"Looking for Mabel").

The behemoth box office was only part of the story. When Mack's tune "Mickey" was released, it sold 500,000 copies in the first four days.[12] A *Mickey* craze hit the nation like a tidal wave. Merchants scrambled to fill the demand. Soon there were *Mickey* hats and *Mickey* dresses. There were *Mickey* lantern slides, shirts, socks, phonograph records, flowers, etc., etc. Store windows soon had all *Mickey* displays.[13] It marked the first time that Fifth Avenue devoted window space to publicize a movie.[14] Hollywood had accidentally stumbled onto the treasure trove of movie merchandising. It was a lesson they would never forget.

The phenomenon that was *Mickey* would make neither Mack nor Mabel the multi-millionaires that—by any fair measure—they deserved to be. Mabel never got a cent beyond her salary. Yet they both found something better than gold. A surprised Mack Sennett found that the world held reverence for him and his work. Writers gave him the title that would never leave him: the King of Comedy. For the rest of his life, as he struggled with finances, health, age and loneliness, he always had that banner above his head. He was not just a comedy producer. To America, and the world, he was the king.

For Mabel, the superstardom she found with *Mickey* reflected her country's collective longing and collective fear. President Wilson boldly strode the world stage with strange new words like internationalism and the League of Nations. Paranoia swept the nation with the Red Scare of 1918, as neighbor reported neighbor for real or imagined sedition. Into this turbulent time came *Mickey*. The quaint film of 1916 became the touchstone experience of 1918. And it took Mabel Normand to the heights of her career. In the fall and winter of 1918 she was the biggest star in the world, featured in the biggest movie in the world. The girl from Staten Island had made it to the pinnacle of show business and millions of working class Americans loved her for it.

But Americans had a very short memory.

17

Mabelescent

People enjoy laughter, but they're not grateful for it. They forget. —Mabel[1]

Mabel burst into Sam's office. *Mickey* was a box office smash and Mabel wanted her due, one way or another.

"I want $5000 a week, *right now!*"

"We have a contract!"

"Change it!"

"I'm not going to change it!"

"Well, I'm not going to work for slave wages!"

She sailed out of his office and slammed the door so hard his furniture rattled. Sam sat with his head in his hands. He knew he wouldn't see his "employee" again for weeks.[2]

On the eleventh hour, of the eleventh day, of the eleventh month of 1918, an armistice was signed between the Allies and Germany at Compiegne, France. Hostilities ceased on the Western Front. When Mabel learned that her brother Claude was coming home, she determined to leave the lot immediately and head back east to see him. Sam caught her just in time. He quickly promised to pay Claude's train fare to Hollywood, if she would just stay and shoot her scenes.[3]

The era of the Great War ended for America, and a new era was about to begin. After the national trauma of World War I, America threw itself a decade-long party that was ultimately known as the Roaring Twenties and the Jazz Age. New Orleans–based creole musicians improvised a subculture of sound that provided a backdrop for the age. Mabel immediately took to jazz, noting, "Some people hate jazz. They are the same people who can't dance."[4] Celebrating victory, celebrating peace, and then celebrating anything at hand; a general silliness would come to permeate the age. Mabel would fit right in. Jazz replaced ragtime, speakeasies replaced saloons, and the Flapper replaced the Gibson Girl.

It wasn't just the youth that were buoyed by the times. Working men with family responsibilities were suddenly willing to extend themselves financially in ways that had heretofore been unheard of. "Buy now and pay later" became a staple of consumerism. Cars, radios and appliances were suddenly affordable. A form of affluence could be had on the installment plan, and the stock market kept rising with no end in sight. It seemed the good times would go on forever.

By now, Mabel was nothing short of an American icon, and she knew it. After the amazing success of *Mickey*, a new word entered the American lexicon: "*Mabelescent* (mey-buhl-es-unt) *adjective*. Bubbly, vivacious, sparkling, in the manner of Mabel Normand." Mabel said she was honored to have a word coined just for her. But, as writer Truman Handy pointed out, "It wasn't an honor; it was a necessity."[5] The world was in love with Mabel, or at least their perception of Mabel. As Mary Pickford noted, "Ovations are given to ideas, not to people."[6]

Mabel with Goldwyn director George Loane Tucker. She insisted on control of her film projects (Marc Wanamaker/Bison Archives).

But by the end of 1918, Mabel was not the spirited tomboy that her fans loved. She was neither bubbly, vivacious nor sparkling. She was an overworked 26-year-old. She had pain in her body, trouble in her heart and Goldwyn Studios on her shoulders.

Mabel's life may well have been happier without *Mickey*. It did not bring her riches; it only intensified her spotlight. And she felt an increased pressure to be Mabelescent for her fans. As Mabel's tuberculosis became worse, her lungs would hurt constantly, and it became easy to fall into the trap of self-medicating. Cocaine may have been prescribed by her doctor. It was a potent pain reliever and it also suppressed the cough reflex. Yet there is no direct evidence that Mabel used cocaine. The most that can be said is that her friends thought she did and said so openly.

Anita Loos remembered, "One of the strange manifestations of Mabel's cocaine addiction was a frenzy for writing letters. She would write to anybody; she used to send long chatty accounts about nothing at all to salesgirls whose names she didn't know—addressing them, for examples, to 'Saleslady in Stocking Department.' I destroyed the letters I got from Mabel, perhaps subconsciously, because they were so disturbing."[7] Actress Claire Windsor recalled, "Cocaine was the only real drug I ever saw Mabel use."[8]

Mabel was wrong about cocaine. But so was America. Despite the medical precautions and the legal limitations, cocaine was considered by most Americans to be safe and non-addictive. While therapeutic on a symptomatic level, cocaine's dangerous effects were little understood, and were most often attributed to either the moral or the physical weaknesses of the user, rather than to the impact of the drug itself.

Cocaine was rampant in the silent film industry. Mabel may have first tried cocaine on the Keystone lot. Keystone was the narcotic-dealing capital of Hollywood, with cocaine being the main attraction. The lot dealer was a man known as "The Count." Eddie Sutherland reported: "There was a man in Hollywood. I don't think I should mention his name. Everybody who took drugs in the industry was started by this man. He was one of the quietest, nicest actors I've ever known. I don't think anybody's ever heard of him. He put Mabel on the junk. Also Wallace Reid and Alma Rubens. He was the pusher. Somebody would have a hangover and he'd say, 'I'll fix your hangover,' you know."[9]

Minta Durfee remembered Mabel's glazed eyes and the deepening lines on her face. There were whisperings about certain "sophisticated" parties that featured cocaine in silver bowls. On the set, her close-ups were reserved for her "good" days. Yet in the Hollywood circus, Mabel was just another sideshow. The movie industry was filled with performers fighting their personal demons.

In 1918, the entire world was celebrating "Mabel Normand" and Mabel wasn't going to be left out of the party. Instead of resting her body, she organized her life. She gathered around her a loyal staff that included her chauffeur Thomas Kennedy, her housekeeper Louella Bender, her secretary Betty Coss and her personal maid Mamie Owens. On the set, she hired a boy to call out once every hour to remind her to take her tonic.[10] But, of all her assistants, none was more vital to her life than her private nurse, Julia Brew Benson.

As Julia remembered it, her first impression of Mabel was that of a dark-haired, pigtailed waif with large brown eyes. Mabel's chest was badly burned by mustard plasters, a popular poultice of mustard seed powder used to treat chest congestion. It also stimulated nerve endings and distracted the body away from more painful areas. Julia tended to her wounds and nursed her back to health. Over time, Mabel and Julia became more than employer and employee. They became true companions and shared a friendship that lasted the rest of their lives.[11]

Mabel's scattered attentions left no room for the press. Soon, journalists requesting an interview received the following reply:

> Miss Normand will pretend perfectly that she is glad that you have chosen to seek her out and invade the privacy of her apartment. Miss Normand will act precisely as if she had never been interviewed before, and will blush and simper and beg you to publish her latest photograph. In fact, Miss Normand will not be herself at all, for she knows that you will much prefer to write of her as an animated doll, squeaking opinions that someone else has thought of for her.
> And in return for this interview Miss Normand makes ten stipulations as follows:
> 1. That you do not say she owns gold furniture.
> 2. Nor that she is whirled hither and thither in a tufted limousine.
> 3. Nor that she has a dog.
> 4. That you do not mention the hundreds of letters she receives.
> 5. That you do not say she adores acting in pictures.
> 6. That you omit descriptions of her clothes.
> 7. That you refrain from saying she loves sports and all-outdoors.
> 8. That you do not advertise her tremendous war work.
> 9. That you do not credit her with interest in sociology and world politics.
> 10. That you do not reveal her passion for the works of Edith Wharton, Mrs. Humphrey Ward and Joseph Conrad.
>
> Finally, Miss Normand will be available for 10 minutes.[12]

Naturally, her desire to keep reporters away backfired; her unavailability made her all the more desirable. But, while Mabel needed rest, Sam needed movies and he was determined to get them one way or another. Mabel had good reason to be bitter and, eventually, incensed at Goldwyn. When it came to business, Sam was ready and willing to forget any and all his promises. Instead of three pictures a year, as agreed, Mabel starred in eight feature films in 1918 alone.[13] In the fall of that year, Mabel starred in two films, *Peck's Bad Girl* and *A Perfect 36*. Set in small town, rural America, *Peck's Bad Girl* tells the story of Mabel getting angry at a bank's refusal to pay her father his wages as a night watchman. In revenge, she causes a run on the bank by announcing that it is insolvent. Saved from reform school by a traveling con woman who hires her to model clothing, Mabel uncovers the woman's plot to rob the bank and redeems herself.

For *A Perfect 36*, Mabel finds a suitcase left behind by a traveling corset salesman and decides to take up the job herself. While traveling through a beachside town, she decides to go for a swim, only to have her clothes stolen. When local law enforcement discover that her suitcase was involved in a jewelry heist, a bathing suit–clad Mabel must find her clothes while being pursued by the police. When the heist turns out to be a publicity stunt, Mabel is off the hook. The movie was shot on location at Sea Cliff, New York. One

All of Mabel's films for Goldwyn were box office hits (Marc Wanamaker/Bison Archives).

local newspaper felt compelled to make the following announcement. "Attention! Mabel Normand, she of the svelte figure, dark eyes and engaging smile, is going to appear at the beach at Sea Cliff in a one-piece bathing suit!"[14] Mabel caught a cold during the shoot that soon turned into pneumonia.

In January 1919, Goldwyn reneged on his promise to shoot exclusively on the East Coast, and announced that Mabel's films would henceforth be shot on his new Culver City, California, lot. While Mabel did begin shooting her next film *Sis Hopkins*, her continuing illness forced the shoot to be suspended for months. Like *Peck's Bad Girl*, *Sis Hopkins* recalled the country charm of *Mickey*. When a wealthy con man visits the Hopkins family farm, he sees a pool of oil that Mabel had accidentally spilled on the ground. Believing the land to be oil-rich, he hatches a plan to gain control of the property by marrying Mabel. When his plan fails, he simply tries to buy the seemingly worthless farm from Mabel's father. Realizing what he is up to, Mabel succeeds in significantly jacking up the price. After he buys the farm, he finds the spilled oil can that started the whole thing.

Still staggered by *Mickey's* returns, Goldwyn tried yet another *Mickey* rehash. In *The Pest*, country girl Mabel is invited by the malicious Blanche Fisher to a party in order to amuse her sophisticated friends. Mabel is humiliated, but the family ring on her finger catches the eye of Blanche's father, Judge Fisher. When Mabel uncovers a plot to kill the judge, he finally remembers the ring. He realizes that Mabel is his real daughter, and that she and Blanche had been switched at birth. Mabel is welcomed into a life of luxury while Blanche is banished from the home.

Mabel's spring release *When Doctors Disagree* featured portly actor Walter Hiers as John Turner, the romantic lead. Hiers' casting was a one-time and failed attempt to reinvent the success of the Fatty and Mabel films. In the film, John gets into a fight, believes that he has killed a man, grabs his uncle's doctor's bag and a railroad ticket and boards a train to evade capture. On the train, Mabel, believing that John is a doctor, feigns illness to attract his attention. Intervening, Mabel's father gives her some chewing tobacco as a remedy. When Mabel accidentally swallows it, she gets sick for real. John, expected to do something, prescribes an operation, and a cooperative engineer stops the train at a nearby sanitarium. After a series of mix-ups, John's uncle shows up to reveal that the man John fought with didn't die, thereby saving John from being a "doctor" and Mabel from being a patient.

Mabel's career continued to be on solid ground, and whatever the merits of a particular film, she never lost her audience. Professionally, it was easy for Mabel to feel annoyed with the royal treatment given to Goldwyn actresses like Geraldine Farrar, Madge Kennedy and Pauline Frederick who weren't necessarily box office stars. And she let her irritation show. Each morning Farrar's male secretary would greet Geraldine in song: "Good morning! How are you?" and Geraldine would sweetly sing back, "V-e-e-ry well! Thank you!" This continued day after day until Mabel couldn't take it any more and responded with a screeching song of her own, featuring lyrics that were both rude and obscene.[15]

But Mabel wasn't finished with Geraldine. With the fixed purpose of annoying her, Mabel began haunting Geraldine's sets and quite openly staring at her. Geraldine complained that she couldn't act with Mabel staring at her, and Sam asked Mabel to leave. Mabel refused. Geraldine had a fence built around her set, only to discover Mabel staring at her through a knot hole. After Geraldine had the knot hole plugged up, she was shocked to look up and see Mabel waving at her from the rafters overlooking the stage.[16]

Perhaps inevitably, a professional challenge appeared. Fed up with Mabel's absences, Sam began sending "Mabel" parts to Madge Kennedy. Madge proved to have a knack for comedy and built herself a following,

Mabel with fellow Goldwyn star Madge Kennedy. The smiles for the camera masked an intense rivalry (Marc Wanamaker/Bison Archives).

much to Sam's delight. Enraged, Mabel began sitting in on Madge's daily rushes, providing the executives present with a stream of commentary on all of Madge's faults as a performer. "Hmph!" Mabel spat. "She saw me do that first." Predictably, Madge sat in on Mabel's rushes, loudly proclaiming, "She saw *me* do that first!"[17]

Pauline Frederick also got on Mabel's nerves. Pauline insisted that she needed a violinist on her set. When Pauline got her violinist, Geraldine Farrar claimed that she needed a string quartet on her set. When Geraldine got her string quartet, Mabel demanded a 17-piece jazz band for her set. And when she got her jazz band, she ordered it to happily blast away, drowning out both Pauline's violin and Geraldine's quartet.[18]

In the summer, Mabel continued her string of hits with *Upstairs*. Mabel portrays a dishwasher in a ritzy hotel. She is pursued by wealthy Lemuel Stallings, who wins her affections after disguising himself as a bellboy in order to meet her. Mistaken for a real bellboy, Lemuel is handed a dress to have cleaned; he gives it to Mabel so that they can go dancing. But the dress belongs to heiress Eloise Barrison. Knowing that Eloise is plotting to elope with his chauffeur, her father alerts the house detective to stop them. Because of the dress, Mabel and Lemuel are mistaken for the couple and are chased into a room by the house detective and the chauffeur. In the ensuing fight, Mabel swings from a chandelier and kicks the chauffeur in the jaw, knocking him out. Grateful, Eloise's father gives her a $5000 reward and Mabel accepts Lemuel's proposal of marriage.

In *Jinx*, Mabel plays a laborer in a circus. She is nicknamed "Jinx" by drunken circus owner Bull Hogarth, who blames her for bringing the circus bad luck. When their star performer Alice, a serpentine dancer, leaves over unpaid wages, Mabel tries to take her place, with disastrous results. She flees from Hogarth's wrath to a local farm where she is saved from a beating by farm boy Slicker, who becomes her hero. Mentioning her drawn appearance, *Variety* wrote, "Noticeable were the closeups. Miss Normand should not have tried to stand the test in a kid role."[19]

Despite her illness, Mabel immediately began work on her next film, *Pinto*. Arizona cowgirl Mabel lives with the five ranchers who raised her after her parents died. Their former ranch partner, Pop Audry, is now living in high society in New York City. In another Goldwyn attempt to "*Mickey*" the plot, the ranchers decide that Mabel should be sent to Pop in the hopes that New York can make a lady out of her. Pop's snooty wife objects and moves out of the house in protest. When Mabel discovers that Mrs. Audry is having an affair, she informs Pop, who by now has become a second father to her. Fed up, and eager to wash his hands of high society entirely, Pop

Mabel on the set of *Jinx*, directed by Victor (Paw) Schertzinger, at the Samuel Goldwyn Studio in Culver City, 1919 (Marc Wanamaker/Bison Archives).

turns over his New York holdings to his wife and moves back to Arizona with cowgirl Mabel.

In a report that must have delighted Mabel, Dr. A.G. Hyde, superintendent of the Massillon State Hospital in Ohio, commented on movie choices of the clinically insane. Said the doctor, "The insane have their movie favorites just as other movie fans have." The inmates' favorite star was Mabel Normand.[20]

After *Pinto*, Mabel finally took an extended break, not releasing another film until July. And when she did, it turned out to be one of her most bizarre, *The Slim Princess*. Mabel portrays the princess of Morevana, a land where, as described in the film's advertising, "fat is the fashion." Because of Mabel's embarrassing slimness, she can't find a husband. The law states that she must marry before her rotund younger sister can marry. When her father forces Mabel to wear an inflatable rubber suit under her clothes, comedic distress ensues when the suit springs a leak. Hearing that America has found a cure for slimness, he sends her there, where she meets and falls in love with Alexander Pike. When she is forced to return home, Alexander follows her. Learning that he is wealthy, her father offers him his esteemed, corpulent daughter. But Alexander wants to marry Mabel instead.

Goldwyn fired the director of Mabel's last five films, Victor "Paw" Schertzinger. The director wasted untold hours playing piano with Mabel on the set, and Goldwyn was furious over the cost. Yet the piano breaks were heaven to Mabel and she demanded that Schertzinger be reinstated. Goldwyn refused. In retaliation, Mabel grabbed a perfume atomizer and backed him into a corner squirting the bottle empty over his face, hair and clothing, "Now you beastly tyrant, take that smell home to your wife and see how you like it." Schertzinger stayed.[21]

In her next film of 1920, *What Happened to Rosa?*, Mabel plays a salesgirl told by a fortuneteller that she is the reincarnation of Spanish dancer Rosa Alvaro. Mabel decides to wear a Spanish dance costume to a masquerade party on a yacht also attended by the man she admires, Dr. Maynard Drew. Completely disguised, she flirts with Maynard. But when she realizes that Maynard's flirtations are for the Spanish dancer rather than for her, she takes off her costume and swims to shore. Discovering the abandoned costume, Maynard believes that she has drowned. Desperate to reconnect with Maynard, the salesgirl fakes an injury. Alone inside the doctor's office, she dons the Spanish dance costume. When Maynard comes in, he is delighted to learn that Spanish dancer and real girl are one and the same.

On May 31, 1920, Mabel began work on her last film for Goldwyn, *Head Over Heels*. In the film, New York theatrical agent Adolphe Menjou takes a trip to Europe, where he spots, and then signs, Mabel, a beautiful Italian acrobat, to a performing contract in America. When she arrives in New York, Menjou is shocked by her unkempt offstage appearance. Seeing his disappointment, Mabel performs an acrobatic routine that nearly demolishes his office. Unimpressed, he sends her to a "beauty hospital" where Mabel reluctantly submits to the beautician's wiles and emerges as a radiant beauty. She immediately captures the heart of Menjou's handsome business partner, played by Mabel's leading man from both *The Slim Princess* and *What Happened to Rosa*, Hugh Thompson.

Head Over Heels brought something new into Mabel's life. Paul Bern was the co-director and he and Mabel became smitten with each other. They went out often and gave other people the impression of a very happy couple. But Paul couldn't tell what Mabel was thinking, and tried to rush into a marriage. One day he dropped to one knee, took out a diamond ring and proposed. Mabel gently declined, but Paul was emotionally devastated. He took the ring and threw it into a canyon. His deeply sensitive nature proved to be his undoing. On July 2, 1932, he married blonde bombshell Jean Harlow. Only two months later he committed suicide over his belief that he was not a worthy husband.[22]

By now Mabel's health and energies were completely spent, and she would not make another film for almost a year. Sam was over-extended too, but his problems were financial. The war had rendered the foreign market effectively dead, and the government had placed heavy restrictions on the use of electricity and fuel. When Washington ordered movie studios to work half-days until the summer months, the Goldwyn lot became a frantic beehive of activity from the first crack of daylight to the early afternoon.[23] Having spent the studio's reserves on new construction, his studio and, indeed, his entire professional life was hanging in the balance. Finally, company controller Melvin Schay arrived to tell Sam that there was no money to meet payroll.

Late one afternoon, Sam sat in his office, nervously going over the figures, then going over them again. Mabel burst into his office, but she wasn't there to demand money. She turned a sack upside down on Sam's desk and poured $50,000 of Liberty Bonds, and commercial real estate deeds onto his desk. "There you are, Sammy, my love," she said. "If that'll tide you over a bit, help yourself. And you needn't pay me any salary till things pick up."[24] This was no gag. A stunned Sam Goldwyn stood there with his mouth open. He looked down at his desk, and saw his salvation scattered before him. "In spite of everything," he later wrote, "she was easy to forgive."[25]

18

Back to Mack

*I thought if I could get her for Molly O' I could
keep her forever.*—Mack Sennett[1]

Mack knew that both the times and the movies were changing. He would forever claim a connection to the common working man. He considered his lowbrow style of comedy a badge of honor. He had seen the artistic heights of filmmaking through D.W. Griffith and, was proud to say, that he had turned his back on it. But those talking points weren't enough any more. There was less demand for one- and two-reel comedies. The real money was in features, with believable characters and developed stories. He had proven that with *Mickey*, and he was determined to duplicate its success.

For months, Mack had been telling everyone that he had a property called *Molly O'* that would be perfect for Mabel. The title was a familiar one: "Molly O'" was a popular song of early vaudeville. Americans everywhere well knew its most popular refrain:

> Oh Molly, my Irish Molly, my sweet acushla dear,
> I'm fairly off my trolley, Molly, when you are near.
> Springtime you know is ring time, come dear, now don't be slow.
> Change your name, go on be game, begorra, wouldn't I do the same.
> My Irish Molly O'![2]

But Mabel was under contract to Sam, and for Mack, that only left Mary Pickford. Mary was the biggest star in Hollywood, and she was the one actress that Mabel didn't seem to resent. They respected and sometimes even *liked* each other. Mary, in a guarded moment, referred to Mabel as "one of the loveliest things I'd ever seen."[3] Mabel, in an unguarded moment, referred to Mary as "a prissy bitch."[4] They remained just as different as they were back in their Biograph days. Mary lived her life enveloped in layers of protection, while Mabel lived hers vulnerably. Mary's domineering mother would never truly leave her, and her husband Douglas Fairbanks demanded an hour-by-hour accounting of her time. Mabel was nothing if not free. She often arrived at public events alone and driving her own car. Mary lived in the splendor of Pickfair, surrounded by a full complement of servants. Mabel lived by herself in an elegant home of her own. Mary's drinking was secretive and insidious, while Mabel's drinking was public, and even joyful.

Mack stood outside Mary's front door at Pickfair. Having written out his sales pitch, he was well prepared. He combed his hair and reminded himself to curb his language.

While Mary was polite, she quickly let Mack know that she in was not interested in his project.[5]

Unbeknownst to Mack, Mabel was growing weary of the petty jealousies and rivalries on the Goldwyn lot. At Keystone, there was only one star dressing room, and she missed being in the center ring. Though she would be loath to admit it, the fact was that Mack's Fun Factory was her emotional home.

For Sam's part, he was at his wits' end with Mabel. Whether fueled by cocaine or her own personality, Mabel's inexhaustibleness had lost its charm for Sam. He had assigned Abe Lehr to have dinner with her at least once a week, just to try to keep her grounded. But being Mabel's night-and-day babysitter had driven Lehr to the edge of a traumatic stress disorder. So when Mack came calling, he found Sam alarmingly receptive. After a brief discussion, he got Mabel on a handshake deal for $30,000.[6] Now he was determined to produce *Molly O'*.

Mabel and Mack soon found themselves nose to nose in his office with a contract between them. Some of the older stage hands said that their meeting was just like the old days. But the only thing that Mabel and Mack were certain of was that this was nothing like the old days. There had been one small crack in the ice. On Mabel's birthday, November 9, he had invited Mabel over for dinner—and Mabel had surprised herself by accepting. Dinner was set for 7:00 p.m. Mabel, in a conscious gesture, was right on time. Mack met her with 11 of her closest friends, who presented her with a silver tea set. Even her favorite director F. Richard Jones was present. And, to everyone's delight, Mack—with a mock formality—presented Mabel with an alarm clock.[7] Mack was elated, and considered it to be a new beginning. But later, in his office, Mabel told him flatly that their relationship would be strictly professional. Of course, a smiling Mack claimed that he understood completely.

Their breakup six years earlier had not changed Mabel and Mack so much as it had exaggerated them. They were two titanic personalities with-

Top: In 1921, Mabel re-signed with Mack Sennett. She told him that their relationship would be strictly professional, but he had other ideas (Marc Wanamaker/Bison Archives). *Bottom: Molly O'* (1922). Mabel disliked "ritzy" people and almost always portrayed working class girls and women (Marilyn Slater/"Looking for Mabel").

out a counterweight to balance their excesses. Mabel was more erratic, unreliable, generous and even lovable. Mack was more driven, eccentric, secretive and even crafty.

Mabel was now earning $4000 a week. But before her signature was dry on the contract, she was making demands of Mack. And, almost before the words came out of her mouth, Mack was agreeing to them. She would have Jones as her director, and the script would be rewritten to her specifications. As for casting, Mack must have gritted his teeth when Mabel said she wanted Jack Mulhall as her leading man. The country club Lothario, whom Sennett had decked a few years before, was now an established star. Jack and Mabel worked well together, which, for Mack, was just another reason to hate him. At least he wasn't Lew Cody. Lew and Mabel had become close friends since appearing in *Mickey*, and had been spotted together at various Hollywood night spots.

In *Molly O'*, Mabel portrays Molly O'Dair, the Irish daughter of a laborer and a washerwoman. She sees a newspaper photograph of the rich

Mabel often embraced her sexuality in films like *Molly O'* (Marc Wanamaker/Bison Archives).

At the *Molly O'* premiere with Mack Sennett (left) and F. Richard Jones (Marc Wanamaker/Bison Archives).

and handsome Dr. John Bryant and is instantly smitten. But her father has already chosen Danny Smith, a rough neighborhood boy, to be her husband. When Molly delivers laundry to a home, the doctor arrives on a house call. They become acquainted and John gives Molly a ride home, much to the displeasure of his fiancée Miriam, who catches the two together.

Later, at a masked ball, John mistakes Molly for Miriam, who angrily returns her engagement ring. Also feeling spurned, Danny arranges for Molly to be put in a compromising situation with John. Molly's father arrives and throws her out of the house. John takes Molly in, but in the morning, when her father discovers her in the doctor's house, he is ready to shoot—until he is told that the couple married during the night. Villain Albert Faulkner lures Molly to a blimp to pay the gambling debt of her younger brother. When she enters, Albert takes the airship aloft and forces himself on Molly. John takes to the sky in a biplane, lowering himself on a rope ladder and landing on top of the blimp. He leaps inside and fights off Albert. When the craft catches fire, he and Molly parachute to safety.

Though in many ways, Mack and Mabel had never been further apart, *Molly O'* would be billed—for the first and only time—as a "Mack Sennett-Mabel Normand Production." It proved to be a huge success. One critic noted, "Anything and everything that may be labelled as funny, thrilling, and sentimental has been poured into *Molly O'*."[8] Another said, "Mabel Normand's *Molly O'* is one of the finest comedies that ever graced the silver screen."[9]

Even more thrilling for Mack was the fact that his foreign markets had returned. The war was over and *Molly O'* could be sent around the globe. Prints of *Molly O'* were retitled overseas and exhibited, leading to huge profits. (Often prints of a film were not returned after their run in a foreign country, instead languishing in vaults. This practice proved to be *Molly O'*'s salvation. For decades it was considered a lost classic. It was rediscovered in the early 1990s in the Gosfilmofund in Moscow. It was carefully restored by UCLA and is now available.[10])

Molly O' was a one-picture deal which was comfortable for both Mabel and Mack. But Mack already had a new property in mind called *Suzanna*. Mabel was happy with *Molly O'* and signed on for the new picture.

19

Gates of Babylon

Hollywood is a crowd of cocaine-crazed sexual lunatics.
—Aleister Crowley[1]

The Jazz Age was a time of Hollywood scandal. Outraging some, fascinating others, it would lead the film industry to blacklists and outright censorship. The early 1920s did not destroy Hollywood so much as it revealed Hollywood. And that allowed Middle America to condemn it and recast it in its own image. Of course it merely substituted one illusion for another. But the moguls needed illusion more than ever just to keep their doors open, doors that by 1922 were called "Gates of Babylon."[2]

A new social experiment was on the horizon. Before January 16, 1919, when the 18th Amendment was ratified, and the subsequent Volstead Act delineated its statues and penalties, over half the states had already voted themselves "dry." And, though millions of Americans thought it beneficial for people to give up drinking, it immediately became clear that they had no intention of doing it themselves. When pre–Amendment stockpiles, local stills, border towns, religious exemptions and doctors' prescriptions proved insufficient to meet the demand, bootleggers and speakeasies eagerly filled the gap between "the spirit is willing" and "the flesh is weak."

For Mabel's part, Prohibition did not affect her drinking habits in any way. Her drinks of choice were provided by upscale, respectable Hollywood bootleggers. And it became the job of her secretary, Betty Coss, to keep Mabel's liquor cabinet fully stocked. A telegram requesting a bootlegger's address and phone number survives:

Dear Betty,
Please give me the address of Freeman's bootlegger. I mean the one you deal with for me and also had [sic] the telephone number you [sic] for tomorrow's Sunday—Please enclose in enclosed envelope I'm very unhappy about my ear

Dr. F and the Dr. who is now treating my ear—the right one—had very bad news for me. Send by town the address of that man also which is most important his telephone [sic] Monday—JFR—Be Happy Betty
I Love You[3]

Mabel's casual attitude about drinking was shared by many Americans. Within 15 years, after making the transition from the ineffective to the futile, the 18th Amendment would be repealed by the 21st Amendment on December 5, 1933.

With the backdrop of Prohibition, American moralists of the '20s were determined to make other changes. They loudly objected to the scandalous behavior of movie stars. The first shock waves did not come from Hollywood at all, but from Paris. On September 10, 1920, actress Olive Thomas died in the American Hospital in Nevilly, France, under bizarre circumstances. Olive, a Hollywood starlet known as "Ollie," was a close friend of Mabel's. She followed her path from modeling to acting. Billed as "The Most Beautiful Girl in the World," she had luminous blue-violet eyes, ivory skin and a face well-suited for the dramatic, Victorian heroines that she often portrayed. Olive was also an international party girl. Her pursuit of high living led her to the perfect playmate in Jack Pickford, whom she would marry in 1916.[4]

After wisely adopting his sister's stage name Pickford, Jack, a substance-abusing womanizer, took full advantage of Mary's standing to gain both starring roles and easy money. Those who knew Jack and Ollie were often afraid for them, as neither possessed an ounce of moderation or maturity. Their relationship seemed to be defined by a series of drunken accidents. A year into their marriage, Jack contracted syphilis.[5]

While on a second honeymoon in Paris, Jack and Ollie spent the evening of September 5, 1920, partying at the notorious nightclub Le Rat Mort (The Dead Rat). Returning to their hotel room at 3:00 a.m., Ollie accidentally took a swig of bichloride of mercury, a topical medication to treat his syphilis. It was a horrific mistake. Bichloride of mercury, when ingested, causes fiery internal burning and acute nephritis, and subsequently attacks all major organs. She was dead in five days.[6] The tragedy struck Mabel to her heart. She spent the following months attending to the needs and wishes of Olive's mother, often driving her to the beach and sitting with her in silence for hours.[7]

Within a year, Mabel would be crushed by the ruin of her longtime friend and confidante Roscoe Arbuckle. On the day before Labor Day 1921, Roscoe, former Keystone director Fred Fischbach and actor Lowell Sherman drove north to the St. Francis Hotel in San Francisco to enjoy the holiday weekend. Booking the adjoining rooms of 1219 and 1220, they prepared for an open house–style party planned for the following day. The guest list was a loose amalgamation of show business friends and studio acquaintances who either lived nearby or happened to be in town. All those invited were told to drop in whenever they pleased. Among those in town—staying at the nearby Paradise Hotel—was a casual acquaintance of both Fischbach and Arbuckle, actress Virginia Rappe. Fischbach invited her over.[8]

Roscoe slept in late that morning, then went out for a drive with friends. With party guests already coming and going, he returned to the St. Francis at about 2:30 in the afternoon. He went into his room to change his clothes and use the bathroom, before joining the party next door. Roscoe was shocked to find an unconscious Virginia Rappe lying on his bathroom floor. With the strong smell of alcohol, a less than surprised Arbuckle picked her up and laid her on one of the room's twin beds. He then withdrew into the bathroom to change.

What happened next will never be known with any certainty. What is known is that Virginia suddenly began screaming and tearing at her clothes. Responding to her cries, party guests rushed in. At first, believing her to be delirious from alcohol, they tried to bring her to her senses and then placed her in a bathtub of cold water. Nothing worked.

Realizing that something was wrong, they got her a room of her own and called the hotel doctor, Olay Kaarboe. By the time he arrived, Virginia had again lapsed into unconscious. Smelling her breath, he concluded that she was passed out drunk; Virginia was left to sleep it off.[9] Unbeknownst to anyone was the fact that Virginia was suffering from a ruptured bladder. By Wednesday night, peritonitis had set in. By Thursday, when she was finally moved to nearby Wakefield Hospital, it was too late. On Friday, September 9, 1921, Virginia died.[10]

On September 11, back in Los Angeles, Arbuckle was arrested and arraigned on charges of rape and murder. During the coroner's inquest the next day, he sat silent and downcast, smoking cigarettes, seemingly oblivious to the throng of onlookers packed into the courtroom and filling the halls outside. When he was told that he would have to stand trial, he slumped in his chair, his hands visibly shaking. He was remanded to cell number 12 on "felony row" at the San Francisco Hall of Justice. Minta and Roscoe were separated at the time of Roscoe's arrest, but she rushed from New York to be by her husband's side.[11]

Before the day was out, theaters across the country announced that they were withdrawing Arbuckle's films from exhibition. This was not part of an organized effort but a financial decision as, under the circumstances, few patrons felt like laughing at Fatty Arbuckle. But the impression it gave was that of an admission by Hollywood that Fatty was almost certainly guilty.

On November 14, 1921, Arbuckle was put on trial in the city courthouse in San Francisco. The intervening months had been the worst of his life. While some believed in his innocence, Henry Lehrman spoke for many when he proclaimed, "This is what comes from taking vulgarians from the gutter and making idols of them"—and adding that if he were ever to see Arbuckle, he would kill him.[12] What was not reported was that Lehrman was Virginia's fiancé. In America, and around the world, the press coverage exploded. Then, as never before, the idea of a film censorship board received both the national spotlight and widespread support among the public at large.

Before the trial, Judge Sylvain Lazarus, finding the evidence flimsy, reduced the charges against Roscoe to manslaughter. Taking the stand on his own behalf, Roscoe impressed everyone with his somber and clear presentation of the facts. Things had calmed down and, for the first time since Virginia's death, Roscoe's acquittal seemed to be a real possibility. On December 5, the seven-man, five-woman jury returned after 41 hours of deliberation to declare themselves hopelessly deadlocked at ten to two for acquittal. Outraged at the intransigence of the two jurors that had voted for conviction, the jury foreman declared the prosecution's case an insult to the intelligence of the jurors and revealed that from the very beginning, one of the jurors had announced that she would vote for conviction until "Hell froze over."[13] Arbuckle would have to be re-tried.

Arbuckle's confidence soared before the second trial. The district attorney's case was falling apart. Witnesses for the prosecution had withdrawn their stories, changed their stories, admitted that they had been forced to perjure themselves, and even left town. Arbuckle breathed a sigh of relief. At the second trial he would not even be called to testify.

On February 3, 1922, the second Arbuckle jury returned to the courtroom after 44 hours of deliberation, to announce that they were intractably deadlocked at ten to two for conviction.[14] To the jurors, Arbuckle's "refusal" to testify was seen as an admission of guilt. To the public, Arbuckle's inability to be acquitted, after two different trials, was seen as proof of guilt. To his friends, Roscoe was a soft-spoken, kind-hearted man. To the public, "Fatty" was a 300-pound brute who had ruptured a woman's bladder under his enormous weight. Arbuckle would again have to be re-tried.

Finally, on April 12, 1922, after only six minutes of deliberation, the eight-man, four-woman Arbuckle jury re-entered the courtroom. They were momentarily stayed from rendering their verdict as the judge warned onlookers against any demonstration whatever. As the courtroom held its collective breath, the decision was handed to Judge Louderback. He read it in succinct fashion, "We find the defendant, not guilty."[15] Arbuckle half rose in his chair and threw his arms around his counsel. Minta, seated in the front row, began to sob. Along with the verdict, the smiling jury issued an extraordinary statement:

> Acquittal is not enough for Roscoe Arbuckle. We feel that a great injustice has been done him. We feel, also, that it was only our plain duty to give him this exoneration. Under the evidence, there was not the slightest proof adduced to connect him, in any way, with the commission of a crime.
> We wish him success, and hope that the American people will take the judgment of 14 men and women, who have sat listening, for 31 days, to the evidence, that Roscoe Arbuckle is entirely innocent and free from all blame.[16]

Mabel was quick to believe that Roscoe would be back. She told the press, "Thank Heaven that the jury has vindicated Roscoe! His fame will only be greater now. I'm glad they went out of their way to place the stamp of approval on him."[17] But, moviegoers no longer cared. In the court of public opinion, Roscoe had been tried and convicted.

And then came Wallace Reid, a blondish, 6'2" matinee idol. Mentored in motion pictures by his father who wrote, directed and acted, "Wally" found immediate success. He specialized in auto race melodrama thrillers like *Double Speed* and *Too Much Speed*, both released in 1921. He also found critical success in the Griffith epics *Birth of a Nation* and *Intolerance*. Women flocked to see his films and Jesse Lasky awarded him a huge contract.

Reid was injured while shooting *Valley of the Giants* in Oregon. Lasky ordered the film to stay in production and a studio doctor began giving Wally morphine injections. Reid became addicted to the drug. Rather than allowing his star to rest and heal, Lasky increased production. When Reid upped his daily morphine injections to continue work, his fate was sealed. Unable to regain his health, he entered a sanatorium and succumbed to influenza on January 18, 1923.[18] Mabel, grief-stricken, told reporters, "When Wally Reid took sick, I suddenly realized the horrible futility of the sort of life we lead. We make big money, but it only brings us headaches and heartaches, sapping our strength and powers of resistance."[19]

Hollywood fought back against the cries for censorship. Their spokesman was director William Desmond Taylor, president of the Director's Association. His agenda was simple: complete freedom for filmmakers. And Taylor would spend much time fighting against the sudden proliferation of "blue" laws cropping up around the country. He helped organize Affiliated

Picture Interests of California, a watchdog committee to fight censorship wherever it appeared. Declaring that Hollywood would not exploit either crime or immorality, he pronounced potential government action to be both unnecessary and redundant.[20] Mabel was happy to help in Taylor's crusade. She told the *New York Dramatic Mirror*, "I am against censorship. The film industry is directed by men of sufficient mental and moral caliber to insure a proper conduct of the profession."[21] Ironically, censorship in Hollywood was cemented in place and debate was quashed when William Desmond Taylor himself was found shot to death on the floor of his bungalow.

20

Different Names

*Bill's friendship was one of the finest
things in my life.*—Mabel[1]

The most important reality about William Desmond Taylor was that there *was* no William Desmond Taylor. His real name was William Cunningham Deane-Tanner, and he was born on April 26, 1872, in Dublin, Ireland. He grew up with an abusive father who was embarrassed, and eventually enraged, that his son needed glasses. Young William began retreating into his books and began a lifetime habit of running away when confronted with painful circumstances.[2] He apparently made his way across France and Germany, and then turned up in Canada. Facts about his early life are hard to come by. In addition to his penchant for travel was his pattern of exaggeration and lies. He claimed to have attended Clifton College in England and then served as a Royal Canadian Mountie.[3] Evidence for either claim is nonexistent. Yet his knack for re-invention served him remarkably well. His vast reading helped him take on other personas, and it led him into a career in acting.

He first went on stage in England in 1890, when he was just 18. He had some success and began putting together a theatrical career. But, one night his father appeared backstage and ended his son's dream. He announced to young William that he was dispatching him to the United States where he would live in a Kansas farm colony for troubled boys.[4]

He lived in the colony for 18 months before running away. With no place to go, he worked his way across the country, taking any job he could find. Soon his longing to be an actor began directing his actions. This time, his father was not there to object. Using the name Cunningham Deane, he began piling up credits. A turn on Broadway led to his meeting actress Effie Hamilton (born Ethel May Harrison); they were married in 1899,[5] and three years later their daughter Ethel Daisy was born. Effie was from a wealthy family, and William suddenly found himself ensconced in a world of luxury. He began a prosperous career as a New York City antique dealer. His customers and colleagues knew him then as Pete Tanner. His elegant, educated manner and affected English accent led most to consider him a true aristocrat, which attracted both business and infidelities with women.[6]

Those who knew him best were disturbed by what they saw. Beset by chronic stomach ulcers, he constantly complained that he couldn't eat. Alternately quiet and erratic, he spent money wildly, isolated himself from his family, and had astonishing lapses in memory. He began to ignore his personal appearance and took on the look and manner of a vagrant. Then, one day, he was gone. Taking the name William Taylor, he bounced in and out of Australia, Alaska and Hawaii, working in whatever menial jobs he could get. His contemporaries remembered him as a man who appeared too elegant for his surroundings.[7]

He made his way to San Francisco where an old friend, actress Eleanor Gordon, and her husband were waiting for him. They found Taylor alone, sick and broke. They took him in and nursed him back to health. They even got him a job: He was paired with Rhea "Ginga" Mitchell in a play on the San Francisco stage.[8]

William and Rhea were a huge hit with audiences. When Thomas Ince of the New York Motion Picture Company spotted the pair, he offered them a job in the movies. Over the next few years, Taylor found a niche playing small screen roles (he was billed as William D. Taylor). Starring in the action adventure feature *Captain Alvarez* in 1917[9] made him a name player. Director Rollin Sturgeon introduced him to Mabel Normand.

Then in his mid-forties, William put down roots in Hollywood, first as an actor and then as a director. While his acting skill was noteworthy, it was as a director that Taylor made his mark. He slowly gained prominence and real prestige within Hollywood. He was known as an Irish gentleman who never raised his voice to either cast or crew. He had endless patience with delays and mishaps and he became an industry favorite. During his career, he directed some of the biggest names in Hollywood, including: Agnes Ayres, Wallace Beery, Frank Lanning, Eugene Pallette, Jack Pickford, Mary Pickford, ZaSu Pitts, Wallace Reid and Constance Talmadge.

When the war broke out he enlisted in the Canadian armed forces. He started out as a private and was soon promoted to sergeant. The memories of his companions were remarkably consistent with others he had known. They recalled that he never mentioned a past life and was often ill with stomach problems. From Nova Scotia, Canada, he went to Britain for further training to become an officer. He was soon known as Captain Taylor.[10] At war's end, he returned to the U.S. to resume his directorial career. The honored war veteran moved easily to Paramount Pictures where he took the name William Desmond Taylor.

In 1919, Taylor directed Mary Miles Minter in the title role of *Anne of Green Gables*. Mary, just 16, fell deeply in love with Taylor. Her infatuation was an ongoing source of conflict between herself and her domineering stage mother, Charlotte Shelby. Infuriated at losing a position of primary influence in Mary's life, Charlotte could not abide Taylor, and would spend years nagging Mary to break it off.

Mary was groomed as a new Mary Pickford "type." And she would forever remember Mabel as being one of the few people she met in Hollywood that was "sweet" to her. They had originally become friends in Hollywood by virtue of having the same French professor, Georges Jaumier. They also shared a mutual affection for William, although of a very different nature.

In 1921 William became engaged to the actress Neva Gerber. Neva, troubled by his private despondency, tried to cheer him up and impress upon him his own importance. But that only worked for so long and the two ended their relationship by mutual consent.[11]

By the fall of 1921 Mabel and William grew closer. They went to movies together, frequented nightclubs and had long discussions about books and current events. The *Los Angeles Times* noted, "Mabel has caught a distinguished-looking one with gray hair this time!"[12]

By the time of the filming of *Suzanna*, Mabel and William had a comfortable friendship. They took each other for granted, and even quarreled. He once asked Mabel why she ignored him when they went out together. Mabel told him to stop being so dramatic. During the fall and winter months of 1921–22, William went to Europe to seek out a specialist for his chronic stomach problems. He returned to America in time for Mabel's studio birthday party, bringing several books that he wanted Mabel to read. William presented Mabel with *The Complete Works of Robert Browning* for Christmas, and then met her again at a New Year's Eve party at the Alexandria Hotel in Los Angeles.[13] He would leave for France soon afterward, and then move on to Great Britain, in another failed effort to find relief for his stomach.

When he left for Europe, he left behind a signed blank check with his houseman, Edward Sands, to use in the event of an emergency. But Sands turned out to be a con man and used the real signature as a model for forgery. Sands accessed Taylor's checkbook and provided himself with a new car and every luxury that attracted his fancy. When Taylor returned, his bank account was drained and Sands was nowhere to be found.[14]

Mabel was a voracious reader and kept herself informed on national and world affairs (Marc Wanamaker/Bison Archives).

Mabel began to sense that something more was wrong. As she recalled it, "He always did the correct thing. Sent flowers, books and candy. But, haven't you had times when all the world seemed false? That's how I felt."[15] She wisely decided to define their relationship in father-daughter terms. William accepted that and, for the rest of his life, he kept a picture of Mabel displayed in his home and another one in the pocket watch he carried with him.

That was the William Desmond Taylor the world knew in early 1922. He sat atop his profession like a shimmering iceberg with so much below the surface. On the evening of February 1, 1922, he had a pleasant visit from Mabel. Only minutes later he had a final name bestowed upon him: murder victim.

Director William Desmond Taylor was murdered on February 1, 1922. Mabel was the last known person to see him alive, casting a shadow over the rest of her life (Marc Wanamaker/Bison Archives).

21

Her Story

I have told the truth!—Mabel[1]

February 1, 1922, was the most important day in Mabel Normand's life. Events of the day overshadowed her career and marked her place in history.

Her story was always consistent. The problem was that too few people believed it.

When the day began, Mabel felt that the struggles in her life were behind her. She remembered, "The whole world and my future seemed cheerful and promising."[2]

February 1 was a cloudy but dry Wednesday. The Los Angeles Basin recently experienced a remarkable cold snap. On January 20 it was 21 degrees, the lowest temperature ever recorded for the area.[3]

Mack gave Mabel the day off and she planned to run errands, but she didn't wake up until noon. She lingered at home until late afternoon. Finally her maid Mamie Owens reminded her of the hour and she quickly dressed. Her chauffeur William Davis loaded some Christmas gifts in her car that she wanted to exchange at Brock and Feagens Jewelry Store. He also put in two silver platters and a vanity bag that Mabel wanted to have inscribed with her monogram. He drove her to the jewelry store on the corner of 4th and Broadway in downtown L.A., arriving at about six, just as they were closing. She tapped on the glass. The clerk was delighted to see the movie star and let her in to take her engraving order.[4]

Davis next drove her to Hellman's Bank, at 6th and Main Street, to deposit some accumulated paychecks and to put some jewelry she had worn over Christmas back in her safety deposit box. (On her way there, noticing that a new Harold Lloyd comedy showing at a nearby theater, she decided to have dinner in town and then see the show.) Once at Hellman's, she was led by a clerk into a small room where he brought out her safety deposit box. She stayed a while and chatted with bank employees who were quite impressed with her gems.[5]

Using the bank's phone, Mabel called Mamie Owens to tell her that she was having dinner in town and then going to a show. Mamie told her that Mack had called and wanted her on the set at eight the next morning. She suggested Mabel have dinner in bed and then allow her to comb Mabel's hair out so she would be rested for the morning. Mabel agreed to the early night. Mamie also said that Taylor had called and that he wanted Mabel to come by his bungalow to pick up a book that he had for her.[6]

Returning to the back of her limousine, Mabel directed Davis to William's bungalow at 404-B South Alvarado Court. It was almost seven. Catching sight of a newsstand, she called for Davis to stop, her eyes going to the latest copy of *The Police Gazette*. The cover photo featured a girl dressed as Salome from the Bible, Mabel felt that both the lighting of the photo, and the angle of the shot, could be an exemplar for Mack of how she wanted to be presented in *Suzanna*. She determined to bring it to the studio with her the next day. She also bought a bag of popcorn and two bags of peanuts, one for her and one for William. Happily crunching her peanuts and dropping the shells onto the floor of her car, she was engrossed in *The Police Gazette*.[7]

As she stepped out of the car, she turned to ask Davis to wait for her and to sweep out the peanut shells. As was his custom, Taylor's front door was standing open and his porch light was on. As Mabel strode up the cement walkway towards the bungalow, his houseman Henry Peavey came outside to tell her that the director was on the phone, making an appointment to meet with actor-director Antonio Moreno the following morning. Mabel waited outside until she heard William say goodbye and saw him hang up the receiver. He then invited her inside.[8]

Mabel hadn't been to Taylor's place for a while—and it was the first time she had ever been there unaccompanied. She commented on the additions of a piano and a Victrola since her last visit. He told her that he was working on his taxes and trying to straighten out his checkbook. He showed Mabel several of Sands' forged checks that had cleared the bank. They both agreed that the counterfeit signatures were remarkably good.[9]

William then handed her the book that he wanted her to read, *Rosa Mundi* by Edith M. Dell, a London author known for novels and short stories of romantic intrigue.[10] Her stories were considered racy for their time. She thanked him, but because of her early call in the morning, she turned down his invitation to dinner and his offer of rice pudding (Mabel's favorite). She finally agreed to stay for a quick drink. Taylor had Peavey mix up some

Orange Blossoms. Equal parts gin, sweet vermouth and orange juice, the cocktail was a favorite in Prohibition Era America.[11] Peavey placed the shaker and two glasses on a tray and carried it in to Mabel and William. Taylor indicated that he wouldn't be needing anything further. Peavey said good night and got his hat and coat. He walked out the front door, stopping at Mabel's car to chat with Davis before leaving the property. During his brief conversation with Mabel that night, William expressed regret that he had sworn out a warrant against Sands. He told Mabel that he feared Sands, and had a premonition that something was wrong.

Then Mabel and William argued. She had her heart set on starring in a production of *The Little Minister* by J.M. Barrie, but Taylor's Paramount Pictures bought the rights. Mabel was livid that Paramount was buying up all the good properties, leaving little for smaller organizations like hers. Mabel would have been brilliant as Bobbie, a fiery girl of noble birth who disguises herself as a gypsy to gain her freedom and protect the common people from the harsh ruling class. Mack knew of Mabel's love for the story and even wrote a treatment for her.[12] But Mack was just too slow with his checkbook.

Then William mentioned that his home had been broken into some time ago. The incident was peculiar: After breaking in the door, the thief didn't take anything of real worth. Instead, the thief took some token pieces of jewelry (leaving many more valuable pieces behind), food from Taylor's larder and a stash of Muratti's Gold Tipped Ariston Cigarettes, an exclusive brand sold in London (Taylor picked them up during his last trip to Europe). Strangest of all, the intruder took the time to walk on Taylor's bed with dirty shoes.[13] When William showed Mabel around his ransacked house, she noticed a stack of letters that she had written him, bound together in his open top dresser drawer. When she asked him why he had kept them, he only smiled. They both were letter writers, and over the years they had exchanged dozens of them, each one replete with the teasing banter that defined their light-hearted friendship. His letters would refer to Mabel as "Blessed Baby," while Mabel would retaliate by referring to him in print as simply "Baby." What alarmed him the most, he said, was that a small pile of the stolen cigarettes were smoked, and then left on his front door stoop, a few nights before.

Then the conversation got around to books, as it always did. They discussed the 1921 American novel *Three Soldiers* by writer-critic John Dos Passos. One of the first important novels about World War I, it took a brutally realistic look at the struggle. Mabel was attracted to it, as her own pacifistic ideals had only been hardened by the recent carnage overseas.[14]

Taylor helped Mabel with her wrap, walked her out to her car and said that he would call her later. He also sent her home with a book critiquing the works of Friedrich Nietzsche. When they arrived at the car, they found Mabel's chauffeur reading her *Police Gazette*, which he quickly tossed into the backseat. The magazine landed next to a copy of Freud's *Interpretation of Dreams*. It tickled Taylor, and he chided her that Freud and Nietzsche were hardly compatible with *The Police Gazette*. He laughed again when he saw the peanut shells that had been swept from the car.[15]

Mabel gave him a quick hug and got into the back seat, and Davis drove her away. Looking through her rear window she saw William waving goodbye, so she jokingly blew kisses at him until he was out of sight. When Mabel got home that night, she ate dinner in bed. She noticed that he didn't call, as he said he would, but thought nothing of it, and went to sleep.

22

The Edge of Murder

I spoke with Mabel. Her voice haunted me all night.
—Adela Rogers St. Johns[1]

The body of William Desmond Taylor was discovered by his houseman Henry Peavey. Peavey arrived at Taylor's home on February 2 at 7:30 a.m. to make the director his usual breakfast. He had stopped at a nearby drugstore to buy a bottle of Milk of Magnesia for the director's stomach trouble. Using his front door key, Peavey let himself in. He was surprised to see Taylor lying flat on his back on the floor. "Mr. Taylor? Mr. Taylor?" Kneeling, Peavey sought to rouse Taylor before suddenly realizing that he was dead.[2] Horrified, he immediately ran out the front door and into the courtyard, screaming for help. Among those he awoke was Chaplin leading lady and Taylor neighbor Edna Purviance. The blonde beauty lived in a two-story bungalow attached to Taylor's.[3]

Edna immediately telephoned Mabel, who was making up at home for the day's shooting of *Suzanna*. Edna told her that Taylor's butler was yelling that William had died; that he had died of heart failure. Mabel thought that there had to have been some kind of mistake. Shocked, and wiping away tears, she asked Edna to find out if it was true and to call her back.[4] Peavey also got on the telephone, calling Charles Eyton, the 51-year-old general manager of Famous Players–Lasky, where Taylor was working at the time. Eyton, Australian-born, a former prizefight referee, raced to Taylor's bungalow to find both Peavey and LAPD Detective Thomas Ziegler at the site.[5]

Taylor was on the floor, directly in front of his writing desk. A tipped-over desk chair was lying across the bottom part of his legs. For a man who had fallen out of his chair, the posture of the corpse was eerie and unnerving. His legs were stretched out straight. His arms were resting at his side, his eyes were closed and his calm, delicate features showed no expression. His lapels and jacket were smoothed and straightened out.[6]

Robbery was immediately ruled out as a motive. A two-carat diamond ring was on his finger. His wallet contained $78. In his pockets were an ivory toothpick, a silver cigarette case and the pocket watch containing a picture of Mabel.[7]

A local doctor arrived at the door asking if he could help. Stepping through the growing assembly of curious neighbors, he knelt down and made a preliminary diagnoses of a stomach hemorrhage being the cause of death. The conclusion made perfect sense. Peavey told the doctor that Taylor had been seeking medical attention for relief from his chronic stomach problems. He opened a cabinet to reveal a shelf of medications, and showed the doctor the bottle of Milk of Magnesia that he had purchased for Taylor that morning. Nobody thought to write down the doctor's name, and when he left he was never heard from again.[8]

Among the crowd was neighbor Douglas MacLean, an actor known as "the man with the million dollar smile."[9] He had his own theory about Taylor's death. He and his wife had heard what sounded like a gunshot during the night. They dismissed it as being the backfire from a car. He urged Detective Ziegler to turn the body over and look for a bullet hole. Ziegler told him that they would wait for people from the coroner's office to arrive. When Deputy Coroner William MacDonald made a thorough examination of the body, he discovered a bullet hole and a small pool of blood on Taylor's left side. William Desmond Taylor had been murdered. Within a few minutes, Edna called Mabel back with an update. Mabel said she was on her way.

Tests would determine that he had been shot with a .38 caliber steel-nosed bullet from a snub-nosed revolver. The bullet had entered midway below his left armpit, pierced his heart, and then continued its upward trajectory into his right shoulder; where it remained.[10] He had apparently been shot while sitting at his desk, as there was an open checkbook and a pen left in their places. The shooter must have been crouching, or even lying down, as the revolver that shot him was no more than a foot above the floor when it was fired. As soon as it was determined that Taylor had been murdered, Captain David Adams assigned every available officer to the case. When Mary Miles Minter arrived, detectives met her at the door and explained that he had been murdered. Mary left in hysterics.

With tears flowing freely, Mabel left her apartment at 3089 West Seventh Street and made the drive west on Seventh before turning north on Alvarado. She parked in front of the house. It all seemed unreal. The police were accustomed to actors and actresses, but Mabel Normand was a movie star, and they were surprised to see her coming up the walk. The body had been removed. It was now a crime scene closed off by a tightening police presence. Mabel explained to the officers that she didn't want to disturb anything, but did want to retrieve a packet of letters that she had written to William over the years. They contained nothing scandalous, she added; she just wanted them kept private. Mabel was allowed inside. When she went into Taylor's bedroom and opened his middle dresser drawer, she was shocked to see that the letters were gone.[11]

When Mabel arrived home she found the police there. She was questioned at length. Getting more upset with each telling, she replayed the previous night's events over and over again, to each successive questioner. There was no escaping the fact that Mabel was the last known person to see Taylor alive. She was understandably a person of interest and, unbelievably, a murder suspect.

A hysterical Mary Miles Minter arrived at Mabel's front door. Officers told her that Mabel was in a state of shock, barricaded in her bedroom and not receiving callers. But Mabel suddenly appeared at the top of the stairs and told them that it was all right. Mary climbed the stairs and instantly the two women fell into each other's arms. Mabel led her into the bathroom. She turned the water on full blast to ensure privacy. They asked each other what they knew and what they suspected, each finding in the other someone who could truly understand.[12]

After the agonizing meeting with Mary, Mabel quickly wrote out a telegram for Mamie Owens to send:

February 2, 1922
Mr. and Mrs. Claude G. Normand c/o
125 St. Mark's Place, Staten Island, NY
   Don't worry Mamma and Papa. Unfortunately I was one of the last to leave Mr. Taylor's house. Soon after that, he was shot. They all know I know nothing about the sad affair, and I will be exonerated entirely.
   Mabel[13]

Mabel's brother Claude left his job at a Staten Island movie theater to call Mabel and offer what help he could. He asked her if she wanted the family to come west to be with her. Mabel said that there was no need. She was already planning her own trip to Staten Island. The home she purchased for her parents seemed like Heaven to her now. Claude's statement to the press revealed the strength of family that she so desperately needed: "We feel that Mabel knows enough to take care of herself, and are confident that she will be cleared."[14]

Mabel's own confidence was waning, and her fragile constitution gave way to fear. She reached out to Mack Sennett: "Hello, Mack?" Mack knew at once that it was Mabel's voice, but it never sounded like this. In anguish, she told him that Taylor had been murdered and that they were blaming her. "Mack, I'm in trouble! I am in serious trouble!" With an uncharacteristic paranoia, she told Mack that she couldn't tell him everything, because the police had tapped her phone line. Mack promised to meet her the next day so they could talk in person, and he pledged to do all he could for her. Mack heard a sigh. "There's nothing for you to do, Mack. Nothing at all. I've never brought you anything but trouble. I just wanted you to know."[15] She silently hung up the phone.

Working for Mack proved to be a godsend. The William Desmond Taylor case was his finest hour. He responded to Mabel's plight directly and with sympathy. He immediately suspended work on *Suzanna*, encouraged her to go east to see her family, and offered to help her financially. He defended her in the press (and would continue to do so for the rest of his life). He knew that Mabel was not capable of murder. Perhaps for the first time, Mabel and Mack shared something that their relationship had always been missing: real friendship.[16]

The Taylor murder couldn't have come at a worse time for the film industry. It validated the voices of those who had been decrying Hollywood's vices. The proverbial last straw, it would lead to the censorship of movies for decades to come. From a business standpoint, millions had been lost on Arbuckle, and the potential losses on Normand would be even more staggering. While Mabel's public had grown accustomed to the tales of her hijinks and misadventures, this was murder. They would never forgive her for that.

Mabel fully cooperated with investigators. She presented her statements in a serious, straightforward manner. She would be questioned, interrogated and cross-examined for hours at a time, then have to do it again. Her timetable was corroborated by Taylor's neighbors and her chauffeur.

At ten on the morning of Saturday, February 4, 1922, Coroner Frank A. Nance held his inquest at the Ivy H. Overholtzer Undertaking Parlor at Tenth and Hill Streets in Los Angeles. The mortuary receiving room was filled to capacity. Six chairs had been arranged in a semi-circle, for use by the all-male jury. After being sworn in, the jurors were led into the next room to view Taylor's body, laid out on a marble slab, covered by a satin sheet which was turned back to reveal his face and shoulders. The inquest, which lasted approximately 45 minutes, did not include Edna Purviance, the MacLeans or anyone else that Henry Peavey roused that morning. As the jury took their seats, all were present and accounted for except for Mabel. More than a little irritated, Nance ordered that a search be made for the movie star. Mabel finally arrived 15 minutes late.[17]

Reporters, newspaper photographers and a teeming throng of star gazers were camped out in front of the building since early morning, waiting for Mabel. Her limousine parked in the back alley behind an ice truck. Police officers met her there and hustled her under a fence and across the property extending behind Overholtzer's. They entered the building through a back door. Police formed a flying wedge to get her through the packed crowd and into a private office that held one table, two chairs and one light. Mabel sat in silent dread and awaited her summons to appear on the witness stand.

After receiving the testimony of Charles Eyton and autopsy surgeon A.F. Wagner, Nance called Mabel to the stand. A large policeman entered the private office and told her that it was time. The officer emerged from the private office and pushed his way through the mob with Mabel sticking close behind. Shaky, she took the stand. Her testimony took only a few minutes.[18]

After being excused, a relieved Mabel stepped down. Smiling politely, she bowed to the jurors, before being surrounded by a police detail. Mabel and her imposing entourage made a dash for the back alley. She got inside her idling limousine and it sped away. At the inquest's conclusion, the jury briefly recessed before issuing its finding: "William Desmond Taylor came to his death on the 1st day of February 1922, by a gunshot wound of the chest, inflicted by some person or persons unknown to this jury with intent to kill or murder."[19]

Mabel was deeply hurt and conflicted. She always despised reporters. But now, she *wanted* to speak. She pleaded with the press to print the key distinction: She was not the last person to see Taylor alive, she was the last person, *other than the killer*, to see Taylor alive. But an edict was handed out by the Hollywood studios: steer clear of Mabel Normand. Studio heads were terrified that the Taylor investigation would expose one scandal after another and kill box office receipts worldwide. Though they released statements of support for law enforcement, and offered a cash reward for the killer, they were eager for the whole thing to go away.

Mabel would not be silent and, despite the pressure from the studios to avoid her, reporters could not resist a story. A major suspect in an infamous murder wanted to be interviewed. Her comments ranged from a wish that the killer receive his due, to a quotation from the Bible. She proclaimed her innocence and asked the public to be fair to her. But the counter-reaction was huge. Calls for her banishment from the screen came from every part of the country.

Then came the funeral. Fearing for Mabel's safety, the Los Angeles Police Department assigned two detectives to protect her. On Tuesday, February 7, 1922, her limousine pulled up in front of the St. Paul's Pro-Cathedral for the memorial service. A crowd of no less than 10,000 surged forward when she appeared. The police fought them back and made a path for Mabel.[20] Her assigned detectives escorted her inside the church, where she was seated up front with many other Hollywood luminaries. The coffin was draped with a British flag with Taylor's British Captain's cap sitting on top. Mary Miles Minter, too grief-stricken to attend, sent a bouquet of Black Prince roses. It sat among the floral arrangements from Rudolph Valentino, Wallace Reid, Gloria Swanson and other stars.

The service was conducted according to the rites of the Church of England. It was a burden that Mabel wanted to bear for William's sake, but she could feel herself weakening and she wept throughout. The service concluded with a male quartet singing "Abide with Me," a Christian hymn written by the Scottish Anglican divine, Henry Francis Lyte, as he lay dying from tuberculosis. Then the minister said a final prayer. Attendants gently laid aside the flowers and the cap atop the casket and the lid was opened. Steeling herself, Mabel joined the line of congregates waiting to say their goodbyes. Both Mamie Owens and Julia Benson, who stood behind Mabel, advised her against viewing the body, and Mabel reluctantly sat down. Then she became uncomfortable with her own retreat. Gathering herself, she returned to the line and resolved to see it through. When the moment came, she allowed herself one glimpse of Taylor's waxen face before bursting into tears. Sobbing uncontrollably, she was helped to a back pew by Julia and Mamie.[21] As bagpipes played the mournful strains of the funeral march, they helped Mabel to her feet and walked her outside. In no condition to join the cortege to Hollywood Memorial Park, Mabel slumped into the back of her limousine and cried.

Things may have calmed down for Mabel were it not for Taylor's houseman Henry Peavey. For the rest of her life Mabel was bedeviled by this strange man. Flush with the press attention, Henry told all who would listen that Mabel was the killer. First, he asserted that Taylor's chauffeur Howard Fellowes told him that he called his boss at 7:30 and got no answer. Therefore, Peavey concluded, Taylor was already dead and that placed Mabel at the scene.

Next he claimed that Mabel visited Taylor the night before the murder. He was certain of this because the rice pudding he made was still in the icebox but was almost completely eaten. When Mabel arrived on the night of the killing, Peavey overheard Taylor offering her some rice pudding. She replied that she did not care for any but had enjoyed it the night before.

Then there was the question of the arguments. Mabel admitted that she and William quarreled during a New Year's Eve party at the Alexandria Hotel. Peavey claimed that he found Taylor at his desk on New Year's morning weeping and writing a letter to Mabel. He gave it to Henry to deliver.

Peavey next claimed that one evening he found a half-crazed Mabel sitting on the floor of Taylor's bungalow with scissors in her hand. She was cutting photos of herself to ribbons. When Peavey questioned her, she cried, "I guess I can cut up my own pictures if I want to!"[22]

But the most disquieting story was the one that Peavey did not report until 1930. If Peavey can be believed, he tried to tell the district attorney at the inquest that he believed the murderer to be Mabel Normand. When he did, he was told to keep his mouth shut and get out of Los Angeles. If he didn't, *he* would be charged with the murder. It was a burden he carried for the rest of his life. He was totally convinced that there was a studio cover-up to protect Mabel. And if that were true, many more facts must be missing from the record.[23]

But Peavey's quest for fame backfired when he was kidnapped by a group of Hearst reporters determined to make him confess. In a bizarre episode, the reporters drove Henry to the cemetery where Taylor's body was resting temporarily. A writer wearing a while sheet leaped up from behind a grave stone, shouting, "I am the ghost of William Desmond Taylor! You murdered me! Confess, Peavey!" Peavey just swore at the reporters and ran off.[24]

By March 8, 1922, 300 persons had confessed to the murder, yet the case was going nowhere. Few believed it was a coincidence. One exasperated writer proclaimed, "The movie interests will spend a million *not* to catch the murderer!"[25]

Claire Windsor was a good friend of Mabel. A popular actress under contract with Paramount Pictures, she specialized in playing high society girls. She was worried about her friend's alleged cocaine use but she knew that Mabel was no killer. When she tried to say so, her world was turned upside down: "I started to defend Mabel—she was my friend—but the second I opened my mouth my picture was plastered across the *Herald* along with my given name and the fact that I had a three-year-old illegitimate son. If I hadn't shut up I would've been out of a job."[26]

The press openly reported that the powerful studios were squelching the investigation. Actors couldn't talk, reporters couldn't write, and police could not arrest. The Arbuckle case caused havoc in Hollywood. This new scandal was could be suicide. Mabel's fate was sealed.

23

Fatal Tales

We have to work from trails that cross and criss-cross.
—Thomas Woolwine[1]

As the weeks and months dragged on, the Taylor murder case remained open and unsolved and the number of theories and suspects multiplied. In the days following the murder, confessions came in to the district attorney's office at the rate of ten per day.[2] And Mabel found herself trapped in a maddening situation. While they would neither accuse her, nor try her, they wouldn't clear her either. D.A. Thomas Woolwine was also in a frustrating position. Mabel was much loved by her public, and only an overwhelming amount of evidence could warrant an indictment against her. Still, Mabel was a Taylor intimate, and the last known person to see him alive. Even if she didn't pull the trigger, Woolwine was convinced that she knew more than she was saying. He also knew that he could never convict her.

Mabel's public identity was inextricably linked with the case. It was an identification that she would never escape. The press that once idolized her, turned against her. She was even mocked in print:

> Mabel sat in her gasoline hack
> Eating peanuts by the sack.
> She heard a shot but would not go,
> Because she loved the peanuts so.[3]

Meanwhile, Roscoe was engulfed in his own scandal. As Minta put it, "We couldn't take a breath without some reporter or detective asking something." The Arbuckles believed that their home was bugged, so the only place they felt safe talking was in the pool house. Mabel told Roscoe and Minta that she didn't understand why the press was out to get her.[4]

The widespread public outcry from civic, political, and religious organizations against Hollywood vice reached a fever pitch. By 1921, censorship bills were sweeping America. In 1915, in a unanimous decision, the Supreme Court decided, in *Mutual Film Corporation v. Industrial Commission of Ohio*, that free speech did not extend to motion pictures.[5] The movie industry was on the ropes. Someone to oversee the morals of the film industry was needed badly. Hollywood had little choice if they wanted to stay in business. The man chosen to fill the role of movie czar was Will H. Hays. Hays was the postmaster general under President Warren G. Harding and the former head of the Republican National Committee. Just as important, he was a Presbyterian elder. On January 4, 1921, he signed a three-year contract to serve as head of the Motion Picture Producers and Distributors of America, at a salary of $150,000 a year.[6]

To establish his authority, Hays set his sights on Arbuckle. On April 19, 1922, as his first act as head of the MPPDA, he banned Arbuckle from the screen.[7] The decision was met with almost universal acclaim. Religious organizations, civic groups, school districts, city councils, and anyone running for office, rushed to go on record as endorsing the move. What was largely unreported was that Hays, showing considerable political backbone, reversed his decision only eight months later. But the American people did not reverse theirs. While now able to work, Roscoe was consigned to a life of directing and appearing in second-rate shorts.

At the time of the murder, Mabel was in the middle of shooting *Suzanna*, a tale of Old California based on a novel by Linton Wells.[8] After being away for weeks, she returned to complete the picture. Onscreen, her arms appeared thinner and her eyes appeared sadder, but Mabel turned in a charming and convincing performance.

Suzanna tells the story of a beautiful girl living on the rancho of Don Fernando. Ramon, the son of the don, wants to marry her but finds himself trapped in an arranged marriage to Dolores, the daughter of Don Diego. Ramon and Suzanna go riding together, but Don Fernando does not approve of their flirting and sends Suzanna away to live at a nearby mission. Don Diego arrives with Dolores, a girl who catches the eye of Pancho, a toreador. They hatch a scheme in which Ramon marries Dolores and then meets his death in a duel, leaving Dolores a wealthy widow and free to marry Pancho. Meanwhile, Suzanna discovers that she is actually Don Diego's daughter and was switched at birth. Pancho tries to provoke Ramon into a duel by proposing to Suzanna. Suzanna, unaware that she is being used, and despairing over losing Ramon, sadly accepts. Both weddings begin but Ramon is overcome by his regret and love for Suzanna. He boldly invades Suzanna's wedding and spirits her away, leading to a chase and a duel with Pancho. True love wins out and Suzanna and Ramon marry.

Suzanna, 1922 (Marc Wanamaker/Bison Archives).

The surviving prints of *Suzanna* are missing two reels, although the film is still enjoyable. Notable sequences include a wild tomahawk dance that Suzanna performs instead of doing her chores. When Don Fernando catches her, she rushes to a Roman Catholic altar and prays in mock earnestness to avoid a beating. When Suzanna is sent away on foot to the mission,

Suzanna proved a modest success despite the controversy over Taylor's death. Mabel was ill and exhausted but determinedly finished the film (Marc Wanamaker/Bison Archives).

we see on film, for one of the few times, the inimitable Mabel Normand walk: quick, pigeon-toed, purposeful and cute.

When *Suzanna* was released, Mack was sure that the murder would kill the film's receipts. But despite the scandal, *Suzanna* was a hit. Mabel's public did not desert her. Moreover, they accepted her transition into subtler performances. The *Chicago Daily News* noted, "There is more of the wistful and less of the comic element in previous Mabel Normand pictures. *Suzanna* classes among the first-rate pictures worth seeing."[9]

As for the Taylor murder, it became a cottage industry in Hollywood. Each investigation proudly proclaimed the killer's identity, and each investigation was promptly ignored by everyone with a different theory. It was indeed a strange tale. The man who appeared to have no enemies clearly had one too many. Police were baffled by the multiplicity of suspects and leads that seemed to wander lost through the Hollywood community, suggesting suspects but never identifying one.

Learned scholars, writers and even eyewitnesses to Taylor's life looked at the same evidence and reached opposing conclusions. Hard facts, assumptions and wild speculation have been woven together into a tight tapestry of suspects, motives, means and pure nonsense. All we are left with is seven main theories, each one begging for the additional evidence that, most likely, will never come.

Theory #1—The Killer Was Mary Miles Minter

In this scenario, Mary was madly, even obsessively in love with William Taylor, but the huge age difference gave Taylor some pause. He took a paternalistic interest in Mary at first, and truly tried to help her. Pouring her heart out to him, she told him about her abusive mother taking her salary and controlling her every move. An embrace here and there led to some light kissing on the cheeks and the forehead. And, before long, the couple found themselves involved. Many nights she would wait until her mother was asleep, then sneak out to see him. Perhaps sensing a soul as troubled as his own, Taylor stopped short of sexual intercourse, which Mary mistook for chivalry. What Bill had no way of knowing was that Mary had a history of psychiatric problems, having attempted suicide twice: once as a child, once as a teenager.

According to this theory, Mary became frustrated with a relationship that was going nowhere. Finally, she could take it no more. Arriving at Taylor's home armed with her mother's revolver, she confronted him and threatened to shoot herself if he did not marry her. William embraced her in an effort to calm her hysteria, and the gun went off. He collapsed to the floor. In a frenzy of panic, she quickly realized that he was dead. Crying, she was afraid to call the police, and too full of love for him to leave the body crumpled where it lay. She laid him straight on his back, closed his eyes, combed his hair, put his arms at his side and smoothed his jacket and pants. She then made her escape.

Theory #2—The Killer Was Charlotte Shelby

Charlotte Shelby, Mary Miles Minter's obsessively controlling mother, pushed Mary into show business, effectively and callously depriving her of a childhood. Charlotte was volatile and cruel. The story is told of Charlotte ripping Mary's favorite doll from her arms and throwing it into the stove, prompting the first of Mary's suicide attempts. Charlotte oversaw Mary's finances and virtually everything else in her life. She was furious when she discovered Mary's romance with Taylor. She owned a .38 caliber snub-nosed revolver, and she knew how to use it. Acquaintances remember well the number of times that she threatened to "blow someone's head off" after they had crossed her in some way.

According to this theory, Charlotte stalked Taylor for weeks, waiting for an opportunity to shoot him. On the evening of February 1, as Taylor walked Mabel to her car, Charlotte, who had been hiding in the shadows, slipped into his house through the open front door and waited. When he came back in, she aimed and shot him in the back.

Theory #3—The Killer Was Mabel Normand

Of all the major suspects in the Taylor murder, Mabel's story was the only one that held up, the only one that didn't change over time. Mabel's visit on the night of the murder was incredibly unfortunate. Had Taylor not asked her to stop by pick up a couple of books, she would have never been on the suspect list. Still, there are those who would see a more sinister motivation for her visit that night.

According to this theory, Mabel and William were secretly engaged to be married. Mabel knew about his romance with Mary, and didn't like it. They began to have heated arguments. Mabel's foul language would fill the air, and was overheard by others. In a jealous rage she cut up all William's pictures of her. When Mabel entered his bungalow on February 1, she had both the motive and the opportunity; and she took it.

Theory #4—The Killer Was Mrs. Ethel Cunningham Deane-Tanner

William Taylor had left his wife and daughter in New York City. His departure consigned them to a life of poverty and shame. One evening, years later, when the pair attended a movie, they were astonished to see "William Desmond Taylor" on the big screen. Ethel turned to her daughter and said, "That's your father!" Even though she had obtained a divorce in William's absence, Ethel was furious at what he had done to them.

As a young woman, Taylor's daughter made the trek to Hollywood and found her father. According to accounts, they had a surprisingly pleasant visit at his bungalow, and she stayed with him for several days. When she returned to New York, she provided her mother with his home address. The ex–Mrs. Taylor now could take her revenge.

Theory #5—The Killer Was Edward Sands

Taylor hired Edward Sands as his secretary and cook soon after moving to Alvarado Court. Sands did well at first. But Taylor trusted him both far too quickly and far too much. Those around Taylor were not as charmed with the man as He was. To many of them, he seemed unbalanced. They were unnerved by his repeated statement that 35 years of life were enough for him, and that he planned to blow his brains out on his 35th birthday.

When Taylor left for Europe to find help for his chronic stomach ailment, he naively signed a blank check and gave it to Sands, to cover any emergencies. Sands gave in to his capacity for self-indulgence. When Taylor filed a formal complaint, Sands vowed revenge. To most people, Taylor's murder seemed like the work of a madman, and Sands was an obvious suspect.

Theory #6—The Killer Was a Hollywood Drug Dealer

Taylor felt deeply protective of Mabel Normand. He took her drug addiction personally, and was determined to help her. She had been at the Watkins Glen Sanatorium in late 1920, allegedly for the treatment of a cocaine addiction. By the winter of 1921, Taylor was shocked to discover that Mabel was again using cocaine. He felt passionately about this issue. While working at Paramount, Taylor had a drug dealer physically thrown off the lot. The rumor was that Mabel's drug dealer was a local peanut vendor.

According to this theory, Taylor caught a drug dealer at Mabel's back door, chased him off the property and subsequently became an informant for U.S. Attorney Tom Green. It didn't take area drug dealers long to figure out who was informing on them, and decided to have Taylor killed.

Theory #7—The Strange Case of Margaret Gibson

On October 21, 1964, a young man named Raphael Long was called to the home of neighbor Pat Lewis, a reclusive old woman. He found her on her back, in the throes of a heart attack. The police were called repeatedly, but they did not arrive for 45 minutes. She then began frantically calling out for a Catholic priest. When none appeared, she urgently began talking. She said that she had been a film actress and claimed that she had murdered William Desmond Taylor. Long was startled, but didn't record her confession as he had no knowledge of the 1922 murder. After her death, Raphael searched public records but found no trace of a movie actress named Pat Lewis. Her real name was Margaret Gibson.

Margaret Gibson began her acting career as a young girl. She was hired by Vitagraph and spent the next six years taking on a wide variety of roles, supporting herself and her mother in the process. For a few months she worked alongside another actor named William Desmond Taylor. In 1915, she left Vitagraph and moved to the Thomas Ince Film Company. Her career came to a halt in 1917 when she was arrested for vagrancy and allegations of drug dealing. Though the charges were eventually dropped, she wisely changed her name to Patricia Palmer. On November 2, 1923, she was arrested again, charged with being part of a national blackmail and extortion operation. Again, after much time and trouble, she escaped charges. When she was free, she fled to Singapore where she met and married an American oil man, Elbert Lewis, and became known as Pat Lewis. In 1940 she returned to the U.S. to be treated for a bladder infection. Before she could return to Elbert, he was killed by Japanese bombers who attacked his oil plant in the early stages of World War II. Without the means to leave the country again, Lewis lived out her life on a widow's pension in a tiny Southern California house. Among her neighbors was the young Raphael Long. When Raphael shared Pat's confession with his mother, she remarked that Pat had long ago told her of the murder that she had committed, after becoming hysterical while watching a local television show about the murder.

24

Sail Away

Mabel Normand is the idol of London!
—San Francisco Chronicle[1]

Suzanna was finished and Mabel had to get away. After a cross-country train trip to reach New York, she was to set sail for Europe on June 13, 1922. Mabel was sailing on Southampton's *Aquitania* of the Cunard Ship Line. She arrived just minutes before departure, planning to board quickly and quietly and just slip away. But the reporters who had staked out the West 14th Street dock weren't there to wish her a safe trip; they asked Mabel about the murder. "Please don't discuss that," Mabel said dejectedly. "I've been running away from that for months."[2] Her destination was Cherbourg and Southampton, England. She took along her friend Juliet Courtial and travelled under the name "Miss Mabel Norman."[3] Her goal was to see London, Paris and Berlin, and have fun.

Mabel's decision to sail on the *Aquitania* was a godsend for the Cunard Line. Only a year after the *Titanic* disaster, the fleet was forced to create the most opulent ship at sea to lure nervous passengers back onto the water. The porters were surprised to find Mabel's trunks so heavy. They discovered that they were loaded with books.[4] As America receded into the distance, Mabel reportedly did a diving exhibition in the ship's diving tank.[5]

A private letter from a passenger commented on Mabel's Atlantic crossing:

> Our stewardess took care of her and had a great deal of admiration for her. I sent my card to her, and, after a very restful day, she called on me in my cabin. No simple young girl could have been more charming. Do you think she knows my story? For she immediately told me I had sad eyes and mentioned Jane Cawl in *Smiling Through*. Of course we wept a little together, and then I whispered my little story to her. She suggested, quite commercially, that if Scribner's would not have me, possibly "Smart Set" would. She also invited me for tea or lunch, and I think she

was a little modest when she did not see me dressed quietly in black, talking to Pasadena friends. I reminded her in another little note of my request for her signature in Charlie's autograph album.

Poor Mabel fell from her pedestal that evening, with much noise, about midnight. Our stewardess ceased to love her and so did I for a short time, but Mabel is very clever and a little note sent me just before leaving the ship very tactfully put her back in my heart. I thought this would amuse you.[6]

When Mabel arrived in London, she wanted to avoid the limelight. She quietly went around seeing the sights and buying things. But that couldn't last forever and word soon got out. One evening, as crowds followed her though the streets, she visited a London pub. She stood politely and answered questions from fans. When Mabel reached out to shake hands with a fan, many more hands reached out to her. The crowd got larger and more intense. Mabel failed to notice that she was in a corner. As the crowd came closer, Mabel became flustered and distressed. At the last moment, a man from Brooklyn, New York, bulled his way through the crowd and carried a frightened Mabel outside to safety.[7]

"London's reception of Mabel Normand, the American movie star, was overwhelming according to a member of Miss Normand's vacation party."[8] Mabel's fan mail in England was about eight to ten thousand letters a day. Mabel remembered, "Little did I realize that I would be recognized, or never for a moment would I have gone. But somehow or other they instantly began calling me 'Mybel' in their quaint Cockney dialect, and instead of a quiet little stroll, it assumed the proportions of a parade!"[9] When Mabel jumped in her car to leave, one ardent English suitor was determined to follow. Mabel caught sight of him instantly and decided to have some fun. She led him on a wild ride through the English countryside all night.[10]

A journalist arrived at Mabel's hotel room at The Ritz expecting a normal celebrity interview. When she came in, Mabel was engrossed in a book. But Mabel had her mind set on experiencing the Limehouse District and announced to the startled writer that she had a taxi waiting and they were going with some friends to see it for themselves. When they got in the taxi, Mabel ordered the driver to take them to "The Slums." She was a huge fan of author Thomas Burke, especially his books *Limehouse Nights* and *Whispering Windows*, and wanted to see firsthand the environment and the conditions he described.[11]

Burke's *Limestone Nights* was a gritty portrayal of poverty and despair in London's Limehouse District, with special attention paid to the Chinatown area. (The narrator of the book is a Chinese character named Quong Lee.) His work, wildly popular in America, inspired D.W. Griffith's classic film *Broken Blossoms*. *Limestone Nights* generated special controversy for its depictions of interracial relationships. Mabel viewed it as a place of unique charm and even romanticism. What she didn't realize was that the Limehouse District was every bit as perilous as the book described. Their taxi crossed the bridge into South London[12] and headed for Limehouse, a place of shoddy buildings, heavy fog and few streetlights. They arrived around 11:00 p.m. "We'd better get out here and walk," their male escort said. "A car in these parts will attract too much attention. I'll tell the driver to wait here."[13]

The group uneasily got out and were not sure where to walk. The only man in the party demanded that Mabel remove her jewelry before they began. But Mabel refused to drop her jewelry in her purse. The group proceeded through the dark Chinatown streets. Their efforts were rewarded when they found a beautiful temple hidden from view.[14]

As before, Mabel caused a near-riot as crowds of people followed her everywhere she went. When she and her party went into a Chinese restaurant, a policeman nervously stood guard outside the door and was quite anxious for the movie star's visit to end. When Mabel and her party came out of the restaurant, a huge throng was waiting and happily shouted at her:

"Mabel! Hello Mabel!"

"What's it like in America, Mabel?"

"Is Mabel you real name?"

"How old are you?"

The group made their way back to a waiting taxi. Mabel reluctantly got inside and headed back to the Ritz.[15] When she arrived at her hotel room, she discovered that a Royal Command Appearance was waiting for her. The hotel staff was ecstatic to give her the news, but Mabel was nervous about it. She found it ironic that her quest for the common experience would lead her to the royal palace.

Mabel arrived at Buckingham Palace a few days before her royal encounter. She was assigned a lady-in-waiting to school her in royal etiquette and to be her escort during the entire process. She planned to wear an evening gown, but was told that a simple dress that extended to the elbows would suffice. She was told not to bring up a topic of conversation unless it was first mentioned by a royal. She was instructed to never turn her back on royalty. Her escort told her that the simplest solution was to wait for the king and queen to stand to leave a room and simply follow them.

Mabel's get-together with the king and queen was cancelled when Sir Henry Wilson, a British war hero, was murdered. His assassination by the IRA caused international turmoil.[16]

24. Sail Away

Mabel couldn't wait to get to Paris. She got the last available seat on a small airplane. She was determined to forget her troubles in a blizzard of alcohol and shopping. Able to speak and read French, she bought gems by the handful and wowed the French in elegant gowns. Other times she put on a soft hat and sunglasses and went about unnoticed. She spent thousands of dollars on frocks and hats. She spent days shopping in the streets of Paris. But soon the word was out that Mabel was in town. Designers came to her. They paraded their creations into Mabel's hotel suite as she sat on the floor and pointed to the ones she liked. Those who were there said that she pointed more often than not.

It was then that Prince Ibrahim of Egypt re-entered her life. The prince was in Paris pursuing good times and beautiful women. Mabel enjoyed their friendship and the two were spotted in the best restaurants. The prince gave her a gold scarab, expensive rugs and assorted jewels and even had two perfumes created to commemorate their love. The scents Oud Save the King and Oud Save the Queen are still available today. But Mabel was firmly against a romance and was not swayed even by the throne of Cleopatra.[17]

From Paris she headed to Monte Carlo. Her first night there she had a run of luck in the casino and had an extra pile of cash to play with.[18] Mabel sailed home in September on the *Majestic*. She was delighted to discover that new star Pola Negri was on the same ship. Pola, a sensation of the German film industry, was so successful that Paramount believed she was cutting into their European profits. They had no choice but to buy out her contract and summon her to Hollywood. Mabel took every opportunity to praise Pola and deflect attention from herself.[19]

When Mabel arrived back in New York in September 1922, she had already decided that she wanted to return to Europe. She planned to spend Christmas 1922 in England with a group of friends. She checked into the Hotel Ambassador, where she found attention of a different sort. Her trunks, wardrobe, jewelry and all other property had been attached and seized from the hotel safe over a bill of $2940 allegedly owed to press agent Perry M. Charles. He claimed that Mabel incurred the debt during her European tour, especially in London, Paris and Berlin. Perry apparently went ahead of Mabel on her tour and arranged publicity and introductions to local reporters, editors and theatrical writers. Perry conceded that Mabel had paid him $1100 but noted that he had spent $1340 on Mabel's behalf. In court, Perry produced two telegrams from Mabel in May 1922 that contained very definite promises of payment:

> Perry Dear—Wire me collect your plan. Received wire this A.M. Wonderful if you are in England when I arrive to meet me. Without you I will be lost. Love

and thanks to the Tates. Is Harry (Tate) paying your passage? Wire details. If you need money, wire me. When do you sail? Might be able to go along. Want you to work for me. Anything you say goes about salary. Might be better your going ahead to fix things up, then return to America with me. London, Paris, Berlin, etc. When arrive New York will telephone you. Love, Mabel.

Perry Dear—Can I phone you anywhere and at what time Wednesday? Send me straight wire. Also insist upon paying for phone. You are beloved by me. Telephone me Wilshire 7226. Love, Perry, always. M[20]

Mabel was not even able to access her jewelry, which was particularly galling to her. A reporter in the hotel lobby was determined to get Mabel to discuss the problem. When he caught sight of her flitting through the lobby in a white, shimmering dress, he tried to catch up with her but could not. He called her in her room. At first she claimed to know nothing about the situation, but then agreed to come down to be interviewed. She descended the stairs with a male escort but quickly changed her mind, and instead ran outside to her waiting limousine.[21]

Mabel did return to Europe. She sailed with a new group of friends on the *Majestic* on December 16, 1922. She promised Mack that she would return by December 27 or 28. In Europe, she met George Bernard Shaw, H.G. Wells and members of the royal family.[22] Mabel insisted that she was doing movie research and planned to film a movie with an English backdrop. She toured European film studios and tried to learn from their methods. Others whom she met in the course of her visits were Sophie Tucker, Max Linder and Marie Dressler. She went to as many movies as she could to determine what kind of Hollywood movies Europeans liked best. Mabel was once again interested in moviemaking. When she returned home she was ready to go to work. And she prayed that the scandal was behind her.

25

To Live Through Pain

Be patient when there's sorrow,
The sun will shine again.
Always, there is tomorrow.
Learn to live through pain.—Mabel.[1]

In the spring of 1923, Mack began preliminary shooting on *The Extra Girl*, starring his new girlfriend Phyllis Haver. Within a month, Phyllis left the picture, the studio and Mack. He then tested Priscilla Bonner, Sigrid Holmquist, Evelyn Brent, Betty Francisco and Virginia Brown Faire. All were unsatisfactory. He finally got Mabel with the promise of $3000 a week and a percentage of the profits. It was another one-picture deal, with the promise of a second deal to star in Sennett's production *Mary Anne*.[2]

The Extra Girl tells the story of movie-crazy Sue Graham, who dreams of travelling to Hollywood and working as an actress. She is in love with Dave Giddings but her father wants her to marry the prosperous Aaron Applewhite. She writes a letter to the studio asking for her chance in the movies but a jealous rival switches the photo she enclosed with that of another girl. Dave spirits Sue away to the train station to avoid a wedding and she leaves for Hollywood. On arrival she learns of the photo switch and only manages to get a job in the wardrobe department. Dave follows her to Hollywood and is hired as a stagehand. She finally gets a screen test which comically goes wrong. Sue loses her job by releasing a lion that runs amok through the studio. But she and Dave marry and find happiness beyond Hollywood dreams.

The film is widely known as an excellent record of filmmaking production in the 1920s, and Sennett's burlesque of his own studio is fun to watch. Mabel's experience making the film was marred by a bout with appendicitis. Rather than admitting herself to a hospital to have her appendix removed, she wanted time to rest and to have fun, promising to take care of the problem after the winter holidays.

On Sunday, August 5, 1923, Mabel was in San Diego enjoying a horseback ride on Coronado Beach. After several miles, her horse got spooked when she turned toward the surf. Breaking into an unbridled gallop, he threw Mabel to the sand and pawed at her. Mabel was left with a broken left collarbone, nerve shock and a bruised left eye. She was transported to Good Samaritan Hospital in Los Angeles.[3] With her arm and shoulder enclosed in plaster, she laid on her back for a week before being discharged to recover at home. Released on November 9, 1923, *The Extra Girl* was a hit. Mabel signed to do a personal appearance tour in support of the film in the coming year.

On January 1, 1924, after a night of heavy drinking, Edna Purviance and her fiancé, 34-year-old Denver playboy Courtland Dines, invited Mabel to join them at Dines' apartment at 325-B North Vermont Avenue. When Mabel arrived, the three embarked upon a round of drinking. For Mabel, it was her last chance to be rambunctious for a while, as she would be entering the hospital the next day to have her long-delayed appendix operation.

At one point, a drunken Dines began chiding Mabel for forgetting to bring his Christmas present, a pair of military hair brushes. Mabel immediately called her friend and houseguest Edith Burns and asked Edith to have her chauffeur, the small, bespectacled, 27-year-old Joe Kelly, get the gift from atop her radiator and deliver it.[4] Genuinely concerned about Mabel, Edith reminded her that she had to report for surgery early the next morning, and suggested that she allow Kelly to drive her home. Kelly, within earshot of the conversation, misunderstood the tenor of the exchange and, according to his own account, ran upstairs to get Mabel's gun from her bathroom cupboard.

En route to Dines' apartment, Kelly convinced himself that the wealthy cad, Courtland Dines, was preventing Mabel from leaving his apartment. Mabel was sitting on the davenport when Kelly knocked on the door. Dines went to answer it.

In the adjoining bedroom with the door open, Edna was powdering her face. As Kelly walked in carrying the package for Dines, Mabel got up to ask Edna if she could borrow her powder puff. Behind her, the two men almost immediately began exchanging angry words, to which Mabel paid little mind. Edna and Mabel were chatting in the bedroom when they heard what they assumed to be firecrackers in celebration of the New Year. Mabel did not even turn around at first. When she finally did, she saw Dines bent over and staggering toward her, clutching his chest with both hands and bleeding profusely. Kelly was nowhere to be seen. "I'm plugged!" gasped Dines, and the two women rushed to his aid.[5] "Can you believe it?" he cried. "That hophead shot me!"[6]

Kelly, who had run to the police station to confess to the shooting, kept repeating that Dines had picked up an almost empty Gaelic Old Smuggler's Scotch whisky bottle to "brain" him, and that he was only defending himself.[7] The facts that came out shortly after Kelly's arrest revealed that he had shot at Dines three times. The first shot had missed, the second grazed his right ear, and the third hit him in the chest.

A court-appointed psychiatrist eventually testified that Kelly had a "deep spiritual love for Miss Normand, and was motivated by a delusion that he needed to protect her."[8] Kelly claimed that he had only done what any gentleman would do. It was also revealed that Joe Kelly was not Joe Kelly. He was Horace Greer, a cocaine addict who had escaped from an Oakland, California, chain gang after serving 15 days of a 75-day sentence and fled to Los Angeles.[9]

Mabel lay in bed that night, curled up to accommodate the pain of her swollen appendix. Sick in body, and sick at heart, she knew what was coming. Again the scandal was spelled out in headlines. In the days ahead, Mabel was so horrified at the press coverage that she refused to pick up a newspaper for a year.[10]

Once again, Mabel was called upon to give a moment-by-moment account of a crime that she had nothing to do with. For many in Hollywood, this was too much, and many sought to distance themselves from Mabel. Even Mack felt the need to announce to reporters that he had no contractual agreement with Mabel Normand. Her upcoming film was cancelled. She would never work for Sennett again.

The movie that Mabel never made, *Mary Anne*, relates the story of a girl who longs for expensive clothes and fine living. She believes in the Law of Opulence, that concentration brings material results. Mack wrote in his production notes:

> She spends all her spare moments longing for wealth, but she finds she loses all her old friends, her personal freedom and finally is in danger of losing her life on account of the money. This shows developmental of her character and brings a real psychological kick to our story. She finally renounces all the wealth and goes back to the happiness which the life she is most familiar brings to her.[11]

Horace Greer-Joe Kelly was unable to come up with $10,000 in bail and was assigned to the county jail to await trial. Miraculously, after being shot at point blank range, Courtland Dines was making a full recovery, as the bullet somehow did not do any great harm. Within days, Mabel would enter the Good Samaritan Hospital, the same hospital where Dines lay, for her operation. It fueled rumors in the press that she had undergone her "so-called operation" to avoid being questioned by authorities.

When Mabel was released from the hospital, she fled to the Ambassador Hotel in Chicago to see her mother. Although Mabel at first agreed to an interview with journalist James P. Sinnot, her mother stepped in and barred the writer from their hotel room.[12] A few months later she and her mother sought even more seclusion at a mountain cabin in Minnesota.[13]

In April, Mabel kept her commitment to make a series of theater appearances to promote *The Extra Girl*. In many states, voices had been raised in Mabel's defense, and the preemptory ban of her films, on both the state and local levels, were slowly being lifted. Her courageous marketing efforts paid

In *The Extra Girl* (1923) the stress began to show on the screen (Marc Wanamaker/Bison Archives).

off, and *The Extra Girl* ended up doing excellent business. But Mack spent a fortune on publicity to offset the scandal. With only a one-picture contract in place, both Mack and Mabel had their freedom.

Mabel's *Extra Girl* personal appearance tour took her to Newark, New Jersey, where she was spotted by theatrical producer Al Woods. He was convinced that her screen presence would translate well to the stage.

But in California, District Attorney Asa Keyes had his re-election to think about, and talking about the Dines shooting was a perfect way to posture for the voters. While Mabel had been cooperating with the investigation from the very beginning, he announced that if she did not return to L.A. to appear as a witness at the Greer trial, she would be banned from working in motion pictures indefinitely. Of course, his argument was erroneous. He had no authority to ban Mabel from anything. But exaggerating his own authority could only enhance his reputation.[14]

Mabel angrily got on a train and took the trip back across the country to California. Astonishingly, upon her return, the June 17, 1924, trial date of Horace Greer became the anticlimax to the entire sordid affair. While he was

The Extra Girl (1923) was Mabel's final feature film, and her last for Mack Sennett (center). F. Richard Jones, also pictured, was the director (Marc Wanamaker/Bison Archives).

charged with assault with a deadly weapon to commit murder, neither Mabel nor Edna had witnessed the shooting. And Dines, claiming that he was too drunk to remember anything, refused to testify. For reasons of his own, Dines did not even want to press charges and was ready to forgive and forget the whole thing.[15] Greer could not be forced to testify. With such a lack of drama, the press immediately put the spotlight on Mabel. Her responses under cross-examination would not only keep the crowded courtroom laughing, but would become a quotable part of Hollywood lore.

When asked if she had told Greer to shoot Dines, Mabel replied, "For Heaven's sake no! Why should I tell anybody to plug anybody, anyhow?"[16] And when she was asked how she could account for Greer's actions, she exclaimed, "He must have been crazy, or wild! I don't know!"[17] Asked how much Dines had to drink, she replied, "He had plenty." And, much to the crowd's delight, when the attorney's badgering finally became too much for her, she turned on him: "You haven't any right to cross-examine me like that! What do you want to be so mean to me for? That isn't the way you were supposed to act! The idea of cross-examining me like that! That wasn't the understanding I had with you!"[18] When Mabel's attorney Milton Cohen objected to her treatment, Judge Charles Crail could only laugh. "This witness seems perfectly able to take care of herself," he said.[19] When the case was submitted to the jury, there was little for them to do but to acquit. Greer was released, but in a bizarre twist, he was re-arrested one hour later on a Prohibition charge.[20] Ultimately, the only one hurt in the case was Mabel.

The *Wisconsin State Journal* printed an editorial that reflected the view of many:

"The Egg"

The action of the Chicago club in refusing to condemn Mabel Normand without a hearing sounds fair enough. The principle is all right. The trouble with it is that Mabel has been having a hearing for several years. She has been widely described in the press as the victim of dope, and as an accomplished bacchanalian. She was involved in the Taylor shooting in a manner that caused her to be closely questioned by officials. Her name has long been associated with the class of riotous livers who are bringing bad fame to their legitimate fellows in the profession. Now she is a witness in another shooting in which her chauffeur wielded the gun, and no worldly-wise person doubts that the affair was the outcome of a drinking party. In all the years Mabel Normand has denied none of these things, so far as we know. Certainly, if they were false, she would've had libel suits instituted against every newspaper in the United States. And her failure to call her critics to account in the courts where her reputation is at stake suggests that the circumstances do not warrant her in bringing the matter to an issue.

While public opinion may justify the view of the Chicago women's clubs that Miss Normand should not be condemned until the Dines shooting case has been tried and evidence legally adduced, it is liable to indulge in a quiet talk, in the plans of the club women, to settle the matter by having Miss Normand come to Chicago to tell her own story. No doubt it will be a good story, fully exonerating her, albeit she may create something of a shock by repeating her reference to her chauffeur as "that egg," language that may cause aristocratic eyebrows in Chicago's 400 to be delicately raised. In any event, it is doubtful that club women throughout the country will agree with the assertion made in the Chicago club, and then in the Normand case, that "We women must stand together." Not every American club woman will care to "stand together" with Mabel Normand.

When Mabel Normand made her second bid for immortality through the medium of the Dines shooting affair, there arose throughout the country a newspaper protest against her further connection with the screen. Mabel was quick to see the handwriting on the wall—the stone wall of public opinion—which Fatty Arbuckle could not pass through from infamy to reinstatement. There was something pitiable about this seared woman's pleading with the reporters for "a chance."

But there was nothing repentant about her plea. She did not comprehend the public verdict that one who lives the life which begets shootings will be connected to shootings. To lay the blame on the "egg," and protesting her own righteousness was the sum of her statement. And if evidence of her unfitness as an entertainer for home people were waning, her failure to censor herself for her familiar part of the story as a dope addict would suffice.

Mabel Normand has weathered enough discreditable notoriety to have retired the average movie star. Probably the impression that she has been making a brave fight to overcome a drug habit has tempered criticism. Doubtless, the sudden cessation of demands for her ostracism was due to a feeling that her case had better await her recovery from what happened with that appendicitis operation, which she underwent immediately after her latest scandal, possibly to escape reporters and win sympathy. At any rate, the fact remains that more than any other actress, Normand's name is taken as the synonym for loose living and licentious habits. It is all right to be wisely merciful, but this country must be merciful to the young generation which is getting much of its outlook on life from the silver screen. They should not be sacrificed to sentimental notions about a woman who has never sacrificed a wayward sensation in defense of her reputation. Mabel Normand is not the victim of persecution. She has been sinned against only by herself. The pitcher has gone too often to the well. Patience has ceased to be a virtue.[21]

In September of 1924, socialite Dorothea Church sued her millionaire husband Norman W. Church for divorce. While her petition accused him of numerous offenses, the most notorious charge was that Mr. Church, while in Good Samaritan Hospital after being involved in an automobile accident in the fall of 1923, had enjoyed some intimate encounters with Mabel while she was convalescing from her Coronado beach horseback riding accident. Specifically, she accused Mabel of running in and out of Mr. Church's room clad only in her nightgown and sharing alcoholic drinks with him. Mabel was livid.[22] "I was bound up like a sore thumb. The only way I would have been able to get around would have been to swing from the chandelier by my teeth!"[23] Again forced to explain something that she had very little knowledge of, Mabel referred the case to her lawyers. "There is a limit to human endurance, and I have reached mine! This is more than I can stand!"[24] On October 10, 1924, her lawyers filed a $500,000 libel suit against Dorothea Church that instantly hit the newspapers. Her lawyers forced Mrs. Church to withdraw her complaint, and thereupon withdrew her suit. But Mabel was furious when Mrs. Church's retraction left her with no recourse. "I don't want her money, but I do want a chance to clear my name in court."[25] But Judge Shaw decided that Mabel had no direct interest in the outcome of the case and therefore was not entitled to intervene.[26] While the matter was concluded, the damage to Mabel's reputation was irreparable. Her protestations of innocence were by now all too familiar to the American public, and no longer taken seriously. Where there was smoke, there had to be fire.

While Mabel always had friends who would remain fanatically devoted to her, she was genuinely hurt by those who now kept her at a distance. As someone who was able to both love and trust completely, disloyalty was something that she wasn't prepared for. She did not harbor any illusions about the Hollywood press corps, but to Mabel her press coverage was mean, hyperbolic and too personal. She was ready for something new, and she was ready to be close to home, on Staten Island. So when Al Woods called to set up a meeting with her at the Ambassador Hotel in Los Angeles to discuss a live theater run, she was more receptive than she might otherwise have been. Despite her concerns about her ability to project her voice across the footlights, she signed to play the lead in the Clifford Grey farce *A Kiss in the Taxi*. Come summer, she listed her house for rent and headed to the East Coast for rehearsals.[27]

In August 1925, she took a New York apartment with a one-year lease.[28] She was shocked to find that the property she was slated to star in was switched from *A Kiss in the Taxi* to *The Little Mouse*. But she was guaranteed $1500 a week and a percentage of the gross receipts.[29]

A musical comedy, *The Little Mouse* was a property that had been rewritten and re-produced under four previous titles: *Oh Diana!*, *Diana of the Movies*, *The Five O'Clock Man* and *The Blue Mouse*. It did not have a single successful run to its credit. When the critics recognized what it was, they hated it all over again. Mabel opened in Hartford, Connecticut, then the production played Ashbury Park, New Jersey, Atlantic City, New Jersey, Washington D.C., Brooklyn, New York, and Providence, Rhode Island, in preparation for its Broadway opening.[30] Mabel knew that projecting her voice was a problem. Voice coaches Laurette Taylor, Willard Mack and Holbrook Blinn reassured her that she was coming along fine.[31] While it was predicted that Mabel's notoriety would bode well for the play's success, one critic made the snide qualification that her connection to Hollywood tragedies and escapades would at least draw the curious if not the elite.

The production was a disaster. Stepping in to try to save the play, Willard Mack completely reworked the second act, but to no avail. After an unmerciful lambasting by the critics, Mabel refused to go on with the play.[32] Woods released her from her contract, and Mabel left for Southern California.

Her friend, the humorist Will Rogers, couldn't resist noting her return. One night, on stage at the Pantages Theatre, he told the crowd, "There was a shooting today in Los Angeles. Mabel Normand must be in town!"[33]

26

Final Frames

*I'm tired of being Cinderella. In fact I'm tired
of being Mabel Normand.* —Mabel[1]

In February 1926—perhaps at the behest of F. Richard Jones (now a vice-president and production supervisor at Roach studios)—Hal Roach signed Mabel to a one-picture deal at his "Lot of Fun."[2] Mabel was not a favorite of Roach's. He considered her off-color humor, smoking and drinking to be a disgrace. He did, however, appreciate her talent; and if she made money for the studio, he would hold his peace. Besides, the commitment was a nominal one. The contract called for her to star in a short comedy at a salary of $500 for the first week and $1000 for each succeeding week.[3] It was understood that if the picture did well, the contract could be extended to include additional shorts and possibly a return to features. Oddly, the contract also included a provision (Mabel would later recall with great amusement) that she "never weigh more than one hundred and eleven pounds."[4]

By the time of her contract with Roach, Mabel felt free enough from her past to joke about the Dines shooting. She stated that before she hired another chauffeur, she was going to give him a "psychopathic examination."[5] Neither Hollywood nor the press was as willing to laugh about it.

Instead of returning to the screen in 1926, Mabel could have retired to a life of comfort and financial security. After the public abuse she'd taken, it would have been easy, even advisable. She had money, loyal friends, no shortage of male admirers and an impressive body of work. Any comeback attempt—especially in three-reel shorts—could only be seen as a sheepish comedown from the heights of *Mickey* and the Mabel Normand Feature Film Company. But Mabel didn't see it that way. She was nobody's victim, and couldn't bring herself to leave the screen on terms other than her own. For good or bad, she was determined to have the last word.

She arrived at the Hal Roach Studio in Culver City on March 8, 1926, to begin *Raggedy Rose*.[6] She was referred to in the press as "former screen star, Mabel Normand."[7] Jones was assigned to supervise her productions. Her co-directors were Richard Wallace and the soon-to-be star Stan Laurel (who also co-authored the screenplay).[8]

In the spring of 1923, District Attorney Asa Keyes, who was known as a friend in Hollywood, went after Mabel again. Like before he wanted to question her about the Taylor murder. A week after filming began on *Raggedy Rose*, a series of announcements from his office shook Mabel to her core. She was placed under police surveillance, perhaps to be summoned and questioned once again about the Taylor murder.[9] Keyes wanted indictments. Like a plot twist in the third act, this could finally destroy everything.

No longer the silent mourner of 1922, nor the exasperated casualty of 1924, Mabel was finally, purely and righteously livid. She shot back with her own announcements that came with unedited speed, and scorched the pages of newspapers nationwide. "This is persecution not prosecution!"[10] "I am tired of being the goat for a bunch of politicians!"[11] "I am innocent, and from now on I'm going to fight back!"[12] In a turnaround worthy of a Keystone chase, a chastened District Attorney immediately, publicly and finally cleared her of all charges.[13] It was, at last, time to make movies.

As *Raggedy Rose*'s title character, Mabel works for a junk dealer, played to Yiddish extremes by Max Davidson. After meeting handsome young millionaire Ted Tudor, she dreams of falling in love. But she is a hungry girl and—in a fit of Harold Lloyd–like logic—tries to get hit by a car, on the premise that a hospital would have to feed her. Uninjured by the car, but knocked unconscious by the angry driver, Mabel is carried into the closest house, which, by sheer luck, is the home of Tudor. He is smitten with the unconscious Mabel and sees to her comfort.

Waking up, Mabel is shocked to find Tudor attending her. When he leaves the room, Mabel is doubly shocked to be assaulted by Tudor's jealous would-be fiancé and her scheming mother. The result is a pillow fight for the ages that ends with Mabel under the bed and the two assailants tumbling out the window into a waiting car. Rushing in at fight's end, Tudor finds Mabel safe and quickly professes his love.

Mabel wasn't feeling well. After her long hiatus from the movies, the 17-day shooting schedule was grueling. Planned as a three-reeler, the finished film was five reels in length and the heavy workload took its toll. Actress Anita Garvin later revealed that Mabel seemed confused at times, and had difficulty finding her mark in front of the camera.[14] But this was a film of which Mabel could be proud. At the end of shooting, a generous Mary Pickford published an open letter in the *Motion Picture World*:

> Welcome back to the screen Mabel Normand. Your return makes us all happy. For you have the gifts, the training, the personality, and the technique—which is the supreme technique—the one which is so sure it does not show. You have that rare thing, the possession above price, the charm of spontaneity!
> The best of luck, Mabel. And welcome back to the screen.
> Mary Pickford[15]

As a side note to *Raggedy Rose*, Oliver Hardy's appearance in the film was canceled after he accidentally burned his arm while cooking a leg of lamb. He was also unable to appear in the subsequent film *Get 'Em Young*, Hardy's role of the butler was taken by Stan Laurel, who had all but retired from performing. Laurel was teamed with Hardy the following year.[16]

Roach was sufficiently satisfied with *Raggedy Rose*, to extend Mabel's contract and increase her salary to $1500 a week. She was rushed into her second Roach film, *One Hour Married*, even before her first one was released.[17]

In *One Hour Married*, a bride's husband is drafted as they emerge from the church and shipped to the western front to fight the war. Unable to bear the separation, she volunteers for the Red Cross, disguises herself as a soldier (complete with mustache) and finds her husband in the trenches. She fights next to him to clean out an enemy machine-gun nest. At the battle's conclusion, Mabel's husband realizes that his trench mate is Mabel, and they are both thrilled when rewarded with a ten-day leave in Paris for a honeymoon.

Filming on *One Hour Married* was begun on June 14, 1926. Upon hearing a blank shot ring out during a battle sequence, Mabel quipped, "I didn't have anything to do that!"[18] While the production itself was a smooth one, it had to be shut down after two weeks when a smoke bomb caught Mabel's military-issue trousers on fire. The extent of her injury was noted a month later when, during an interview, a reporter wrote that she sat gingerly on a pillow, still nursing a burn.[19]

On the morning of Friday, September 17, 1926, radio listeners tuned into KFWB's *The Breakfast Club* were treated to a surprise announcement: Hollywood man-about-town Lew Cody began, "Fellows, I went to a party last night—it was a wedding party. I married Mabel Normand." A sudden gasp arose and then a roar of applause. Cody's many friends encircled him with congratulations all around.[20]

Their relationship had begun as that of two buddies engaged in a series of jibes and pranks. When they were together, their endless bantering could render onlookers breathless with laughter. It was not surprising that on Sep-

26. Final Frames

In September, 1926, Mabel impulsively eloped with Lew Cody. It was a troubled marriage that over time developed into a loving relationship (Marc Wanamaker/ Bison Archives).

tember 15, 1926, in the midst of a drunken and riotous party, Lew, with a dramatic flourish, flung himself at Mabel's feet and asked for her hand in marriage. Was he serious? With Lew, as with Mabel, it was hard to tell. The surprise came when Mabel said yes. Egged on by a staggering congregation of partiers, the two were "married" in a mock, and thoroughly camp, ceremony. That could—and perhaps should—have been the end of it. But the "newlyweds" began to like the idea of getting married, and they impulsively decided to make it legal. Driving to Ventura from Los Angeles, they roused a clerk, got a marriage license and proceeded to the home of Judge Malvern Dimmick, who had to find his pants to perform the ceremony. His 18-year-old daughter Ruth served as the witness.[21] The next day, Mabel told reporters that they would honeymoon at home. (In fact, the couple had little choice. Mabel's new film *The Nickel-Hopper* was set to begin shooting the next morning.) As for Mack Sennett, this was the finish. He and Mabel never saw or spoke to each other again.[22]

Filming began on *The Nickel-Hopper* on September 18, 1926. It was co-written by Stan Laurel and directed by F. Richard Jones, a combination that promised a good result. But the narrative itself was a mix of tired ideas and disjointed situations. In the first half, Mabel takes in both laundry and children during the daytime, while working in a dance hall at night. By Mabel's own account, a Nickel-Hopper was a girl who got two and a half cents per dance, for dancing with anything from a "Piute Indian to a hardboiled Eskimo." Her dancing scenes are filled with predictable gags, from having her toes stepped on by outsized feet, to fending off the advances of an amorous sailor. Mabel's reactions get about as much humor out of these situations as anyone could have.

The second half involves Mabel's attempt to deal with her wildly overprotective father. Leaving the dance hall after work, Mabel misses the last streetcar of the night due to the advances of a young Boris Karloff. Now stranded, she is rescued by a wealthy young gent who gives her a ride home. Awakened by the car's arrival, and angered by the late hour, her father appears. Mabel spots her dad and quickly tells the young man that she lives on 625 *Park* Street, not Lark Street, and the couple drives away. The owner of 625 Park Street (Jimmy Finlayson, in a superbly overacted performance) mistakes Mabel, the young man and her pursuing father for burglars, and calls the police.

Mabel transcends the poor material at times but, except for some flashes of playfulness while being tossed about the dance floor, she does not appear to be herself. *The Nickel-Hopper* could have been cut into two Keystone one-reelers, and neither would have been worthy of Mabel. Its only truly funny moments are provided by a clean-shaven Oliver Hardy, going wild on the drums as the nickel-hoppers dance by.

Settling into married life, neither Mabel nor Lew showed any immediate intentions to accommodate a spouse. They kept separate homes and separate bank accounts.[23] At first, those around Mabel and Lew treated their union with the same indifference that they themselves seemed to have. Many of Mabel's friends considered the marriage a mistake. People assumed that either a quick annulment or quick divorce would be forthcoming. But their mutual affection began to tell. With advancing illness, Mabel found it increasingly difficult to concentrate and focus. Patient and accommodating, Lew was often found on the set standing by, watching, helping her however he could. The marriage was not traditional, but to both of them, it became real.

On October 12, 1926, shooting began on Mabel's fourth Roach film, the Cinderella story *Anything Once*. A prince, glancing in the window of a tailor shop, falls instantly in love with a working-class Mabel. She returns

Mabel with Max Factor on the set of *Anything Once*, one of her final films (Marc Wanamaker/Bison Archives).

his flirtations. Forming a plan, she appropriates the Marie Antoinette costume that she is mending and attends the prince's ball. She wins his heart but informs him that, rather than living happily ever after, she must first be wooed and won.

Mabel is well-served by the energetic mugging of co-stars Jimmy Finlayson and Max Davidson, who both seem quite at home in this fast-moving and entertaining farce. Regrettably, there is no way to watch *Anything Once* without feeling bad for Mabel. Her makeup is heavy. The merits of both her performance, and the film itself, are completely obscured by the story of struggle and decline written on her face. Sadly, the story she is trying to tell is not as compelling as the story she was trying to hide. Mabel was not Cinderella any more.

As if racing against time, Roach immediately put Mabel into another production, *Should Men Walk Home?* Professional thief Mabel and her partner in crime (Creighton Hale) execute a plan to crash an elegant party and steal a valuable jewel. Most of the footage concerns itself with Mabel and Creighton sneaking about the mansion while avoiding the family and a detective assigned to guard the jewel. Once again, the bulk of the belly laughs are provided by Oliver Hardy, whose character has very little to do with the film's story but much to do with its entertainment value. Mabel was not called upon to portray a teenager and it must have been a happy departure for her. It might well have foreshadowed a new direction in her career.

Mabel was visibly wasting away. Her life, energies and presence seemed to be spiraling into an ever-diminishing orbit. Some say she regretted her marriage to Lew. There was speculation in the press about divorce. But by 1928, they shared Mabel's Beverly Hills home. In December 1928, Lew left for a European vaudeville tour. Mabel missed him and knew they would be apart for Christmas. She wanted to do something special for her husband. MGM cameraman George Nogel assisted her in creating a private film for Lew. It was a project that Mabel wrote and directed. The film (now lost) was shipped to Lew just in time for Christmas.[24]

On some days she was too weak to get out of bed until mid-afternoon. On other days she couldn't get out of bed at all. Day and night, hot and cold, hungry and thirsty—they began to lose their meanings. The need to keep breathing became a chore to be done by exertion rather than by reflex.

When Lew came home he was a solicitous and loving companion. He sat for hours by her bedside, reading to her and talking to her, until he was exhausted himself. They talked about movies and moviemaking and about the advent of "talkies"—a reality that Mabel could hardly believe. They even discussed the idea of making a sound film together when Mabel was well enough—though it is doubtful that either of them believed it would happen. Julia Benson held a low regard for Lew, and his devotion came as a surprise to many of Mabel's friends. A former medical student, Lew knew the dire realities of Mabel's advancing tuberculosis before she did. When she insisted on seeing her x-rays, he substituted those of a healthy patient, so as not to alarm her.[25]

On September 11, 1929, Mabel left her home for the last time and was moved to Pottenger's Sanatorium in Monrovia. The extent of the care that she now needed, required hospitalization. While Pottenger's was the best facility of its kind in the country, little hope could be extended. A sputum examination by Dr. Pottenger confirmed that Mabel had tuberculosis. She was rarely without consolation. Julia's loving heart made her a ready source of comfort and care for Mabel, and she was an inspiration to the many who witnessed her unremitting attentiveness.

Mabel made her final films, several shorts with Hal Roach, in 1926–27 (Marc Wanamaker/Bison Archives).

In addition to flowers, cards and letters, telegrams were received from around the world. Among the well-wishers were Hollywood royalty: John Barrymore, Harold Lloyd, Stan Laurel, Oliver Hardy, Hal Roach, D.W. Griffith, Blanche Sweet, Ben Turpin, Thomas Ince, Gloria Swanson and many others.

When Mabel forbade Lew from bringing her costly gifts, he brought her charming trinkets instead. The gifts were not as important as the packaging. Mabel had a childlike love of opening presents. Even in her weakened state she wouldn't allow the nurses to open the packages from Lew. As one visit with Mabel came to an end, he bent to kiss her goodbye. She could not resist some black humor. "Lew, I want you to buy me an ambulance. It's the only way to travel. You can lie down, smoke, and, if you get in an accident, you're all undressed and ready for the morgue."[26] He left the room in tears.

Plagued with the heart problems that would soon take his life—something he never told Mabel—Lew's health began to give way under the strain. And, on February 21, at his forty-sixth birthday party—given by friends to cheer him up—Lew collapsed. Doctors insisted that he needed complete bed rest, and Lew reluctantly complied. Still, he could not disappoint Mabel. On the night of February 22, propping himself up in bed, he called the hospital. Told by Julia that Mabel was sleeping, he instructed her to tell Mabel that he would be there in the morning, and that he would bring lots of presents.[27] He never saw Mabel alive again.

27

A Tender Goodbye

Her last press notices will be beautiful.—Will Rogers[1]

It was all over. A fade to black filled the room with the unassailable memories of late nights and joyful days. They were only shadows now. Vibrant, ingenuous and always in motion—but shadows still. Within herself, Julia had no doubt that Mabel had reached Heaven. A perfect place for unaffected love. She kissed her friend goodbye, knowing that a large part of her own life had gone with her.

Soon roused by a sense of calling, Julia marshaled her energies. She called Lew. Decisions had to be made. She contacted Renackers Mortuary, a local Monrovia funeral home that Pottenger's had used before.[2] It would do, for now. With bowed proficiency, Renackers' attendants transferred Mabel's small frame onto a stretcher and carried her down the hall toward the exit. It was a cold day in Los Angeles, barely rising above 60 degrees, and the chilly night air braced them as they stepped outside. Exhaling fog with each breath, they walked to the open back door of the landau-embossed hearse. They set Mabel's stretcher atop the wood-framed rollers, pushed her body inside and closed the door.

Word of Mabel's passing spread by word of mouth through Hollywood the next day. Mabel's corpse was embalmed at the Cunningham & O'Connor Mortuary at 1031 South Grand Avenue. Julia, as loyal as ever, lovingly brushed and styled Mabel's hair for the last time. She gently snipped small locks of hair and spoke to her friend soothingly.[3] Hundreds of fans stood outside. Lew Cody arrived at the parlor, deeply shaken. He finally chose a silver and bronze casket for his wife.[4] The undertakers sent someone over to Bullock's Department Store for a black veil, along with black undergarments and black slippers.[5] An ivory crucifix given to Mabel by Mrs. Sinnott lay upon her breast.

The newspapers wrote tribute pieces and the adjectives were fitting; "lovely," "much-loved," "adorable." A loose chronology of her career was usually included: Griffith to Sennett, Sennett to Goldwyn, Goldwyn to Sennett, and Sennett to Roach. And then, the scandals. The murder, the shooting, the libel. It was all recalled and re-embellished in rapt detail. "Purported," "asserted" and "claimed." "Exposed," "disclosed" and "admitted." The language told a story of its own. Mabel Normand was dead, but the questions were very much alive. In a few years, the stories that hid her from succeeding generations were all that was left.

Responding to gathering reporters, a shocked Lew made the only public statement he would ever make about his wife's death: "The suddenness of Mabel's passing is a great shock. I was with her only a few hours before she passed and, so far as I know, she had no premonition that the end was near. We all felt in our hearts, however, that we would probably lose her. My wife exhibited great courage in her struggle to remain with us, but neither she, nor any of us, have control of such things."[6]

Tributes to Mabel poured in. From Mary Pickford: "The screen has lost its most spontaneous comedienne, and I, a loyal friend." From Charlie Chaplin: "I am deeply grieved over the loss of a dear friend."[7] Mack Sennett stated, "She was a wonderful character, very generous, and a marvelous little woman. I am deeply pained to hear of her death."[8]

With no need for an autopsy, her body was prepared for burial. Despite hundreds of calls asking him to do so, Lew would not permit a public viewing. Mabel would have approved of his decision. Mabel was dressed for burial in a pink chiffon dress. Around her neck was a strand of pearls. A rosary from Pope Leo was entwined in her hands. Finally, Mabel's face was adorned with a veil.

By Wednesday, Mabel's family—Mary, Claude Jr. and Gladys—were on their way from Staten Island by train. As the family drew closer, a funeral date of Friday, February 28, was selected.

The funeral began at 11:00 a.m. The scene outside was bedlam. Police had to call on two reserve units to restore order. Traffic lines were set up two blocks away. Thousands of people camped and waited outside the Cunningham and O'Connor chapel. *The Los Angeles Record* noted, "The film world, from its highest to its most obscure, paid its last tribute to the girl who, in another day, made millions laugh."[10]

It was cloudy and cold outside, as thousands crowded around the mission-style parish church, waiting, watching and grieving. Inside, Mabel's family—having arrived only 90 minutes before the service—sat in the appointed pews. Gladys and Claude Jr. were ashen-faced and emotional.

Mother Mary, only two weeks after the death of her husband, clung to Lew for support. The sanctuary was ornate, with sweet peas and pink and white roses fronting the altar. The casket was overlaid by lilies of the valley and maiden hair ferns.[11] One writer observed, "It was a funeral such as Los Angeles never saw before—not even on the day they buried the beloved Valentino, or the popular Barbara La Marr, or the tragic Wally Reid."[12]

Those in attendance comprised a living history of a still-emerging industry: Marion Davies, Marie Dressler, Louise Fazenda, Creighton Hale, Jean Hersholt, Leatrice Joy, Norman Kerry, Harold Lloyd, Mildred Davis, Mae Marsh, Jack Mulhall, Marshall Neilan, Mary Pickford, Ruth Roland, Constance Talmadge, Ben Turpin.[13] Father Michael J. Mullins, pastor of the Church of the Good Shepherd in Beverly Hills, led a funeral mass that was surprisingly short. He spoke for 20 minutes on Mabel's great heart.

Yet the business of making movies went on. Across town, a young King Vidor was set to pitch a script about Billy the Kid to Irving Thalberg. When he arrived at the studio, Thalberg motioned him into a black limousine. He remembered,

> Suddenly the car made a right turn and came to an abrupt halt. Quite a crowd was gathered on the sidewalk. A number of limousines similar to ours were parked ahead of us. I realized that we were at the main entrance of a funeral parlor.
> "Whose funeral?" I wondered.
> We were shown to reserved seats at the front. I noticed a grim-faced Lew Cody.
> I passed a note to Eddie Mannix reading: "Whose funeral is this?"
> "Mabel Normand," he wrote back. "Don't you read the papers?"[14]

As the service came to an end, Mabel's casket was led outside by honorary pallbearers, a group of men who loved her but could not save her: Roscoe Arbuckle, Paul Bern, Charlie Chaplin, Douglas Fairbanks, World War I flying ace and Hollywood stunt flier Art Goebel, Samuel Goldwyn, theater owner Sid Grauman, D.W. Griffith, Superior Court Judge William P. James, character actor Eugene Pallette (who had appeared with Mabel in her final film *Should Men Walk Home?*), Mack Sennett and Ford Sterling.[15] Behind the casket walked Lew Cody, Mary Normand, Gladys Normand and Julia Benson.

The assembled guests got into their automobiles for the procession to Calvary Cemetery on Whittier Boulevard. The long column moved slowly through the Los Angeles streets, and were met at the cemetery by another large gathering of fans held back by the police. The pallbearers and attendants carried Mabel's casket up the two tiers of stairs that led into the new

The pall bearers at Mabel's funeral include Sam Goldwyn, Mack Sennett, D. W. Griffith, Arthur Goebel, and Douglas Fairbanks, 1930 (Marilyn Slater/"Looking for Mabel").

Calvary Mausoleum chapel. It was there that Father Mullins said the final rites over Mabel's body. Denied access to the mausoleum by the police presence, the crowd was unwilling to leave, and gathered around the building's exterior. They were hoping for a glimpse of the final act. When the rites were concluded, the Hollywood luminaries began filing out. Lew, Mary, Gladys and Julia lingered at the casket. Each one bent over and kissed it. Then they hugged and comforted each other. When they finally departed, the body was placed in a temporary receiving vault in the chapel basement until a crypt could be selected.[16]

Lew was the administrator of Mabel's will and estate. The creditors included the Renacker Company's fee of $25 for the handling of the body. Then there was the itemized bill from the Pottenger Sanatorium for $414.03. Cunningham & O'Connor submitted a bill of $4,288.70, including $3,775 for the silver bronze casket, $45 for a burial dress (not used), and $66 for a veil and slippers.[17] In her will, Mabel left Lew the sum of one dollar for the reason that he was able to earn his own support. Her devoted employee Julia Benson received $10,000 for her services.[18] Everything else was left to Mary Normand.

Mabel was finally entombed in Calvary Mausoleum, Block 303, Crypt D-7. Her inscription reads:

Mabel Normand-Cody
1895–1930
"Rest in Peace"

She wouldn't have minded the wrong birth year at all.

Epilogue

> *To criticize is easy. But to view the errors of our fellow beings with human tolerance and a kindly heart is much more difficult—and much more wonderful. Au 'voir, Mabel*[1]

The legacy of Mabel Normand is the most ironic of all film stars. She is remembered for the scandals in which she played no part, and forgotten for the triumphs in which she did. The unsolved murder of William Desmond Taylor left a blood trail through history that stained Mabel's place as the first great screen comedienne.

The notice that she has received by film history has been scant and random. In the classic film *Sunset Boulevard* (1950), the name of the leading character, Norma Desmond, was said to be a combination of the names Mabel Normand and William Desmond Taylor. Mabel was given cursory mention in a succession of books, that generally became less accurate as the years went by. She was portrayed in the highly-fictionalized Broadway musical *Mack and Mabel* (1974), and depicted in films like *Chaplin* (1992) and *Forever* (1992)

Mabel Normand was a movie star. She was loved by millions of people who never knew her but were certain that they did. But Mabel's deepest impact was upon the lives of those who knew her best. Mack Sennett never married and died in 1960 at the age of 80. In the mid–1950s, as he worked on his autobiography with Cameron Shipp, Mack was forced to take stock of his life in print. He was proud of his studios and proud to be the creative force behind more than 1000 films. He was proud to be known as The King of Comedy. But Mack was old and sick and way past kidding himself. "The most important thing in my life," he wrote, "was a girl."[2]

Appendix A: Filmography

This filmography was culled from many important sources including William Thomas Sherman's *Mabel Normand: A Sourcebook to Her Life and Films*, 6th edition; the work of Marilyn Slater; Brent E. Walker's *Mack Sennett's Fun Factory: A History and Filmography of His Studio and His Keystone and Mack Sennett Comedies, with Biographies of Players and Personnel*; and Simon Louvish's *Keystone: The Life and Clowns of Mack Sennett*, Library of Congress.

The Indiscretions of Betty
Vitagraph (1 reel)
Released March 29, 1910
Cast: Mabel Normand

Betty overspends herself into trouble.

Over the Garden Wall
Vitagraph (1 reel)
Released June 10, 1910
Cast: Maurice Costello, Florence Turner, Mabel Normand

Boy meets girl and they fall in love at a dance. But he is a military officer and is shipped off to the Philippines. Ten years later, they find themselves living side by side.

Willful Peggy
Vitagraph (2 reels)
Released August 29, 1910
Cast: Mary Pickford, Henry Walthall, Claire McDowell, Mabel Normand

A peasant girl is forced to marry a noble lord. She dresses as a man and makes her escape.

Troublesome Secretaries
Vitagraph (½ reel)
Released April 21, 1911
Cast: John Bunny, Mabel Normand, Alec B. Francis

Betty, an office secretary, charms all the men, so the boss seeks to hire an old man to work for him. Ralph, Betty's secret fiancé, disguises himself as an old man to be with her.

Betty Becomes a Maid
Vitagraph (1 reel)
Released April 21, 1911

Cast: Mabel Normand, John Bunny, Ralph Ince

Betty and her older sister vie for the attention of a young millionaire. But the young man is smitten with Betty. Eventually she agrees to marry him and her father consents.

Picciola

Vitagraph (½ reel)
Released May 3, 1911
Cast: Mabel Normand, William Humphrey

Mabel, a girl from the first French Empire, visits her sick father, a political prisoner. A magical plant grows in his cell and restores him to health. The plant also affects the emperor's mind and her father is soon released.

His Mother

Vitagraph (½ reel)
Released May 9, 1911
Cast: Mary Maurice, Maurice Costello, Mabel Normand, Hazel Neason

When a Man Is Married His Trouble Begins

Vitagraph (½ reel)
Released May 16, 1911
Cast: Mabel Normand, James Morrison, Elvin R. Phillips

A young reporter trades cameras with a colleague. When his wife finds pictures of another woman taken with the camera, she is furious until the colleague appears and explains the situation.

A Dead Man's Honor

Vitagraph (1 reel)
Released May 23, 1911
Cast: Maurice Costello, Mabel Normand, Julia Swayne Gordon

The Changing of Silas Warner

Vitagraph (1 reel)
Released June 10, 1911
Cast: Maurice Costello, Mabel Normand

Two Overcoats

Vitagraph (½ reel)
Released June 24, 1911
Cast: John Bunny, Flora Finch, Mabel Normand, William Shea

The Subduing of Mrs. Nag

Vitagraph (1 reel)
Released July 14, 1911
Cast: Mabel Normand, John Bunny, Flora Finch

The Diving Girl

Biograph (½ reel)
Released August 21, 1911
Cast: Fred Mace, Mabel Normand, William J. Butler, Verner Clarges, Robert Harron, Donald Crisp, Eddie Dillon, Dell Henderson

Mabel and her uncle arrive at a seaside resort. She and some friends plan to go swimming, but her uncle disapproves and locks her in her room. A friend lets her out and she is soon on the high board doing series of trick dives.

How Betty Won the School

Vitagraph (½ reel)
Released August 22, 1911
Cast: Mabel Normand

Betty, a seminary student, is ostracized by the girls at her school. When she captures a burglar, she suddenly finds herself popular.

The Baron

Biograph (619 feet)
Released August 31, 1911
Cast: Mabel Normand, Dell Henderson, Joseph Graybill, Grace Henderson

A waiter dresses well and cons people into believing he is wealthy. He uses a disguise to borrow money and impress an heiress (Mabel). Another waiter shows up and reveals the truth.

Her Awakening
Biograph (1 reel)
Released September 28, 1911
Cast: Mabel Normand, Kate Bruce, Harry Hyde

A beautiful girl won't introduce her boyfriend to her mother because of his shabby appearance. After her mother is killed in a car accident, she is filled with regret.

The Squaw's Love
Biograph (1 reel)
Released September 28, 1911
Cast: Mabel Normand, Dark Cloud, Dorothy West, Alfred Paget

Gray Fox is in love with the chief's daughter, Wild Flower. When he asks the chief's permission to marry her, he is banished from the tribe. His friend White Eagle brings Wild Flower to him. White Eagle's jealous fiancée follows them and hurls Wild Flower off a cliff. After she is rescued, the lovers escape together.

The Making of a Man
Biograph (1 reel)
Released October 5, 1911
Cast: Mabel Normand, Dell Henderson, Blanche Sweet, William J. Butler

A girl, in love with a traveling actor, runs away to join him but is ultimately sent back home.

The Unveiling
Biograph (1 reel)
Released October 16, 1911
Cast: Mabel Normand, Robert Harron, Grace Henderson

A wealthy college boy returns home, but soon frequents nightclubs. A gold-digging showgirl tries to marry him but his mother threatens to kill herself and cut him off financially if they marry. The boy realizes the true motive of the showgirl and calls off the relationship.

Through His Wife's Picture
Biograph (½ reel)
Released October 23, 1911
Cast: Mabel Normand, Fred Mace, Eddie Dillon

Mabel attends a masquerade ball where she believes her husband has gone in pirate costume.

Why He Gave Me Up
Biograph (706 feet)
Released December 4, 1911
Cast: Fred Mace, Mabel Normand, Eddie Dillon, William J. Butler

Fred is happy to get away from his wife Mabel and go to the beach. Mabel shows up as part of a swimming club.

Saved from Himself
Biograph (1 reel)
Released December 4, 1911
Cast: Mabel Normand, Fred Mace, Eddie Dillon

A young man tries to provide for his fiancée and gambles his money in the stock market. He loses everything and contemplates a robbery, but his fiancée stops him from committing the crime.

The Eternal Mother
Biograph (1 reel)
Released January 11, 1912
Cast: Mabel Normand, Blanche Sweet, Edwin August, Kate Bruce

A young man divorces his wife for another woman. He soon discovers his new wife is not who he thought she was.

When the new spouse becomes ill, the first wife cares for the lady and her infant, prompting the man to see his mistake.

The Mender of Nets
Biograph (1 reel)
Released February 15, 1912
Cast: Mabel Normand, Mary Pickford, Charles H. West, Marguerite Loveridge Marsh

Tom, a young fisherman, is engaged to Grace (Mabel). Then a mender of nets (Mary Pickford) catches his eye. Grace is heartbroken and her brother swears vengeance. But the beautiful mender of nets intervenes and tells Tom to return to his fiancée.

The Fatal Chocolate
Biograph (½ reel)
Released February 19, 1912
Cast: Mack Sennett, Mabel Normand, Charles H. West, Dell Henderson

Mabel has three suitors, two "country boy" brothers and her true love from the city. The city boy dares the brothers to prove their love by placing three chocolates on the table and telling them that one is poisonous.

A Spanish Dilemma
Biograph (1 reel)
Released March 11, 1912
Cast: Fred Mace, Mack Sennett, Mabel Normand, Dell Henderson

Brothers Jose and Carlos draw cards to see who will court Senorita Mabel.

The Engagement Ring
Biograph (½ reel)
Released March 11, 1912
Cast: Mabel Normand, Eddie Dillon, Dell Henderson, Kate Bruce, Fred Mace

Harry intends to buy Alice (Mabel) an engagement ring, but a rival tries to stop him.

Hot Stuff
Biograph (½ reel)
Released March 21, 1912
Cast: Mack Sennett, Mabel Normand, Dell Henderson, Kate Bruce, Fred Mace

Mark (Mack Sennett) gets his revenge on his rival for Mabel's love by pouring Tabasco sauce into the taffy he is making.

Oh, Those Eyes!
Biograph (½ reel)
Released April 1, 1912
Cast: Mabel Normand, Eddie Dillon, Dell Henderson

Gladys' (Mabel) beauty attracts men in her father's office and on the street. She receives two proposals but declares she must have her father's consent. The two suitors stage a mock duel to see which one Gladys prefers. But Gladys is found petting a bear.

Help! Help!
Biograph (½ reel)
Released April 11, 1912
Cast: Mabel Normand, Charles H. West, Frank Evans, J. Jiquel Lanoe, Mack Sennett

Mabel reads of burglaries in the newspaper. When her husband leaves for work, she is scared by something behind her curtain. She calls her husband and he races home to discover that it was only a puppy.

The Brave Hunter
Biograph (½ reel)
Released April 22, 1912
Cast: Mabel Normand, Mack Sennett,

Dell Henderson, William J. Butler, Kate Bruce

At a party, Mabel meets a big game hunter from Africa. He encounters a bear and runs away terrified. Mabel plays with the bear and leads it away. The hunter tears his clothes and puts on makeup so that it will appear as though he fought the bear. Then Mabel arrives with the tame bear.

The Fickle Spaniard

Biograph (½ reel)
Released May 2, 1912
Cast: Mabel Normand, Fred Mace, Claire McDowell, William J. Butler, Eddie Dillon

A Spanish girl (Mabel) falls in love with a Spanish musician. His former love catches him with her and a chase ensues.

The Furs

Biograph (½ reel)
Released May 2, 1912
Cast: Mabel Normand, Dell Henderson, Kate Bruce, William J. Butler, Mack Sennett

Mabel and her mother-in-law compete for the attention of her son. Mabel takes shopping money and buys some furs. Then she pawns the furs and gives the pawn ticket to her husband. He buys back the furs, a large one for his mother and a small one for Mabel.

When Kings Were the Law

Biograph (1 reel)
Released May 20, 1912
Cast: Mabel Normand, Wilfred Lucas, Harry Hyde, Dorothy Bernard, J. Jiquel Lanoe, Claire McDowell

Mabel is an extra in a royal court scene.

Helen's Marriage

Biograph (½ reel)
Released May 23, 1912
Cast: Mabel Normand, Eddie Dillon, Frank Opperman, Grace Henderson, Fred Mace

Helen and Tom try to elope, but her father catches them and forbids it. The couple pretends to act in a movie wedding scene. Her father doesn't realize it is real until it is too late.

Tomboy Bessie

Biograph (½ reel)
Released June 3, 1912
Cast: Mabel Normand, Mack Sennett, Kate Toncray, William J. Butler, W.C. Robinson

Andrew (Mack Sennett) wants to marry his sweetheart Cissie. But her father won't consent unless he can entertain Cissie's bratty little sister Bessie (Mabel). Bessie makes Andrew give her a piggyback ride and uses him for target practice.

Neighbors

Biograph (363 feet)
Released June 13, 1912
Cast: Mabel Normand, Fred Mace, Frank Evans, Sylvia Ashton, William J. Butler, J. Jiquel Lanoe, Frank Opperman, Kate Toncray

Two wives get into a dispute over a bicycle. The two husbands agree to a duel. The duel degenerates into a comic chase. The husbands make amends, to their wives' relief.

Katchem Kate

Biograph (636 feet)
Released June 13, 1912
Cast: Mabel Normand, Fred Mace, Jack Pickford, Vivian Prescott, Tony O'Sullivan

After attending a school for detectives, Kate is awarded a gun, a badge and a false mustache. She follows a suspicious character, discovers a gang of bomb-makers and calls the cops.

A Dash Through the Clouds
Biograph (742 feet)
Released June 24, 1912
Cast: Mabel Normand, Fred Mace, Philip Parmalee, Sylvia Ashton, Jack Pickford, Eddie Dillon

Mabel is enamored with a daring young pilot, much to her boyfriend's displeasure. Mabel goes for a ride with the pilot. She returns for another ride the next day and rescues her boyfriend from the air after he gets in trouble with some Mexican townsfolk.

The Tourists
Biograph (½ reel)
Released August 5, 1912
Cast: Mabel Normand, Charles H. West, William J. Butler, Grace Henderson, Frank Evans, Kate Toncray

Mabel arrives with a train full of tourists in Albuquerque, New Mexico, but misses the train when it leaves. She then offends the Native American women by flirting with their men.

What the Doctor Ordered
Biograph (617 feet)
Released August 5, 1912
Cast: Mabel Normand, Mack Sennett, Kate Toncray, Jack Pickford, Eddie Dillon

A hypochondriac is taken to a resort in the mountains. But the party gets lost in a snowstorm. They are rescued, but a young boy in their party tumbles over the snowy cliffs and needs to be rescued himself. Mack then tumbles over the same cliff.

An Interrupted Elopement
Biograph (½ reel)
Released August 15, 1912
Cast: Mabel Normand, Eddie Dillon, William J. Butler, Ford Sterling, Elmer Booth, Charles Gorman

Bob is rejected by Alice's father when he asks for her hand. Bob and his friends plan an elopement. He sends Alice a note to meet him on Elm Avenue, so they can go to the minister to be married. When the note is discovered by her father, he rushes to the minister's house. When he arrives, chaos ensues. Alice's father finally consents to the marriage.

The Tragedy of a Dress Suit
Biograph (½ reel)
Released August 15, 1912
Cast: Mabel Normand, Dell Henderson, Eddie Dillon, Ford Sterling, Kate Bruce, William J. Butler

Mabel is a young heiress at a large estate. A young man meets her at a party and hopes to impress her. He steals a dress suit to fit in with the partygoers. But at the party, the suit's owner arrives to claim his suit and ends his chances with Mabel.

He Must Have a Wife
Biograph (½ reel)
Released September 5, 1912
Cast: Mabel Normand, Gus Pixley, William J. Butler, Ford Sterling, Kathleen Butler

Harry must get married to get a $25,000 inheritance from his uncle.

Cohen Collects a Debt
Keystone-Mutual (½ reel)
Released September 23, 1912

Cast: Mabel Normand, Ford Sterling, Mack Sennett, Fred Mace

Cohen, a second-hand clothing store salesman, receives $1000 under false pretenses. He then must hide from a crafty bill collector.

The Water Nymph

Keystone-Mutual (½ reel)
Released September 23, 1912
Cast: Mabel Normand, Mack Sennett, Ford Sterling, Gus Pixley

Mack and Mabel are a couple in love. Ford Sterling plays Mack's father who wants to go to the beach. Mack tells Mabel to flirt with him as a joke. Mabel changes into her swimsuit and does a series of trick dives. After their swim, the two meet for church, where Mack reveals the prank.

Riley and Schultz

Keystone-Mutual (½ reel)
Released September 30, 1912
Cast: Mabel Normand, Mack Sennett, Ford Sterling, Fred Mace

Two policemen, vying for the love of a girl, both try to impress her by catching an escaped convict.

The New Neighbor

Keystone-Mutual (½ reel)
Released September 30, 1912
Cast: Mabel Normand, Fred Mace, Ford Sterling, Mack Sennett

A jealous husband misinterprets his neighbors' attempt to save his wife from an intruder. When he finds himself in court, he discovers the judge is his new neighbor.

The Beating He Needed

Keystone-Mutual (½ reel)
Released October 7, 1912
Cast: Mabel Normand, Fred Mace, Ford Sterling, Frank Opperman

A weak young man is sent west by his father to force him to grow up. A fight turns out to be the thing he needed.

Pedro's Dilemma

Keystone-Mutual (½ reel)
Released October 7, 1912
Cast: Mabel Normand, Mack Sennett, Ford Sterling, Fred Mace, Victoria Forde, Nick Cogley

Mack and Mabel are a couple trying to elope. Mabel's friend wears a disguise, which confuses her disapproving father.

The Ambitious Butler

Keystone-Mutual (½ reel)
Released October 21, 1912
Cast: Mabel Normand, Fred Mace, Ford Sterling, Victoria Forde, Frank Opperman, Alice Davenport

A butler tries to win Mabel's heart by pretending to a count. His plan backfires when a chef identifies him.

The Flirting Husband

Keystone-Mutual (½ reel)
Released October 21, 1912
Cast: Mabel Normand, Ford Sterling, Fred Mace, Victoria Forde, Frank Opperman, Alice Davenport, Mack Sennett

Mrs. Smith is angry at her flirtatious husband. Her friends trick her husband into playing Blind Man's Bluff where his wife is waiting.

At Coney Island

Keystone-Mutual (½ reel)
Released October 28, 1912
Cast: Mabel Normand, Mack Sennett, Ford Sterling, Gus Pixley

land. Mabel is whisked away by a charming Ford Sterling, who has a wife and children.

Mabel's Lovers

Keystone-Mutual (½ reel)
Released November 4, 1912
Cast: Mabel Normand, Fred Mace, Ford Sterling, Alice Davenport

Mabel, tired of all the attention she receives at the beach, makes her bathing suit appear lumpy and unattractive. Mr. Black (Ford Sterling) sees her doing it and tries to court her in spite of her appearance.

At It Again

Keystone-Mutual (½ reel)
Released November 4, 1912
Cast: Mabel Normand, Fred Mace, Mack Sennett, Alice Davenport

A woman hires detectives to follow her unfaithful husband. The detectives accidentally follow the police chief instead, and mistakenly catch him cheating.

The Deacon's Troubles

Keystone-Mutual (½ reel)
Released November 11, 1912
Cast: Mabel Normand, Ford Sterling, Fred Mace, Mack Sennett

A morality campaign is led by a town deacon. He tries to keep a dancer from performing her act. But when he has his picture taken with a girl at an amusement park, he is the subject of scandal.

A Temperamental Husband

Keystone-Mutual (½ reel)
Released November 11, 1912
Cast: Mabel Normand, Ford Sterling, Henry Lehrman, Laura Oakley

A jealous husband mistakes his wife's brother for a lover.

The Rivals

Keystone-Mutual (½ reel)
Released November 18, 1912
Cast: Mabel Normand, Mack Sennett, Fred Mace, Ford Sterling

Mabel is in love with Fred. When she is robbed, Fred disappears and Mack comes to her aid.

Mr. Fix-It

Keystone-Mutual (½ reel)
Released November 18, 1912
Cast: Mabel Normand, Mack Sennett, Fred Mace, Ford Sterling

Mack, a shy Romeo, sends his friend to give Mabel flowers and gifts. But his friend uses the gifts to claim Mabel for himself.

A Desperate Lover

Keystone-Mutual (½ reel)
Released November 25, 1912
Cast: Mabel Normand, Fred Mace

Fred is in love with Mabel. He uses disguises in his quest to stay out of trouble so he can win her heart.

Pat's Day Off

Keystone-Mutual (½ reel)
Released December 2, 1912
Cast: Mabel Normand, Mack Sennett, Fred Mace

Pat has a raucous argument with his wife. Police are called to settle the dispute. Then Pat fakes a suicide to get attention.

Brown's Séance

Keystone-Mutual (½ reel)
Released December 2, 1912
Cast: Mabel Normand, Fred Mace

Two unfaithful men and their wives go to see a fortune teller. The men must pay off the medium to keep her from revealing details to their wives.

A Midnight Elopement
Keystone-Mutual (½ reel)
Released December 9, 1912
Cast: Mabel Normand, Ford Sterling, Fred Mace

Mabel's father tries to use his shotgun to put a stop to Mabel and Fred's elopement. When his gun goes off in the justice of the peace's office, he must consent to the marriage to avoid jail time.

A Family Mixup
Keystone-Mutual (½ reel)
Released December 16, 1912
Cast: Mabel Normand, Mack Sennett, Fred Mace

Two errant husbands begin to flirt with each other's wives, who have never met each other. The women get even by flirting with each other's husbands.

Mabel's Adventures
Keystone-Mutual (½ reel)
Released December 16, 1912
Cast: Mabel Normand, Fred Mace

Fred dances in drag in a burlesque show. Mabel disguises herself as a boy to gain admittance. A magician drops a stolen necklace into Mabel's pocket, setting off a chase.

The Duel
Keystone-Mutual (½ reel)
Released December 30, 1912
Cast: Mabel Normand, Mack Sennett, Fido the dog

A count and a duke vie for the attention of Mabel. They finally decide to fight a duel.

Mabel's Stratagem
Keystone-Mutual (½ reel)
Released December 30, 1912
Cast: Mabel Normand, Fred Mace, Alice Davenport, Arthur Tavares, Chester Franklin

Mabel loses her job as a secretary due to the jealousy of the boss' wife. Mabel gets her job back disguised as a boy.

Saving Mabel's Dad
Keystone-Mutual (½ reel)
Released January 6, 1913
Cast: Mabel Normand, Fred Mace

Fred, Henry and George all pursue Mabel. George capsizes Mabel's dad's boat so he can pretend to rescue her father and win Mabel's heart.

How Hiram Won Out
Keystone-Mutual (½ reel)
Released January 13, 1913
Cast: Mabel Normand, Ford Sterling

Country boy Hiram with city boy Alfred compete for Mabel's affection. Alfred rescues her from the water and wins Mabel's heart, but Hiram tries to get her back.

For Lizzie's Sake
Keystone-Mutual (¾ reel)
Released January 20, 1913
Cast: Mabel Normand, Ford Sterling

A frustrated suitor ties Mabel to the rocks at the beach to get her to agree to marry him. But her true love rescues her in time.

The Mistaken Masher
Keystone-Mutual (½ reel)
Released January 27, 1913
Cast: Mabel Normand, Ford Sterling, Mack Sennett, Alice Davenport

George catches another man with his girl and challenges him to a boxing match. The other man is actually a champion boxer.

The Deacon Outwitted
Keystone-Mutual (½ reel)
Released January 27, 1913
Cast: Mabel Normand, Ford Sterling

Betty's father is a minister. Betty wants to marry her sweetheart Harold. But after an argument with Harold's father over a horse, the cleric objects to the wedding.

Just Brown's Luck
Keystone-Mutual (½ reel)
Released February 3, 1913
Cast: Mabel Normand, Fred Mace, Alice Davenport

Brown's wife and mother-in-law agree to go for a ride with a man. But they run into Brown at a restaurant.

The Battle of Who Run
Keystone-Mutual (1 reel)
Released February 6, 1913
Cast: Mabel Normand, Mack Sennett, Fred Mace, Ford Sterling, Nick Cogley

A Civil War Union officer (Sennett) and his commanding officer (Sterling) compete for the love of Mabel.

Mabel's Heroes
Keystone-Mutual (½ reel)
Released February 13, 1913
Cast: Mabel Normand, Mack Sennett, Fred Mace, Arthur Tavares

In a park, Mabel must contend with many young men trying to get her attention. They each hire would-be robbers to hold up and dispose of their rivals.

A Tangled Affair
Keystone-Mutual (½ reel)
Released February 24, 1913
Cast: Mabel Normand

Henry and Ned both seek Mabel's affection. Henry mistakenly kidnaps Mabel's father in a bag that was intended for Ned.

A Red Hot Romance
Keystone-Mutual (½ reel)
Released February 27, 1913
Cast: Mabel Normand, Fred Mace, Ford Sterling

Antone and Gomez pursue a beautiful girl in a Spanish village. But Gomez and his villainous friend dangle Antone from a cliff.

A Doctored Affair
Keystone-Mutual (½ reel)
Released February 27, 1913
Cast: Mabel Normand

Young Tillie (Mabel) wants to elope with her love Harry. Her father locks her in her room to prevent them from eloping. Harry outwits her father by disguising himself as a doctor.

The Sleuths at the Floral Parade
Keystone-Mutual (½ reel)
Released March 6, 1913
Cast: Mabel Normand, Mack Sennett, Fred Mace, Ford Sterling, Beverly Griffith

Fred and Mabel plan to ride in a car in the Rose Parade. But Mack is jealous and locks Mabel away and rides in the car himself.

A Strong Revenge
Keystone-Mutual (1 reel)
Released March 10, 1913

Cast: Mabel Normand, Mack Sennett, Ford Sterling, Nick Cogley, Laura Oakley, Dot Farley

A shoemaker and grocer both want Mabel. The shoemaker puts limburger cheese in his rival's shoe to ruin his chances with Mabel at a party.

Foiling Fickle Father

Keystone-Mutual (½ reel)
Released March 13, 1913
Cast: Mabel Normand

A father and son both try to win Mabel's hand. The son finds a new girl for his father so he is free to elope with Mabel.

The Rube and the Baron

Keystone-Mutual (½ reel)
Released March 20, 1913
Cast: Mabel Normand, Mack Sennett, Fred Mace, Nick Cogley, Arthur Tavares

Mabel is set to marry a baron whom her father has selected for her. A persistent Mack still tries to win her heart.

Twelve O'Clock

Keystone-Mutual (1 reel)
Released March 27, 1913
Cast: Mabel Normand, Fred Mace, Mack Sennett

Mabel is kidnapped by an Italian rogue who rigs a gun to fire at her at exactly 12 o'clock. Mack arrives just in time to rescue her.

Her New Beau

Keystone-Mutual (½ reel)
Released March 31, 1913
Cast: Mabel Normand, Fred Mace, Mack Sennett

The daughter of a prominent judge (Mabel) gives her boyfriend (Mack) her father's watch to be repaired. But Mack loses the watch leading to a series of complications.

Hide and Seek

Keystone-Mutual (½ reel)
Released April 3, 1913
Cast: Mabel Normand, Ford Sterling, Nick Cogley, Hale Studebaker, Helen Holmes, Charles Avery

Mabel plays hide and seek with a young girl at her father's office. She thinks the girl has hidden in a locked vault. The police arrive but the girl turns up safely.

Those Good Old Days

Keystone-Mutual (1 reel)
Released April 7, 1913
Cast: Mabel Normand, Fred Mace, Mack Sennett, Ford Sterling, Laura Oakley

In King Fizzle's small kingdom, the peasants use the king's infidelity to blackmail him into granting them better living conditions.

A Game of Poker

Keystone-Mutual (½ reel)
Released April 10, 1913
Cast: Mabel Normand, Ford Sterling

A dishonest gambler (Sterling) keeps a royal flush in his pocket. He enters a card game, but his cheating ways are soon discovered.

Father's Choice

Keystone-Mutual (½ reel)
Released April 10, 1913
Cast: Mabel Normand, Fred Mace, Ford Sterling

Mabel's father tries to stop her from eloping with Fred. The two lovers start a fire as a decoy and blacken their faces with ash to disguise themselves.

Bangville Police
Keystone-Mutual (½ reel)
Released April 24, 1913
Cast: Mabel Normand, Fred Mace, Nick Cogley, Dot Farley, Charles Avery

Farm girl Mabel spies two strangers, leading to a chain of mistaken identity events.

The New Conductor
Keystone-Mutual (½ reel)
Released April 28, 1913
Cast: Mabel Normand, Ford Sterling, Carmen Phillips, Helen Holmes, Evelyn Quick

A streetcar conductor begins stealing fares. He is eventually caught by the transportation inspector.

His Chum the Baron
Keystone-Mutual (½ reel)
Released April 28, 1913
Cast: Mabel Normand, Ford Sterling, Rube Miller, Nick Cogley

Mr. Smith lends a baron a suit but soon demands it back at a party. The baron is left to deal with people in his underwear.

That Ragtime Band
Keystone-Mutual (1 reel)
Released May 1, 1913
Cast: Mabel Normand, Ford Sterling, Raymond Hatton, Nick Cogley, Alice Davenport

Prof. Smelts, a band conductor, kicks out a trumpet player who is in love with Mabel. Later, during a performance, he has vegetables hurled at him.

A Little Hero
Keystone-Mutual (½ reel)
Released May 8, 1913
Cast: Mabel Normand

Mabel's cat tries to eat her canary but her dog comes to the rescue.

Mabel's Awful Mistake
Keystone-Mutual (1 reel)
Released May 12, 1913
Cast: Mabel Normand, Mack Sennett, Ford Sterling

Mabel is set to get married until she learns that her future husband is a bigamist. To get revenge, he ties her to a saw, but the police arrive just in time.

Hubby's Job
Keystone-Mutual (½ reel)
Released May 19, 1913
Cast: Mabel Normand, Fred Mace

Pretending to be single to get a job as a secretary, Mabel soon has to contend with the advances of her boss.

The Foreman of the Jury
Keystone-Mutual (1 reel)
Released May 22, 1913
Cast: Mabel Normand, Ford Sterling, Fred Mace, Hale Studebaker

A jury foreman is surprised when his case involves the thief who stole a necklace he gave Mabel.

Barney Oldfield's Race for a Life
Keystone-Mutual (1 reel)
Released June 2, 1913
Cast: Mabel Normand, Mack Sennett, Ford Sterling, Barney Oldfield

When Mabel rebuffs the advances of a villain, he and his cohorts tie her to the railroad tracks. She is saved just in time.

The Hansom Driver

Keystone-Mutual (½ reel)
Released June 9, 1913
Cast: Mabel Normand, Mack Sennett, Ford Sterling, Alice Davenport

Mabel, tired of her boyfriend Mack, agrees to elope with Ford. But the cab they take to make their getaway, turns out to be Mack's.

The Speed Queen

Keystone-Mutual (1 reel)
Released June 12, 1913
Cast: Mabel Normand, Ford Sterling, Nick Cogley

Mabel is Nellie, the judge's daughter. When her father becomes sick, Nellie races to bring home his medicine and catches the attention of two cops. One of them is Mabel's love, the other a former love.

The Waiters' Picnic

Keystone-Mutual (1 reel)
Released June 16, 1913
Cast: Mabel Normand, Ford Sterling, Roscoe Arbuckle, Nick Cogley, Bert Hunn

Louis and Oscar seek Mabel's attention. At a picnic, Louis tries to poison Oscar's drink. The solution ends up at Mabel's place and Louis must race to keep her from drinking it.

For the Love of Mabel

Keystone-Mutual (1 reel)
Released June 30, 1913
Cast: Mabel Normand, Roscoe Arbuckle

Mabel has a number of potential suitors. They all use trickery and schemes to outwit the others.

The Telltale Light

Keystone-Mutual (1 reel)
Released July 10, 1913
Cast: Mabel Normand, Roscoe Arbuckle

Moral crusaders band together to stop the spooning of young people in public. Mabel's searchlight soon catches the moralists spooning themselves.

A Noise from the Deep

Keystone-Mutual (1 reel)
Released July 17, 1913
Cast: Mabel Normand, Roscoe Arbuckle, Nick Cogley, Edgar Kennedy, Al St. John, Charles Avery

Mabel falls into the water while bicycling. Her father's choice for a son-in-law runs to get help while her true love Bob saves her.

Love and Courage

Keystone-Mutual (½ reel)
Released July 21, 1913
Cast: Mabel Normand, Roscoe Arbuckle

Country girl Mabel's boyfriend competes with another for her affection.

Professor Bean's Removal

Keystone-Mutual (1 reel)
Released July 31, 1913
Cast: Mabel Normand, Ford Sterling, Roscoe Arbuckle

Prof. Bean and his daughter Mabel are both music lovers. But their noisy horn playing drives the neighbors crazy. Finally they awake to find their house being pulled away by moving trucks.

The Riot

Keystone-Mutual (1 reel)
Released August 11, 1913
Cast: Mabel Normand, Roscoe Arbuckle, Charles Inslee, Alice Davenport

A feud between two neighborhood leaders, Cohen (Arbuckle) and Inslee, erupts into a full-scale riot. Mabel plays Cohen's daughter.

Baby Day

Keystone-Mutual (½ reel)
Released August 25, 1913
Cast: Mabel Normand, Ford Sterling

A baby is accidentally left on a park bench. A man, believing the baby was abandoned, takes it in and eventually enters it in a baby contest.

Mabel's New Hero

Keystone-Mutual (1 reel)
Released August 28, 1913
Cast: Mabel Normand, Roscoe Arbuckle, Charles Inslee, Virginia Kirtley

Mabel and her friends go to the beach where "Handsome Harry" pesters them. Roscoe intervenes and fights Harry until the police arrive. When Harry sets Mabel aloft in a balloon, Mabel must shimmy down the rope to save herself.

Mabel's Dramatic Career

Keystone-Mutual (1 reel)
Released September 8, 1913
Cast: Mabel Normand, Mack Sennett, Ford Sterling, Roscoe Arbuckle

Mabel is discovered for the movies. When Mack goes to see her performance, a villain from the screen begins threatening him, causing chaos in the theater.

The Gypsy Queen

Keystone-Mutual (1 reel)
Released September 11, 1913
Cast: Mabel Normand, Roscoe Arbuckle

When Fatty (Roscoe Arbuckle) leaves gypsy queen Mabel for another woman, she ties him to a tree and begins threatening him with a snake.

What Father Saw

Keystone-Mutual (½ reel)
Released September 15, 1913
Cast: Mabel Normand

Mabel's father Blodgett uses his telescope to spy on Mabel and discovers she is with a young man he doesn't approve of.

The Fatal Taxicab

Keystone-Mutual (1 reel)
Released September 18, 1913
Cast: Mabel Normand, Ford Sterling, Roscoe Arbuckle, Charles Inslee

Ford makes unwelcome advances on Mabel. Fatty (Roscoe Arbuckle) tries to stop him but Ford escapes in a taxi, leading to a wild chase.

When Dreams Come True

Keystone-Mutual (1 reel)
Released September 22, 1913
Cast: Mabel Normand, Ford Sterling, Roscoe Arbuckle, Hank Mann

Ford becomes drunk and accidentally switches his suitcase with that of a snake charmer. The snake is discovered at home, causing Mabel to become hysterical.

The Bowling Match

Keystone-Mutual (1 reel)
Released September 29, 1913
Cast: Mabel Normand, Ford Sterling, Charles Inslee, Edgar Kennedy

Two rivals for Mabel decide to settle their differences with a bowling match.

The Speed Kings

Keystone-Mutual (1 reel)
Released October 30, 1913
Cast: Mabel Normand, Ford Sterling, Earl Cooper, Teddy Tetzlaff, Roscoe Arbuckle, Barney Oldfield

Mabel's father has chosen Earl Cooper to be his son-in-law but Mabel has her eye on Teddy Tetzlaff. They decide to race over Mabel, but her father sabotages Teddy's car. At the finish, Teddy is still Mabel's choice.

Love Sickness at Sea

Keystone-Mutual (1 reel)
Released November 6, 1913
Cast: Mabel Normand, Ford Sterling, Mack Sennett, Nick Cogley

Mabel and her father take a sea voyage. Father brings along his choice of a suitor for Mabel, but her true love is on board also.

A Muddy Romance

Keystone-Mutual (1 reel)
Released November 20, 1913
Cast: Mabel Normand, Ford Sterling, Charles Inslee, Minta Durfee

Mabel rejects Ford and wants Charles to be her sweetheart. The two try to get married in a rowboat but Ford drains the lake.

Cohen Saves the Flag

Keystone-Mutual (1 reel)
Released November 27, 1913
Cast: Mabel Normand, Ford Sterling, Henry "Pathe" Lehrman, Nick Cogley, Dot Farley

During the Civil War, Cohen and Goldberg compete for Mabel. When Cohen exhibits bravery in battle, Goldberg is jealous and makes Cohen's actions look cowardly.

The Gusher

Keystone-Mutual (1 reel)
Released December 15, 1913
Cast: Mabel Normand, Ford Sterling, Charles Inslee, Bert Hunn, Hank Mann

An oil man promises to marry Mabel when he strikes oil. He is sold a well that turns out to be a gusher after all and they marry. Later, a jealous rival sets the well on fire.

Fatty's Flirtation

Keystone-Mutual (1/2 reel)
Released December 18, 1913
Cast: Mabel Normand, Roscoe Arbuckle, Minta Durfee, Hank Mann, George Jeske

Fatty's (Roscoe Arbuckle) unwanted attention to Mabel puts the Keystone Cops on his trail.

Zuzu, the Band Leader

Keystone-Mutual (2 reels)
Released December 24, 1913
Cast: Mabel Normand, Ford Sterling, Charles Inslee, Nick Cogley, Edgar Kennedy

Mabel is enamored with band leader Ford, but he rejects her. She convinces his rival Caesar to blow him up.

The Champion

Keystone-Mutual (1 reel)
Released December 27, 1913
Cast: Mabel Normand, Henry "Pathe" Lehrman

At a horse race track, Mabel's boyfriend is kidnapped. Mabel comes to his rescue.

A Misplaced Foot

Keystone-Mutual (2/3 reel)
Released January 1, 1914
Cast: Mabel Normand, Roscoe Arbuckle, Minta Durfee

A flirtatious Mabel uses her foot under the table to flirt with her boyfriend, leading to confusion and misunderstanding.

A Glimpse of Los Angeles

Keystone-Mutual (⅓ reel)
Released January 1, 1914
Cast: Mabel Normand

Mabel comically leads the viewer to historic places in Los Angeles.

Mabel's Stormy Love Affair

Keystone-Mutual (1 reel)
Released January 5, 1914
Cast: Mabel Normand

Mabel has two rivals who battle over her.

Won in a Closet

Keystone-Mutual (1 reel)
Released January 22, 1914
Cast: Mabel Normand

Mabel and Charles are in love. When their parents hear them coming, they hide in a closet as a prank, but Mabel panics and calls the police.

Mabel's Bear Escape

Keystone-Mutual (1 reel)
Released January 31, 1914
Cast: Mabel Normand

Mabel is chased by three bear cubs.

Mabel's Strange Predicament

Keystone-Mutual (1 reel)
Released February 9, 1914
Cast: Mabel Normand, Charlie Chaplin, Chester Conklin, Alice Davenport

Charlie pursues Mabel through a hotel. She accidentally locks herself out of her room in her pajamas. She hides under Chester's bed. Chester arrives and is shocked to find Mabel there.

Love and Gasoline

Keystone-Mutual (1 reel)
Released February 21, 1914
Cast: Mabel Normand

A love story with racing as a backdrop.

Mack at It Again

Keystone-Mutual (1 reel)
Released April 6, 1914
Cast: Mabel Normand, Mack Sennett

Mack tries to lose weight to please his girlfriend Mabel.

Mabel at the Wheel

Keystone-Mutual (2 reels)
Released April 18, 1914
Cast: Mabel Normand, Charlie Chaplin, Harry McCoy, Chester Conklin, Mack Sennett

Mabel and her boyfriend argue. She goes off with villainous Charlie on a motorcycle ride. But Mabel falls off into a puddle. Charlie looks for her at the racetrack. He sabotages the boyfriend's car and a battle ensues.

Caught in a Cabaret

Keystone-Mutual (2 reels)
Released April 27, 1914
Cast: Mabel Normand, Charlie Chaplin, Harry McCoy, Chester Conklin, Edgar Kennedy, Alice Davenport

Charlie is a waiter who poses as a gentleman to impress Mabel, a high society girl.

Mabel's Nerve

Keystone-Mutual (1 reel)
Released May 16, 1914
Cast: Mabel Normand

Mabel tries to stop her boyfriend from getting on a dangerous horse named Suicide. She gets on the horse herself and is taken on a wild ride.

The Alarm
Keystone-Mutual (2 reels)
Released May 28, 1914
Cast: Mabel Normand, Roscoe Arbuckle

The town police department and fire department are strong rivals. They finally meet at a public park where a fire truck is sent over a cliff.

The Fatal Mallet
Keystone-Mutual (1 reel)
Released June 1, 1914
Cast: Mabel Normand, Charlie Chaplin, Mack Sennett, Mack Swain

Chaplin, Sennett and Swain engage in a wild slapstick battle over Mabel.

Her Friend the Bandit
Keystone-Mutual (1 reel)
Released June 4, 1914
Cast: Mabel Normand, Charlie Chaplin, Charlie Murray

A thief poses as French aristocrat Count De Beans to crash a society party.

Mabel's Busy Day
Keystone-Mutual (1 reel)
Released June 13, 1914
Cast: Mabel Normand, Charlie Chaplin, Chester Conklin, George "Slim" Summerville

Mabel tries to sell hot dogs at an auto race track. Charlie is a pest who gives away Mabel's hot dogs. Mabel calls the police.

Mabel's Married Life
Keystone-Mutual (1 reel)
Released June 20, 1914
Cast: Mabel Normand, Charlie Chaplin, Mack Swain, Eva Nelson

Mabel wants her husband Charlie to protect her from a bully who turns out to be a professional boxer.

Mabel's New Job
Keystone-Mutual (2 reels)
Released July 16, 1914
Cast: Mabel Normand, Alice Davenport, Charles Parrot, Chester Conklin

Mabel has trouble with her job. She is fired which leads her into a false suicide attempt.

The New York Girl
Keystone-Mutual (2 reels)
Released August 6, 1914
Cast: Mabel Normand, Mack Sennett, Chester Conklin, Frank Hayes, George "Slim" Summerville

Mabel, a New York City girl, tries to find love with a country boy but soon leaves him for a city boy.

Those Country Kids
Keystone-Mutual (1 reel)
Released August 20, 1914
Cast: Mabel Normand, Roscoe Arbuckle, Al St. John, Frank Opperman, Alice Davenport

Mabel and Fatty (Roscoe Arbuckle) are a couple in love but her father disapproves. Local boy Al St. John wants Mabel for himself. A brick-throwing fight ensues.

The Masquerader
Keystone-Mutual (1 reel)
Released August 27, 1914
Cast: Mabel Normand, Charlie Chaplin, Charlie Murray, Roscoe Arbuckle

Charlie is asked to leave a movie

theater. He returns disguised as a woman and causes trouble.

Mabel's Latest Prank

Keystone-Mutual (1 reel)
Released September 10, 1914
Cast: Mabel Normand

    Mabel is bothered by a man in a park. When she gets hired as a maid, she discovers that the husband of the lady who hired her is the same man who pestered her.

Mabel's Blunder

Keystone-Mutual (1 reel)
Released September 12, 1914
Cast: Mabel Normand, Harry McCoy, Charles Parrot, Charles Bennett

    Mabel sees her fiancé with another woman. She doesn't know that it is actually his sister. She decides to dress as a chauffeur and spy on them. Meanwhile, Mabel's brother impersonates Mabel, which causes the boss to flirt with her. Eventually all is revealed.

Hello, Mabel

Keystone-Mutual (1 reel)
Released October 8, 1914
Cast: Mabel Normand, Mack Swain, Alice Davenport, Harry McCoy

    Mack Swain flirts with a hotel telephone operator (Mabel). At the same time, Mabel's boyfriend is caught flirting with Mack's wife.

Gentleman of Nerve

Keystone-Mutual (1 reel)
Released October 29, 1914
Cast: Mabel Normand, Charlie Chaplin, Chester Conklin, Mack Swain

    Mabel and her boyfriend Chester attend the auto races. Charlie contends with a local bully. When Mabel catches Chester flirting with another woman, she soon goes off with Charlie.

His Trysting Place

Keystone-Mutual (1 reel)
Released November 9, 1914
Cast: Mabel Normand, Charlie Chaplin, Mack Swain, Phyllis Allen

    Mack Swain and Charlie get into a fight in a restaurant. They mistakenly leave with each other's coats. Mabel discovers a flirtatious note and reacts violently toward a confused Charlie.

Tillie's Punctured Romance

Mack Sennett Productions (6 reels)
Released November 14, 1914
Cast: Charlie Chaplin, Mabel Normand, Marie Dressler

    Charlie and Tillie (Marie Dressler) run off and elope, taking with them her father's money. In the city, Charlie gets Tillie drunk and deserts her with the money. He connects with his old girlfriend, Mabel. But when Charlie reads in the newspaper that Tillie has inherited millions from her uncle, he tracks her down and talks her into allowing him to live in her uncle's luxurious villa. Mabel arranges to be hired as a maid. The uncle suddenly appears alive and well, calls the police and has them all thrown out.

Fatty's Wine Party

Keystone-Mutual (1 reel)
Released November 21, 1914
Cast: Mabel Normand, Roscoe Arbuckle, Syd Chaplin, Mack Swain

    Syd is a waiter at a large party thrown by Roscoe for his friends. Roscoe finds himself short of cash when it comes time to pay the bill.

The Sea Nymphs

Keystone-Mutual (2 reels)
Released November 23, 1914
Cast: Mabel Normand, Mack Sennett, Mack Swain, Roscoe Arbuckle, Minta Durfee, Alice Davenport

Roscoe meets Mabel on a cruise to Catalina and falls for her, much to the chagrin of his wife, mother-in-law and Mabel's father.

Getting Acquainted

Keystone-Mutual (1 reel)
Released December 5, 1914
Cast: Mabel Normand, Charlie Chaplin, Mack Swain, Phyllis Allen

Charlie and Mabel meet in a park and begin flirting. They draw the attention of a cop.

Mabel and Fatty's Wash Day

Keystone-Mutual (1 reel)
Released January 4, 1915
Cast: Mabel Normand, Roscoe Arbuckle, Harry McCoy, Alice Davenport

Mabel and Roscoe are sent by their domineering spouses to do the laundry. But they meet and soon decide to leave the laundry and go off together.

Fatty and Mabel's Simple Life

Keystone-Mutual (2 reels)
Released January 18, 1915
Cast: Mabel Normand, Roscoe Arbuckle, Al St. John

Al wants Mabel for his wife. His father offers to forgive Mabel's family's debt if they marry. But Mabel has her heart set on Fatty (Arbuckle).

Fatty and Mabel at the San Diego Exposition

Keystone-Mutual (1 reel)
Released January 23, 1915
Cast: Mabel Normand, Roscoe Arbuckle, Glen Cavender, Minta Durfee

Fatty (Roscoe Arbuckle) and Mabel tour the Exposition in style with a motorized cart. Mabel gets jealous when she catches Fatty watching hula dancers.

Mabel, Fatty and the Law

Keystone-Mutual (1 reeler)
Released January 28, 1915
Cast: Mabel Normand, Roscoe Arbuckle, Harry Gribbon, Minta Durfee

Two couples take a walk in the park. Despite **No Spooning** signs, Harry flirts with Mabel. When the cops arrive, they hide. Fatty (Roscoe Arbuckle) flirts with Harry's wife, leading to embarrassment when they are all taken to the police station.

Mabel and Fatty's Married Life

Keystone-Mutual (1 reel)
Released February 11, 1915
Cast: Mabel Normand, Roscoe Arbuckle, Glen Cavender, Al St. John

An organ grinder's monkey escapes into Mabel's home. She is terrified as the monkey makes the curtains move, mistaking the animal for a burglar.

That Little Band of Gold

Keystone-Mutual (2 reels)
Released March 15, 1915
Cast: Mabel Normand, Roscoe Arbuckle, Ford Sterling

Roscoe and Mabel get married but Roscoe continues his wild ways and he and his wife separate. He tries desperately to win Mabel back. They finally reconcile outside the courthouse.

Wished on Mabel

Keystone-Mutual (1 reel)
Released April 19, 1915
Cast: Mabel Normand, Roscoe Arbuckle, Alice Davenport, Joe Bordeaux

Mabel and Roscoe flirt despite her mother's presence and make their escape. A thief steals the mother's watch. Roscoe is able to return it to Mabel's mother.

Mabel and Fatty Viewing the World's Fair at San Francisco

Keystone-Mutual (1 reel)
Released April 22, 1915
Cast: Mabel Normand, Roscoe Arbuckle, Mayor James Rolph, Jr.

Mabel and Fatty (Roscoe Arbuckle) view the attractions of the fair and are welcomed by Mayor Rolph.

Mabel's Wilful Way

Keystone-Mutual (1 reel)
Released May 1, 1915
Cast: Mabel Normand, Roscoe Arbuckle, Edgar Kennedy, Alice Davenport

Mabel flirts with Fatty at an amusement park. He soon gets in trouble with Mabel's mother.

Mabel Lost and Won

Keystone-Mutual (1 reel)
Released June 3, 1915
Cast: Mabel Normand, Owen Moore, Alice Davenport, Dora Rogers

Mabel and Owen become engaged at a housewarming party. But flirtations abound and Mabel catches him with another woman. Then the woman's husband arrives with her four children.

The Little Teacher

Keystone-Mutual (2 reels)
Released June 21, 1915
Cast: Mabel Normand, Owen Moore, Mack Sennett, Roscoe Arbuckle, Bobby Dunn

A teacher (Mabel) arrives at a new school. Two students (Mack and Roscoe) try a series of pranks. That night Mabel discovers her clothes were stolen by Mack. Her fiance Owen arrives and gives Mack his just deserts.

My Valet

Keystone-Triangle (4 reels)
Released November 7, 1915
Cast: Mabel Normand, Mack Sennett, Raymond Hitchcock, Fred Mace, Frank Opperman

A wealthy young man learns that his family has arranged for him to get married. He lets his valet take his place. He changes his mind when he finds out that the girl is beautiful. But now he must compete for her hand with a French count.

Stolen Magic

Keystone-Triangle (2 reels)
Released November 28, 1915
Cast: Raymond Hitchcock, Mabel Normand, Mack Sennett, Alice Davenport

A fakir (Raymond Hitchcock) convinces a group of partygoers that he has magical powers. He is pursued by someone who believes that he has a holy parchment of great value.

Fatty and Mabel Adrift

Keystone-Triangle (3 reels)
Released January 9, 1916
Cast: Mabel Normand, Roscoe Arbuckle, Al St. John, Frank Hayes, May Wells

Newlyweds Fatty (Roscoe Arbuckle) and Mabel are given a seaside cottage by her parents. But her jilted boyfriend and his friends tries to sabotage their new home by pushing it adrift in the ocean.

He Did and He Didn't

Keystone-Triangle (2 reels)
Released January 30, 1916
Cast: Mabel Normand, Roscoe Arbuckle, William Jefferson, Al St. John

Mabel's school chum Jack arrives at Fatty (Roscoe Arbuckle) and Mabel's place. Fatty is immediately jealous. A scene of Fatty killing Mabel turns out to be a bad dream caused by lobsters the three had for dinner.

The Bright Lights

Keystone-Triangle (2 reels)
Released February 20, 1916
Cast: Mabel Normand, Roscoe Arbuckle, William Jefferson, Al St. John

Mabel is talked into leaving home by the promise of a stage career. Fatty (Roscoe Arbuckle) sets out to rescue her.

Gaumont Graphic Newsreel #39

Released May 22, 1916
Cast: Mabel Normand, Roscoe Arbuckle, Chester Conklin

Dodging a Million

Goldwyn (6 reels)
Released: January 28, 1918
Cast: Mabel Normand, Tom Moore, J. Herbert Frank, Shirley Aubert

Mabel inherits a million dollars from a distant relative. She splurges on clothes and moves to the Ritz Hotel. She soon runs into trouble with bill collectors and a plot involving poisoning.

The Floor Below

Goldwyn (6 reels)
Released March 10, 1918
Cast: Mabel Normand, Tom Moore, Helen Dahl, Wallace McCutcheon, Jr., Lincoln Plumer

Mabel portrays a fun-loving and irresponsible "copy boy" for the local newspaper. After being fired, she works with a reporter to investigate a series of robberies.

Joan of Plattsburg

Goldwyn (5 reels)
Released May 5, 1918
Cast: Mabel Normand, Robert Elliott, William Frederic, Joseph Smiley, Edward Elkas

Orphan girl Mabel imagines that she is Joan of Arc. While reading in a cellar, she hears the voices of spies plotting against the government, leading her to thwart the plan and save the day.

The Venus Model

Goldwyn (5 reels)
Released June 16, 1918
Cast: Mabel Normand, Rod La Rocque, Alec B. Francis, Alfred Hickman, Edward Boulden, Edward Elkas

Kitty O'Brien (Mabel) works in a bathing suit factory. Despite her errant ways, she designs a hugely popular bathing suit called "The Venus Model" that saves her employer and leads to love.

Back to the Woods

Goldwyn (5 reels)
Released July 28, 1918
Cast: Mabel Normand, Herbert Rawl-

inson, T. Henderson Murray, Arthur Housman, James Laffey

A city girl (Mabel) moves to the woods to live the country life. She catches the eye of young writer Jimmie Raymond, who arranges for her to be kidnapped so he can come and save her. Later, she has him kidnapped to see how he likes it. In a scuffle, he is accidentally shot. She nurses him back to health and they discover a love for each other.

Stake Uncle Sam to Play Your Hand

Goldwyn (1 reel)
Released August 1918
Cast: Mabel Normand, Pauline Frederick, J.W. Herbert, Madge Kennedy, Tom Moore, Mae Marsh

This was a wartime fund-raising commercial for Liberty Bonds. Mabel plays a girl who buys a bond to help Uncle Sam at the poker table.

Mickey

Mack Sennett Productions, Mabel Normand Feature Film Company (7 reels)
Released August 11, 1918
Cast: Mabel Normand, Lew Cody, Wheeler Oakman, Minta Durfee, George Nichols, Minnie Devereaux, Laura La Varnie, Tom Kennedy, Edgar Kennedy, William Colvin, Joe Bordeaux

Mickey is an orphan sent from a California mining camp to the New York residence of her aunt, who hopes to turn her into a lady. But she is forced to become a servant when her aunt learns she is poor. Ultimately she is rescued by Herbert Thornhill, her lost love from the mountains and they marry.

Peck's Bad Girl

Goldwyn (5 reels)
Released September 9, 1918
Cast: Mabel Normand, Earle Foxe, Corinne Barker, Blanche Davenport, Riley Hatch, Leslie Hunt

Mabel portrays Minnie, a delinquent turned New York model. One night she discovers two men tunneling into a bank vault. After some confusion, she is recognized as a heroine.

A Perfect 36

Goldwyn (5 reels)
Released October 28, 1918
Cast: Mabel Normand, Rod La Rocque, Flora Zabelle, Leila Romer, Louis R. Grisel, Edward Bernard

Mabel is fired from her job as a paper hanger and a saleswoman. She finally gets a job as a bathing beauty. But when her clothes are stolen, she must go through a series of misadventures to find them.

Sis Hopkins

Goldwyn (5 reels)
Released February 9, 1919
Cast: Mabel Normand, John Bowers, Sam De Grasse, Thomas Jefferson, Nick Cogley, Eugenie Ford

Mabel is Sis Hopkins, a country girl sent to the city to get an education at a girls' school with predictable fish-out-of-water results.

The Pest

Goldwyn (6 reels)
Released April 20, 1919
Cast: Mabel Normand, John Bowers, Charles Gerrard, James Bradbury, Jr., Alec B. Francis, Leota Lorraine, Pearl Elmore

Mabel is Puckers, a mischief-making part of a country family that runs a local ferry boat. With Puckers in charge, the ferry service degenerates.

When Doctors Disagree
Goldwyn (5 reels)
Released May 25, 1919
Cast: Mabel Normand, Walter Heirs, George Nichols, Fritzi Ridgeway, Alec B. Francis, James Gordon, Pomeroy Cannon.

During a May Day celebration, Millie the trouble-maker (Mabel) steals the Maypole. Later on a train, she meets a carpet layer pretending to be a doctor. Millie fakes illness to get his attention. She swallows a plug of chewing tobacco which puts her in a hospital. But Millie wants out and escapes to the maternity ward leading to confusion.

Upstairs
Goldwyn (5 reels)
Released August 3, 1919
Cast: Mabel Normand, Cullen Landis, Hallam Cooley, Edwin Stevens, Robert Bolder

Mabel plays a hotel kitchen worker who is called upstairs to the grand ballroom and quickly learns to be a "lady."

Jinx
Goldwyn (4,069 feet)
Released September 28, 1919
Cast: Mabel Normand, Cullen Landis, Florence Carpenter, Ogden Crane, Clarence Arper

Mabel works for a traveling circus. She is called "Jinx" because everything she tries to help with goes wrong. She flees the circus and is taken in by an orphanage. But the circus boss discovers her and tries to do her harm before "Slicker" Evans, also known as "The Wild Man," comes along and saves her.

Pinto
Goldwyn (5 reels)
Released February 1, 1920
Cast: Mabel Normand, Cullen Landis, Edward Jobson, George Nichols, Edythe Chapman, Richard Cummings, George Kunkel, John Burton, Manuel R. Ojeda, Dwight Crittendon, Billy Elmer, Hallam Cooley

Pinto (Mabel), a western cowgirl, goes east and immediately gets in trouble with a snobbish hostess. But her host, a ranch owner, sympathizes with her and she rewards him by catching his wife in an affair. He returns to his ranch with Pinto by his side.

The Slim Princess
Goldwyn (6 reels)
Released July 4, 1920
Cast: Mabel Normand, Hugh Thompson, Tully Marshall, Russ Powell, Lillian Sylvester, Harry Lorraine, Pomeroy Cannon, Kate Lester

Mabel is the princess Kalora of a faraway country where heavy women are prized. Her younger sister cannot marry before her but Kalora cannot find a suitor. She wears a heavy suit at a party but the ruse is soon discovered. A young, rich American pursues the princess and eventually wins her hand.

What Happened to Rosa?
Goldwyn (4148 feet)
Released April 23, 1921
Cast: Mabel Normand, Hugh Thompson, Tully Marshall, Doris Pawn, Eugenie Besserer, Buster Trow, Adolphe Menjou

Mayme Ladd (Mabel), a department store clerk, visits a bogus fortune-teller and imagines herself to be a Spanish beauty named Rosa. Her friends believe that she is delusional, yet it is her new identity that leads her to capture the attention of a handsome young doctor.

Molly O'

Mack Sennett Associated First National (7588 feet)
Released December 1, 1921
Cast: Mabel Normand, Jack Mulhall, George Nichols, Lowell Sherman, Eddie Gribbon, Anna Hernandez, Jacqueline Logan, Albert Hackett, Ben Deeley, Carl Stockdale

Molly O'Dair (Mabel), a laborer's daughter, is in love with handsome young Dr. Bryant. But her father has already chosen Danny Smith, a local boy, to be her husband. Dr. Bryant is engaged to the wealthy, snobbish Miriam Manchesteer. Molly's father discovers her infatuation and forbids her from seeing the doctor or attending his charity masked ball. Molly sneaks out to attend the dance and is kissed by the doctor before removing her mask. Molly's father banishes her from the house. He arrives at the Bryant house the next day to retrieve his daughter only to discover that they were married during the night. Later, Molly is tricked into a blimp airship and kidnapped, leading to a daring rescue by her new husband.

Oh, Mabel Behave

Triangle-Photocraft Productions (5 reels)
Released January 20, 1922
Cast: Mabel Normand, Owen Moore, Ford Sterling, Mack Sennett, George Ovey, Alice Davenport, Dora Rogers

Mabel plays an innkeeper's daughter. Squire Peachem pursues her, but Mabel already has a love interest in Randolph Roanoke. Peachem schemes to keep the couple apart but love wins out.

Head Over Heels

Goldwyn (5 reels)
Released April 1922
Cast: Mabel Normand, Hugh Thompson, Russ Powell, Raymond Hatton, Lionel Belmore, Adolphe Menjou, Lilyan Tashman

An American theatrical agent invites an Italian acrobat (Mabel) to come to America. Upon seeing her old-fashioned style of dress, they send her to a beauty hospital. When she re-emerges in stylish garb, she is put into the movies where she finds true love.

Suzanna

Mack Sennett-Allied Producers and Distributors (7940 feet)
Released December 24, 1922
Cast: Mabel Normand, George Nichols, Walter McGrail, Winifred Bryson, Leon Bary, Minnie Devereaux, Eric Mayne

Two old California land owners, Don Diego and Don Fernando, want their children to marry. But Ramon, Don Fernando's son, wants to marry a peasant girl named Suzanna and Don Diego's daughter Dolores comes home with a new boyfriend, named Pancho. Later it is discovered that Suzanna and Dolores were switched at birth, giving Suzanna the freedom to marry Ramon and Dolores is free to marry Pancho.

The Extra Girl

Mack Sennett-Associated Exhibitors (5750 feet)
Released October 28, 1923
Cast: Mabel Normand, George Nichols, Ralph Graves, Anna Hernandez, Vernon Dent, Ramsey Wallace, William Desmond, Charlotte Mineau, Eric Mayne, Carl Stockdale, Charles K. French

Sue Graham (Mabel) is a film-crazy girl who wants to be in the movies. She sends her photo to the studio but a rival switches Sue's photo with that of another girl. Sue is summoned to Hollywood but turned away when the picture swap is revealed. She finds a job in the wardrobe department. Her parents join her in California, but lose all their money at the hands of a swindler. Sue's boyfriend Dave arrives at the studio and gets a job as a studio hand. After Sue tracks down the swindler, her career as an actress begins. But she gives it up for a happy marriage and children.

Raggedy Rose

Hal Roach–Pathé (3 reels)
Released November 7, 1926
Cast: Mabel Normand, Carl Miller, Max Davidson, James Finlayson, Anita Garvin, Laura Lorraine

Raggedy Rose (Mabel), a junkman's daughter, dreams of marrying a wealthy young doctor. But a socialite is also after him. Rose tries to get hospitalized in order to be well-fed. She finally manages to be put in the young doctor's home and is pleased when he treats her. Rose and the socialite end up in a physical tussle. But the doctor intervenes and expresses his love for Rose.

The Nickel-Hopper

Hal Roach–Pathé (3 reels)
Released December 5, 1926
Cast: Mabel Normand, Michael S. Visaroff, Theodore von Eltz, Jimmy Anderson, Margaret Seddon, Boris Karloff, Oliver Hardy, James Finlayson

Paddy (Mabel) is a dance instructor required to dance with all comers. She is the daughter of a laundress worker and babysits because she is behind in rent. One customer is too forward. She meets a nice man and invites him home. Her father sends him away. Paddy is distraught. The next night Paddy can't find a ride home. A handsome man brings her home. But Paddy gives him the wrong address to avoid her father. She admits her folly. A cop arrives and sorts out the confusion. Paddy and the handsome man marry.

Anything Once!

Hal Roach–Pathé (2 reels)
Released January 2, 1927
Cast: Mabel Normand, James Finlayson, Max Davidson, Theodore von Eltz, Nora Hayden, Gustav von Seyffertitz, Leo White

A socialite's manager is offered a million dollars if he matches her up with a prince. After a facelift, she is told not to move her face by the facelift doctor. Mabel works at a laundry and must deliver a gown for a costume ball to the socialite's house. But the oblong box proves difficult to deliver. It is thrown from a streetcar and ruined. When it's delivered, the socialite has a fit and tosses it away with her wig. The prince stops by and is smitten by Mabel. She takes the gown and wig and goes to the costume ball herself. The socialite arrives and chaos ensues. Finally, the prince chooses Mabel.

One Hour Married

Hal Roach–Pathé (2 reels)
Released January 2, 1927
Cast: Mabel Normand, Creighton Hale, James Finlayson, Noah Young, Syd Crossly, Clarence Geldart

Right after their wedding, as Mabel and her new husband leave the church, he is taken away to fight in France. She becomes a Red Cross nurse and is shipped overseas where she looks for him. She dresses as a soldier and finds her husband in a trench. Together they clean out a machine-gun nest. Then her husband discovers that his new buddy is actually his wife.

Should Men Walk Home?

Hal Roach–Pathé (2 reels)
Released January 14, 1927

Cast: Mabel Normand, Creighton Hale, Eugene Pallette, Oliver Hardy

Hitchhiker Mabel is picked up by a professional burglar. They become jewel thieves who crash a society party to steal a valuable jewel.

Appendix B: Last Will and Testament of Mabel Normand

    I, Mabel Normand-Cody, resident of Beverly Hills, in the County of Los Angeles, State of California, being of sound mind, and fully understanding all my obligation toward members of my family and other persons, do make, publish and declare this, my last will and testament, in the manner following, to-wit:

    I, give, devise and bequeath unto my mother Mary Drury Normand, all the property that I possess, of whatever kind and however situated, and without restriction or condition of any kind whatsoever.

    To my husband, Lew Cody, I give the sum of one dollar, only, for the reason that he is capable of earning his own support.

    All of the property that I possess or own at the date of the making of this will is my own separate property and is the result of my own personal efforts.

    In witness whereof I have hereto set my signature on the 12th day of February 1927, at Beverly Hills, California, and declared this to be my last will in the presence of the witnesses whose names appear below.

Appendix C: Transcript of Coroner's Inquest William Desmond Taylor Murder Case, February 4, 1922

Coroner Nance and Detective Sergeant Ziegler present.

Frank A. Nance: Please state your name.
Normand: Mabel Normand.
Nance: Where do you reside?
Normand: 3089 West Seventh.
Nance: What is your occupation?
Normand: Motion pictures.
Nance: Miss Normand, were you acquainted with Mr. Taylor; the deceased in this case?
Normand: Yes.
Nance: Did you see him on the evening before his death occurred?
Normand: Yes, I did.
Nance: And where did you see him?
Normand: Will I tell you when I went in there and when I came out?
Nance: Did you see him at his home?
Normand: Oh, yes.
Nance: And you were with him about how long on that occasion?
Normand: I got there about seven o'clock, and left at a quarter to eight.
Nance: And when you left his place, did you leave him in the house, or outside?
Normand: No, he came down to my car with me.
Nance: Where was your car?
Normand: Right in front of the court.
Nance: On Alvarado Street?
Normand: Yes, on the hill.
Nance: He accompanied you to your car?
Normand: Yes.

NANCE: Was he still there when you drove away?
NORMAND: Yes, as my car turned around, I waved my hand at him: he was partly up a little stairs there.

Mabel illustrated the wave with her white-gloved hand.

NANCE: At the time you were in the house, was anybody also in the house?
NORMAND: Yes, Henry, his man.
NANCE: Henry Peavey?
NORMAND: Yes.
NANCE: Do you know whether Mr. Peavey left the house before you did or not?
NORMAND: Yes, he did. He left about, I should say about 15 or 20 minutes before I left; but stopped outside and spoke to my chauffeur. We came out later.
NANCE: No one else except Henry Peavey was there?
NORMAND: That was all.
NANCE: What time was it you say you left him … drove away from his place?
NORMAND: I left him on the sidewalk about a quarter to eight.
NANCE: Did you expect to see him or hear from him later that evening?
NORMAND: Yes, he said—he had finished his dinner—he said would I go out and take dinner with him? And I said, "No." I was tired; I had to go home and get up very early. He said he would call me up in about an hour.
NANCE: Did he call you?
NORMAND: No, I went to bed. If he called me…. I was asleep. When I am asleep he tells my maid not to disturb me.
NANCE: Was that the last time you saw him, when you left him about a quarter to eight?
NORMAND: That was the last time.
NANCE: Have you any questions, gentlemen? That is all, you may be excused.

Taylor's houseman Henry Peavey took the witness stand.

NANCE: Please state your name.
PEAVEY: Henry Peavey.
NANCE: Where do you live?
PEAVEY: I live at 127 East 3rd.
NANCE: What is your occupation?
PEAVEY: Cook and valet.
NANCE: Mr. Peavey, were you employed by Mr. Taylor, the deceased in this case?
PEAVEY: Sir?
NANCE: Were you employed by the dead man in the case?
PEAVEY: Yes sir.
NANCE: How long have you been working for him?
PEAVEY: About six months.
NANCE: Were you in his house on the evening when he was found dead there?
PEAVEY: Yes sir.
NANCE: What time did you leave the house?
PEAVEY: I figured it was about a quarter past, when I left the house.
NANCE: Where was he when you left?
PEAVEY: He was sitting in a chair facing Miss Normand. She was sitting in a chair just the same. They were discussing a red-backed book.
NANCE: In what part of the house were they?

PEAVEY: They were near the dining room, where you enter the dining room from the living room.
NANCE: That is a two-story apartment, is it not?
PEAVEY: Yes sir.
NANCE: And on the ground floor, how many rooms?
PEAVEY: The living room, dining room and kitchen.
NANCE: The entrance to this apartment is immediately into the front there, is it not? The front room, rather?
PEAVEY: The front room, yes sir.
NANCE: They were seated?
PEAVEY: Near the dining room there, in the living room, near the entrance to the dining room.
NANCE: When you went out, which way did you go out? At the front or at the back?
PEAVEY: I went out the front way. I always lock up the back door when I go out. I always lock the back door screen; it has a hook on the inside. I use the front door to come out all the time.
NANCE: Did you carry the back door key with you?
PEAVEY: No sir. I always turn it in the door, and leave it just as it is.
NANCE: Now, when did you next see Mr. Taylor?
PEAVEY: The next morning, when I went to work.
NANCE: What time are you in the habit of coming to work?
PEAVEY: I am usually there about half past seven.
NANCE: What time did you arrive there the next morning?
PEAVEY: At just half past seven.
NANCE: What day was that?
PEAVEY: Thursday morning.
NANCE: On arriving there, what did you do?
PEAVEY: I picked up the paper. First, I stopped in a drug store, on the corner of 5th and Los Angeles to get a bottle of medicine; Milk of Magnesia. He usually takes that every morning, I bought that on my way out. I picked up the paper, and unlocked the door. The first thing I saw was his feet. I looked at his feet a few minutes, and said, "Mr. Taylor." He never moved. I stepped a little further in the door, and seen his face, and turned and ran out and hollered.
NANCE: Who did you summon? Who did you call to?
PEAVEY: I don't know.
NANCE: You just made a lot of noise to attract all the attention you could?
PEAVEY: Yes sir.
NANCE: Several people came, did they?
PEAVEY: Yes sir. I think Mr. Desmond, and the gentleman who owns the court was the first.
NANCE: You mean Mr. Jessurun?
PEAVEY: Yes sir.
NANCE: Who else came?
PEAVEY: And Mr.—you see, I don't know their names—I just seen them. The two gentlemens next door. Mr. MacLean and Mr.... I can't think of the other gentleman's name, right next door to us.

Nance: You didn't come back there, after you had gone away, when Miss Normand was there with Mr. Taylor?
Peavey: No sir.
Nance: When you went out, was anybody around the place?
Peavey: Only Miss Normand's chauffeur. He had his lights all on, inside the limousine, cleaning it. I hit him on the back and stopped and talked to him a few minutes.
Nance: When you first opened the door, did you see any furniture overturned, or any sign of a disturbance in the house?
Peavey: Nothing more than a chair—that was sitting next to the wall—that had been pushed out a little bit, and his feet was under this chair. The rest of the furniture around the house and room was just as I left them when I went away that evening.
Nance: And did you notice whether anything had been taken off of his body, or not; any jewelry?
Peavey: I didn't notice that; I didn't touch him at all.
Nance: Do you know whether he wore any valuable jewelry?
Peavey: Yes sir, he had a wristwatch and another watch with a lot of little trinkets on it, and a thing you stamp checks with to keep anybody from making the check any bigger, and a lead pencil.
Nance: Did he have a diamond ring?
Peavey: Yes sir, he had a large diamond ring that he wore.
Nance: Do you know whether he had it on that evening?
Peavey: Yes sir, he was dressed just as when I went that evening, as I found him the next morning.
Nance: Was the ring on his finger the next morning?
Peavey: Yes sir. His other jewelry, that I had put away the night before, was just as I had put it away, up in the dresser drawer.
Nance: You didn't find anything taken from the apartment?
Peavey: No sir, it was just as when I left it, when I found it. The rug was a little bit kicked up. It looked like he had pushed it with his foot.
Nance: There was no other disturbance there?
Peavey: No sir. Even the living room table that I had moved aside—the rocking chair would hit the table, and I moved the table so the rocking chair would not hit the table—it was just as I left it.
A Juror: Were any of the windows up at night?
Peavey: No sir, we had those little long pins that runs in the windows. The windows upstairs in his bedroom were up. The windows downstairs I always locked with this peg that slipped in the window.
Nance: Were they still that way in the morning?
Peavey: They were still that way in the morning. The lights were burning just as I had left them that night. Two lights; one in the living room and one in the dining room.
Nance: That is all, you may be excused.
 Detective Sergeant Thomas Ziegler was the last witness to be called.
Nance: Please state your name.
Ziegler: T.H. Ziegler.
Nance: Where do you live?

ZIEGLER: 25 North Hill.
NANCE: What is your occupation?
ZIEGLER: Police officer.
NANCE: Mr. Ziegler, were you called to the premises where the deceased was found dead?
ZIEGLER: I was.
NANCE: When did you arrive there?
ZIEGLER: A little before eight o'clock the morning of February 2nd.
NANCE: Will you state what you found when you got there?
ZIEGLER: I found the deceased, Mr. Taylor, lying just inside of the door, on his back. His hands, one of them, apparently to the side of his body, and the other, lying outstretched; and blood pouring from his mouth. He was lying with his head to the east, flat on his back, dead.
NANCE: Was his body rigid and cold?
ZIEGLER: It was.
NANCE: Indicating he had been dead for some time?
ZIEGLER: Yes sir.
NANCE: Did you see any evidence of a disturbance in the house?
ZIEGLER: Not any.
NANCE: Who was there when you arrived there?
ZIEGLER: The owner of the building, Mr. MacLean, another movie actor, and Mr. Peavey.
NANCE: You mean the owner of the building, Mr. Jessurun?
ZIEGLER: Yes sir, and Mr. MacLean, and another man I don't know.
NANCE: One of the adjacent tenants of the building?
ZIEGLER: Yes sir, living next door, east of Mr. Taylor.
NANCE: Did you question any of those persons, as to whether they had heard any gunshot the night previous?
ZIEGLER: I did.
NANCE: What did you learn?
ZIEGLER: I learned that from Mrs. MacLean, that, along about fifteen, or perhaps ten minutes to eight, the night before, she heard a shot. She thought it was a gunshot. She went to her front door and opened the door, and saw a man standing in Mr. Taylor's door. She looked at him, and he stood and looked at her; and he walked down the steps, turned to the left, and going around the end of the building, which is to the east; and out into the street.
NANCE: Into what street?
ZIEGLER: Which is Maryland, I think.
NANCE: Did Mr. Jessurun tell you he heard a shot?
ZIEGLER: I think he did.
NANCE: Did he say he didn't try to investigate it?
ZIEGLER: He did not. He didn't know but what it was an automobile making a noise.
NANCE: Did Mr. MacLean endeavor to investigate it?
ZIEGLER: Not that I know of. And Mrs. MacLean's maid also heard a shot.
NANCE: Did they say why they didn't attempt to investigate the cause of the shot?
ZIEGLER: They did not.
NANCE: Did you find any weapon about the room where the deceased was lying?

ZIEGLER: I found a weapon in the room above.
NANCE: Where was it?
ZIEGLER: In the front bedroom in the dresser drawer, lying on a sort of box.
NANCE: Did you investigate to see whether the clothing was powder burnt or not?
ZIEGLER: I did not. That was investigated, I understand, later.
NANCE: Did you ask any of the persons who were called by Henry Peavey, the valet, whether there was any weapon there when they first came into the room?
ZIEGLER: Yes sir, we looked for everything of that kind.
NANCE: Have you formed any conclusion whether it was possible this shot could have been fired by the deceased himself?
ZIEGLER: Impossible.
NANCE: Have you any questions, gentlemen?
A JUROR: Was the revolver found upstairs loaded?
ZIEGLER: It was. It had five shells in it; it had not been shot of late.
A JUROR: Was it the same caliber bullet as was found on the deceased?
ZIEGLER: This was a .32 automatic Savage.
A JUROR: In the drawer upstairs?
ZIEGLER: Yes.
A JUROR: What was the number of the bullet that was found?
ZIEGLER: I understand it was a .38. I haven't seen it.
NANCE: That is all, you may be excused. That is all the evidence we will take in this case. All but the jury will be excused.

Appendix D: Transcript of Mabel Normand's Testimony at Arraignment of Horace Greer, aka Joseph Kelly, January 22, 1924, Los Angeles Courthouse

Attorneys Shelley, Hahn, Conlin, and Heinecke present.

The Court: To the spectators in attendance, unless there is absolute quiet I will clear this courtroom. State your name please.
Normand: May I sit down?
The Court: Yes. State your name, please. Just state your name in full.
Normand: Mabel Normand
   Attorney Shelley took up the direct examination.
Shelley: Where do you reside, Miss Normand?
Normand: 3089 West Seventh Street.
Shelley: What is your occupation?
Normand: Motion pictures.
Shelley: Do you know one Horace A. Greer, also known as Joe Kelley?
Normand: Yes, sir.
Shelley: Did you know him on the first day of January, of this year?
Normand: Yes, sir.
Shelley: Did you know one Courtland Dines on that day?
Normand: Yes, sir.
Shelley: Do you know where Mr. Dines lived at that time—325B North Vermont Street, in this city?
Normand: Yes, sir, that is correct.
Shelley: What time did you first go there?
Normand: I left my house about ... after five.

SHELLEY: And what time did you arrive at Dines' apartment?
NORMAND: About ... well, from the time it takes from where I live at 3089 West Seventh to South Vermont, where Mr. Dines resides; the exact time of that I cannot recall.
SHELLEY: And did you see Kelley or Greer at the time you first arrived at Dines' apartments?
NORMAND: He drove me there.
SHELLEY: Now, did Greer stay there, or leave after he drove you there?
NORMAND: No. He drove me there, and he was undressing my Christmas tree at my house, and I told him to come back and call for me, and also told him that perhaps Miss Purviance might come back to my house with me, so he left with the understanding that he was to come back for me in about an hour and a half; perhaps not that long.
SHELLEY: About what time was it you next saw Greer after he drove back to your house?
NORMAND: It was about 45 minutes.
SHELLEY: And that would make it what o'clock?
NORMAND: What?
SHELLEY: What time was it?
NORMAND: It was still daylight when Joe, Mr. Kelley, drove me over to my house; over to Mr. Dines' apartment. Then, when I again saw him, it was not with the understanding of taking me home, only that he was to bring over a Christmas gift that Mr. Greer insisted upon.
SHELLEY: Do you fix the time when you knew Greer—you knew Greer as Kelley at that time, did you?
NORMAND: Yes, he was going under the name of Kelley from the Pierce Arrow people.
SHELLEY: Was it dark when Greer came back to Dines' apartments?
NORMAND: I don't remember.
SHELLEY: Do you remember—can you fix the time when he came back there?
NORMAND: Yes.
SHELLEY: How long was he gone as nearly as you can remember?
NORMAND: About.... I was there about 45 minutes.
SHELLEY: I think it would be better, Your Honor, if we could draw a rough diagram, for the purpose of clearing up the testimony.
Deputy District Attorney S.S. Hahn spoke up.
HAHN: No objection to that, clarifying the situation.
THE COURT: You will find a blackboard back there.
SHELLEY: The place marked "D" is a davenport just outside of the door; the place marked "T" is a table in the center of the room; the place marked "B" is the breakfast table; the place marked "H" is the door into the kitchen; the place marked "E" is the door into the bedroom; "C" is a closet; "J" is the bathroom, "I" is the door into the bathroom. Now, when Greer came back the second time; that is, when he came back the first time, and after he drove away from there, where did you first see Greer?
NORMAND: The bell rang, and Mr. Dines asked who was there, and he said, "Joe." He was sitting at the little breakfast table, as near as I can remember, and Miss Purviance was in the bedroom and I got up.
SHELLEY: Where were you sitting at the time?

NORMAND: On the davenport, and I got up. Oh, no, I am making a mistake. Mr. Greer came in and had this package.

SHELLEY: Wait a moment. When he said "Joe," did he then open the door or did somebody go to it?

NORMAND: I am quite sure that Mr. Dines opened the door.

SHELLEY: Tell us what was said and done from that time on.

NORMAND: Well, Mr. Greer, or Mr. Kelly as I knew him, Joe, came with this package, which I had already telephoned for, because he was not to call for me for an hour and a half. And ... you will not allow me to tell that, of course. Unfortunately, I am not allowed to tell that.

HAHN: Just a moment, Miss Normand. We move that be stricken out as not responsive that you are not allowed to explain. We will allow everything to be explained legally.

THE COURT: It will be stricken out.

NORMAND: I see. Well, he came in with a box, which included some military brushes that Miss Purviance had given him Christmas Day. And there was this talk between them. I got up and went over and spoke to Miss Purviance in the door.

SHELLEY: You mean the door "E"?

NORMAND: The door where the bedroom was, and asked her for her powder puff. She was powdering her face and all that sort of thing, and the next thing I heard were shots. I thought they were firecrackers, and I made absolutely no objection to them because I am rather used to firecrackers and all that sort of thing around the studio.

SHELLEY: Now, when you got up off the davenport, had Joe Greer come into the room?

NORMAND: Yes, he was there, and he was speaking with Mr. Dines.

SHELLEY: How far had Joe come into the room, when you turned and walked away towards the bedroom?

NORMAND: Well, I couldn't say just as near. He was already in conversation with Mr. Dines.

SHELLEY: Did Dines close the door when Joe ...

NORMAND: I don't remember that.

SHELLEY: Were you in the living room at the time you heard the shots?

NORMAND: I was in the room that goes between. In the bedroom and the living room. Between the two doors.

SHELLEY: From the time that Greer came into the room, how long was it before you got up off the davenport and started into the bedroom?

NORMAND: Well, I remember Joe coming in, and about.... I had delivered the message over the telephone, to give him, the box of brushes, to Mr. Dines. Mr. Dines started to talk to Joe. What their conversation was, I don't know because I got up ...

THE COURT: Just a moment. You are volunteering too much, Miss Normand. Will you read the question, Mr. Reporter?

HAHN: We are not objecting to that question.

THE COURT: Well, I am, I don't want to encumber the record.

NORMAND: It was not a second.

SHELLEY: Then from the time until the shots were fired, you did not look toward Greer or Dines?
NORMAND: No, sir.
SHELLEY: When you first looked toward them, what was their position; how far inside the door was Greer?
NORMAND: Mr. Greer wasn't there. Mr. Dines was all full of blood, and was like this [indicating that Mr. Dines was bent over with his hands on his chest].
SHELLEY: Wait a minute; just go back to when Greer came in, that is what I am asking now. When Greer first came into the room there, how far into the room did he go when you last saw him?
NORMAND: Well, he was quite close to Mr. Dines, and handing him the package.
SHELLEY: And that was the last you saw of him?
NORMAND: That was the last I saw of him.
SHELLEY: After the shots were fired, did you look toward where Greer and Dines were?
NORMAND: No, because I did not, first ... it never entered my mind to look.
HAHN: Just a moment. We move that that be stricken out as not responsive.
THE COURT: The last part will be stricken out.
SHELLEY: How soon was it that you saw Greer or Dines after that?
NORMAND: I did not see Mr. Greer. I saw Mr. Dines like this [again illustrating Mr. Dines was bent over with his hands on his chest].
SHELLEY: How soon was that after you heard the shots fired?
NORMAND: Well, it must have been ... just as soon as we took the thing seriously. That is, there must have been something happened.
HAHN: Just a minute. We move that that be stricken out as a conclusion.
THE COURT: Stricken out. State the time if you can.
SHELLEY: Within a few seconds or minutes, or how long?
NORMAND: Seconds.
SHELLEY: Where was Dines after you saw him after the shots were fired?
NORMAND: He was sort of staggering.
SHELLEY: Where?
NORMAND: Near the window.
SHELLEY: Which window, will you illustrate?
NORMAND: The back part of his apartment. I mean by that that, there is a front and a back.
SHELLEY: Was he near the table, the dishes, the breakfast table?
NORMAND: Well, I think so.
SHELLEY: This is entrance, you know [indicating on diagram]; there is the bedroom.
NORMAND: Yes, I know. He was near that
SHELLEY: Back toward the kitchen?
NORMAND: No, because he was coming sort of toward us. And he said, I have this ...
HAHN: Just a minute. We object upon the ground it is hearsay, what he said, in the absence of the defendant.
SHELLEY: Greer wasn't there at that time, I take it?
NORMAND: No, he was not. I didn't see Mr. Greer.
SHELLEY: Was he close or not, do you remember, to the outside door?
NORMAND: He was close, but it was locked or half opened.

Shelley: During your visit, just before and up to the time that you heard the shots fired, was there anyone else in that apartment except you and Dines?
Normand: Mr. Dines.
Shelley: When you saw Greer immediately after the shots were fired, what was his condition?
Normand: I did not see Mr. Greer after the shots were fired.
Shelley: Mr. Dines?
Normand: Mr. Dines was leaning over like this [illustrating] holding himself like this [illustrating] and all full of blood.
Shelley: And what part of his body was he holding?
Normand: Up here, on the top part [indicating].
Shelley: Had his hands up to his breast?
Normand: Yes.
Shelley: I will show you a small automatic pistol, and ask you if you ever saw that before.
Normand: I have seen it, yes. I have had it for six years.
Shelley: You recognize the pistol then, do you?
Normand: I don't know.
Shelley: Well, I mean did you have one similar to that?
   Deputy District Attorney Clarence Conlin rose to speak.
Conlin: Object to that as incompetent, irrelevant and immaterial.
Normand: I told you I can't remember. All I am telling you ...
Hahn: Wait a minute, madam. Please don't volunteer an answer.
Shelley: We ask that this be marked plaintiff's exhibit A.
Conlin: Objected to as for identification.
The Court: It may be marked for identification.
Shelley: Did you have an automatic pistol similar in appearance to that, previous to the time that your were in Dines' apartment?
Normand: Yes, for years; for six years.
Shelley: Where was it the last time you saw that automatic pistol that you had previous to the time that you were at Dines' apartments?
Normand: A little stand near my bed, a little stand; a little nightstand that has a lamp, you know.
Shelley: Do you remember how long before you were at Dines' apartments or the last time you saw that gun?
Normand: I haven't seen it or taken notice of it for months and months.
Shelley: Well, as far as you know it was there on that day?
Hahn: Wait a minute. Objected to on the ground—wait a minute, Miss Normand. We object to that on the ground it is leading and suggestive.
The Court: Objection sustained.
Shelley: How long previous to this time had you known Mr. Dines?
Normand: I have known him ever since Miss Purviance introduced me to him, which was about ... perhaps a year ago.
Shelley: How long had you known Miss Purviance?
Hahn: We will object to that on the ground it is incompetent, irrelevant and immaterial, and nothing to do with this case as to how long she knew Miss Purviance.
The Court: Overruled. You may answer.

Normand: I have known Miss Purviance for years.
Shelley: How long had you known Greer?
Normand: The day after my birthday, which was November 10th, and on the 11th I engaged him. That was the first time I met Mr. Greer.
Shelley: That was 1923?
Normand: Yes sir.
Shelley: Did you have any conversation with Greer when he first drove you to the apartment?
Normand: None whatsoever, except to call for me later.
Shelley: What was that conversation?
Normand: It was this; to undress my Christmas tree—which he was doing when I was leaving. And, when I left him at Mr. Dines' apartment, "Why, I have a long way to walk up." I said, "Perhaps I will bring Miss Purviance back with me. I don't know what they're going to do tonight—Miss Purviance—because I was going to be alone tonight."
Shelley: That was what you said to Greer, was it?
Normand: I think so.
Shelley: Now, did you say anything to him about when he was to come back?
Normand: No, I did not.
Shelley: I show you a box containing some brushes and a comb, and ask if you ever saw them before, as far as you know.
Normand: Yes, I believe I did Christmas day, but I paid no attention to it.
Shelley: When Greer came to the apartment, what size of bundle did he have with him?
Normand: A small box like that, wrapped in white paper with the name on it, or something like that.
Shelley: Did you look at the name?
Normand: I could recognize it if you would show it to me.
Shelley: I mean, did you at the time?
Normand: No, indeed I did not.
Hahn: I move that answer to the last question be stricken out. If she did not see the name on the package, it is a dead moral certainty that she don't know that it was there.
The Court: Strike it out.
Shelley: I show you a piece of white wrapping paper with some writing on it and ask you if you are familiar with that writing?
Normand: Yes. That is Mrs. Burns' writing. That is paper from my house.
Shelley: Mrs. Edith Burns?
Normand: Yes, sir.
Shelley: And she was at that time your housekeeper and companion?
Normand: No, not exactly. She was just one who would come over and stay at my house. She had no other place to go, and she would stay. I have my housekeeper and my maid and everything else that are all with me.
Shelley: Is this piece of paper that was around the package that Greer had at the time he came back similar in appearance to the paper I have just shown you?
Normand: Yes, sir. It seems to be the same piece of paper. It seems to be the same piece that was around that box.

SHELLEY: Previous to the time you went to Dines' apartments that afternoon had you seen Mrs. Edith Burns?

NORMAND: Yes. She was in my house all day.

SHELLEY: She was at your house when you left, then?

NORMAND: Yes, all day. She had slept there the night previous; New Year's Eve.

SHELLEY: Between the time you first went to Dines' apartments and the time you heard the shots fired, did you or Dines talk over the telephone from Dines' apartments?

NORMAND: Yes, sir, we did.

SHELLEY: Who talked first?

NORMAND: I did, because when I arrived …

SHELLEY: Did you ring up someone, or did someone ring you up?

NORMAND: No, I telephoned.

SHELLEY: During that time did anyone else talk over the phone from the Dines apartment?

NORMAND: Yes, Mr. Dines did, and finished the conversation with Mrs. Burns—which I did not hear.

Attorney Hahn then took up the cross-examination of Normand.

HAHN: Miss Normand, directing your attention to this map, or diagram, rather, we understood you to testify on direct examination that Mr. Dines was about here; indicated by the letter B; is that right?

NORMAND: What does the letter B mean? Is that the bed?

THE COURT: The breakfast room.

HAHN: No, it does not mean the breakfast room.

NORMAND: There is no breakfast room in the house.

SHELLEY: The letter B is the breakfast table.

HAHN: The breakfast table was at the back end of the room, is that right, going towards the kitchen?

NORMAND: Going towards the kitchen.

HAHN: Going towards the kitchen?

NORMAND: Yes, sir.

HAHN: We have here a diagram that to go to the kitchen you have to go around a wall and come around here to the letter E, which is the entrance into the kitchen?

SHELLEY: The letter E is the bedroom.

HAHN: Where is the kitchen entrance?

NORMAND: There is the breakfast table, and there is a swinging door that leads right into the kitchen.

HAHN: A swinging door goes through this wall?

NORMAND: I don't know. It could not go through the wall.

HAHN: How do you go into the kitchen; by going around a wall?

NORMAND: Right next to it.

HAHN: Right next to it?

NORMAND: Yes, sir, it is right next to it.

HAHN: From the position you have indicated here, so far as you can remember, could you see Greer and Dines from the position where you were standing?

NORMAND: No, I did not.

HAHN: That is good. You did not see them at all, what transpired between the two parties?
NORMAND: No, I did not.
HAHN: You did not see what Mr. Dines had in his hands all the time, did you?
NORMAND: No, sir.
HAHN: You did not pay any attention?
NORMAND: I did not see it.
HAHN: You were busy with Miss Purviance is that right?
NORMAND: Yes, sir.
HAHN: And that was your purpose in going into the bedroom, was to go and see Miss Purviance?
NORMAND: Yes, sir.
HAHN: And you really don't know how long they did argue there, do you?
NORMAND: No, I don't.
HAHN: It is your impression that it was a few seconds, is that right?
NORMAND: Yes, sir.
HAHN: But you could not, under oath, say how long it did take to argue between them?
NORMAND: No, sir.
HAHN: And you could not say what Mr. Dines did say to Greer, and Mr. Greer say to Mr. Dines?
NORMAND: No, sir.
HAHN: And you don't know whether Mr. Dines threw a bottle at him, or not?
NORMAND: No, sir.
HAHN: Thank you, that is all.
On redirect examination, Shelley asked:
SHELLEY: Miss Normand, calling your attention to exhibit C, in the center of the living room there, at the time that you left the davenport and walked to the bedroom, when Greer had just come in the room, did you notice what was on that table C, or had you noticed before that time?
NORMAND: No, sir, I did not.
SHELLEY: Did you notice whether or not there was a large bottle on that table?
HAHN: I object to that as leading and suggestive. She said she did not remember.
THE COURT: Objection sustained.
SHELLEY: Now, if the court please, a witness may say that they did not notice particularly what was on a table, and still they may know that it is not a hobby horse on that table, or something that is a noticeable object there, so I think I may ask this witness the question I asked, did she notice whether or not there was a bottle on that table.
HAHN: Miss Normand is an intelligent witness.
SHELLEY: And Mr. Hahn is an intelligent attorney, and there are some other intelligent people sitting in the courtroom. I insist, your Honor, I have a right to ask her whether or not she noticed a large bottle on that table.
HAHN: We also insist that it is leading and suggestive and we are willing to abide by the court's decision.
SHELLEY: Counsel for the defense has brought out the point, you did not notice Dines throw a bottle at Greer. Now we, the People, certainly have the right to

ask this witness whether or not there was such an object as that in plain view on the table, before this witness.

Conlin: He may have had it in his pocket.

The Court: I think it would be proper for you to ask this witness if there was a bottle of any kind in that room.

Hahn: But she testified that she did not see anything on that table.

Shelley: My question was did she notice anything particularly.

The Court: I will sustain the objection to the question as asked.

Shelley: As I understand, then, the ruling of your honor, refuses to let me ask the witness whether she noticed a bottle on the table?

The Court: No; you can't ask her if she noticed a bottle there in that room. I don't think that would be a proper question inasmuch as the bottle has been brought out here, but to call her attention to any particular place after she said she didn't remember anything of that bottle, or words to that effect, wouldn't be proper.

Shelley: At any time after Greer came back the second time and Dines went to the door, did you see Dines with a bottle in his hand?

Normand: No, sir.

Shelley: During the time that Greer and Dines were there, and when Greer came back the second time, did you see in the living room any bottle?

Normand: No, I didn't notice any bottle.

Shelley: That is all.

Hahn: Miss Normand, let me ask you one question, with your Honor's permission. As I understood from cross examination that you didn't pay any attention as to whether there were any bottles around there?

Normand: I did not.

Hahn: And you could not say that there were not bottles?

Normand: No, sir, I cannot.

Hahn: And as I understood you, you don't know whether Mr. Dines threw a bottle at Greer or not?

Normand: No, sir; I never saw that part.

Hahn: You never saw that part. Thank you very much. That is all.

Shelley: Was there anything on the table at that time? That is, the table in the center of the room?

Normand: No, the table is on the side of the room.

Shelley: Now, on that table in the center of the room, the table T, was there at the time that Greer came back anything that you remember on that table?

Normand: No, there were a lot of little cigarette ends, which were all over the place, but on the table I saw nothing, and then, I don't remember …

Shelley: On the table B, in the kitchen, at the time that Greer came back the second time, do you remember what was on that table?

Normand: I do not.

Shelley: That is all.

Hahn: That is all.

The Court: Miss Normand, did you see Mr. Greer enter the room at all that evening just before the shots were fired?

Normand: No, sir, I don't remember.

The Court: Did you see him there at the door?

NORMAND: No, your honor, because the doorbell rang and I heard Mr. Dines say, "Just a minute."
THE COURT: You didn't see Mr. Greer at all then immediately after the shots?
NORMAND: No, sir. No, sir, I didn't, your honor. I just can't recall.
THE COURT: Did you see him?
NORMAND: After that I just can't recall, but …
THE COURT: Did you see him?
NORMAND: Because they were all talking about everything "New Year's," you know?
THE COURT: Who do you mean by "all"?
NORMAND: Mr. Dines, Miss Purviance, just before she had entered the other room, they were all talking about people and New Year's Eve.
THE COURT: Mr. Dines went back to the breakfast table, and you went to him.
NORMAND: No. When the doorbell rang he was standing, it seemed to me, so far as I can recall, near the breakfast table.
THE COURT: And you were where?
NORMAND: I was sitting on that couch. The doorbell rang. Mr. Dines said, "Who is it?" and Joe answered.
CONLIN: Just a minute, object to that as a conclusion of the witness and incompetent, irrelevant and immaterial unless she is qualified to know his voice.
THE COURT: All right. What was said by the party at the door?
NORMAND: Not a thing.
THE COURT: "Joe?"
NORMAND: Yes, Mr. Greer.
CONLIN: Object to that and move that the answer be stricken as not responsive.
THE COURT: Stricken out. Did you recognize the voice of the person who said "Joe"?
NORMAND: Well, I think I ought to be rather used to it.
THE COURT: Did you recognize who was there?
NORMAND: Well, I think I did.
THE COURT: And who was there?
NORMAND: Joe.
THE COURT: That is the defendant here?
NORMAND: Yes, sir.
THE COURT: But you didn't see him at all?
NORMAND: No, I didn't.
THE COURT: All right. Just at what point did you leave the room, or did you leave the room first?
NORMAND: No, Mr. Dines went to the door. Mr. Greer had a box.
THE COURT: No, whoever it was, did you see him with the box?
NORMAND: Yes, I did. I saw him with the box. I mean…. I don't know whether I saw him with the box or not. Anyway, I got up and went over and spoke to Mr. Dines, who was in the room.
THE COURT: Now, we want to know did you see him, or did you not see the defendant? That is what I want to know.
NORMAND: Yes, I did. I saw Joe in there.
THE COURT: Where was he? That is all right. Now where was he?
NORMAND: Entering the door with the box like this [illustrating].
THE COURT: And where, at that time, was Mr. Dines?

NORMAND: Near the table. Mr. Dines, at that time, was at the table.

THE COURT: All right, take the chalk and show us now; make a mark where each one of them was?

NORMAND: I can't draw a picture, your honor.

THE COURT: You can make a cross?

NORMAND: I can make it where it is.

THE COURT: Where the figure A is, is the door, supposed to be the entrance to the building?

NORMAND: Well, this place [indicating on diagram].

THE COURT: All right, show us where Mr. Greer was when you saw him with the box?

NORMAND: He was there [indicating on diagram].

THE COURT: All right. Now, show us where Mr. Dines was at the same time.

NORMAND: Now, what does D mean?

THE COURT: That is where you were sitting; that is the couch.

NORMAND: All right, that is fine. T for Tommy is what?

THE COURT: That is the table.

NORMAND: And B is the little breakfast table [indicating on diagram].

THE COURT: Well, now let us know where you saw him?

NORMAND: Well, as near as I can recollect, I am sure he was near there, because I ...

THE COURT: All right, never mind why.

NORMAND: I got up, and I went [looking at diagram] where is the bedroom?

THE COURT: Where you see the D there is the door.

NORMAND: I went that way [indicating on diagram].

THE COURT: All right. Now, about how far is it from where you saw Mr. Greer, to where you saw him at that time?

NORMAND: From here to where that gentleman is sitting, your honor.

THE COURT: How far is that, counsel?

CONLIN: About 12 feet.

HAHN: About 12 or 15 feet.

THE COURT: Is that stipulated?

SHELLEY: Ten to 15 feet.

HAHN: Ten to 15 feet, something like that.

THE COURT: Did you leave the room?

NORMAND: Yes, Joe ...

THE COURT: You went into the bedroom, then?

NORMAND: Into the bedroom.

THE COURT: Where were you when you heard these shots?

NORMAND: Still in the doorway.

THE COURT: Just where?

NORMAND [looking at diagram]: Where is the doorway? Because I am getting a little mixed up on that.

THE COURT: Where E is.

NORMAND: There is the doorway [indicating on diagram]. There is where I was.

THE COURT [indicating]: This is the bedroom.

NORMAND: All right, that is where Miss Purviance was.

THE COURT: Did you meet her?

NORMAND: Yes, I did.
THE COURT: And how far apart were you and Miss Purviance at that time?
NORMAND: Well, there is a closet ...
THE COURT: Just answer the question. How far apart were you?
NORMAND: Well, just like this [illustrating]; because that is a long mirror.
THE COURT: Four or five feet?
NORMAND: I can't tell the feet. Like this [illustrating].
THE COURT: How far is that, counsel?
CONLIN: About four feet.
THE COURT: Is that all right, Mr. District Attorney?
HEINECKE: About four feet.
THE COURT: All right. And you and Miss Purviance were talking?
NORMAND: Yes, talking. Back here, I was this way [indicating on diagram].
THE COURT: Which way was your back—towards Mr. Greer?
NORMAND: Yes, sir.
THE COURT: At the time the shots were fired?
NORMAND: Yes, your Honor.
THE COURT: And you went right on talking with Miss Purviance, didn't turn round, for some seconds?
NORMAND: I thought they were firecrackers.
THE COURT: Is that correct?
NORMAND: Absolutely correct.
THE COURT: But when did—when you did look around, where was Dines?
NORMAND: He was near the table.
THE COURT: Show us on the map.
NORMAND: Oh! Is that the table [indicating]?
THE COURT: Yes, that is the table.
NORMAND: Well, it seems to me ... we were so excited when we saw the blood ...
THE COURT: Never mind, now.
NORMAND: That is the only way I can explain, your Honor.
THE COURT: Don't explain it at all. Show us.
NORMAND: It seemed as if he was coming towards us, and we both rushed towards him, and he was all bent over like this [illustrating].
THE COURT: All right; you have told us that. Now, where was Mr. Greer—do you know?
NORMAND: I didn't see Mr. Greer.
THE COURT: He had gone?
NORMAND: He had already left.
THE COURT: That is all. Any further questions?
CONLIN: Do you know whether Mr. Greer had left the room before these reports like firecrackers went off?
NORMAND: No, sir; I do not.
CONLIN: How long prior to the time of these shots did you see Mr. Greer?
NORMAND: Well, it all happened so quickly, I can't recall that, or answer it correctly.
CONLIN: Well, do you know whether it was one minute, or two minutes, or three minutes or how long it was?

NORMAND: Hearing these reports like firecrackers?
CONLIN: When you came out of the bedroom?
NORMAND: Well, I know it was ...
CONLIN: You came out of the bedroom?
NORMAND: Well, I know it was.... I asked Miss Purviance, I had time to ask her for her powder puff.
CONLIN: In other words—did you use the powder puff?
NORMAND: No, I asked her for it. She was using it before that long mirror which goes in the closet.
CONLIN: You stood in the doorway until Miss Purviance got through using it?
NORMAND: I never used it, because in the meantime the shots were fired.
CONLIN: Well, when you went into the bedroom—or when you were standing in the door?
NORMAND: I was standing in the doorway.
CONLIN: You couldn't see what happened in the room, could you, what happened between Mr. Dines and Mr. Greer?
NORMAND: I couldn't see.
CONLIN: Well, then, you don't know how long Mr. Dines and Mr. Greer were talking, do you?
NORMAND: I do not.
CONLIN: It may have been two or three or four minutes, may it not?
NORMAND: It was longer, perhaps.
SHELLEY: Did you, after the shots were fired, when you came back in, or at any time before you left the apartment, see an automatic revolver?
NORMAND: No, sir.
HAHN: Just a minute—she has answered, "No, sir," all right. She said, "No."
SHELLEY: That is all.
HEINECKE: Another question, Miss Normand. You stated when you went in there, you saw Mr. Dines and he was standing in this position [illustrating]. Now you mean he was bent over and had both hands on his chest?
NORMAND: I can't answer that correctly because I know he was this way [illustrating], all full of blood.
HEINECKE: Now, you are indicating that he was stooping with his head over?
NORMAND: Yes.
HEINECKE: And with his hands on his chest?
NORMAND: And he said, "I have been plugged." That is the only way I remember.
HAHN: Wait a minute, madam, wait a minute. Objected to as hearsay, what he said, and no proper foundation laid. It hasn't been shown that Greer was there.
NORMAND: No, Mr. Greer wasn't there.
THE COURT: The objection is overruled.
NORMAND: Pardon me.
THE COURT: I think that is part of the res gestae—near enough. Will you indicate, if you can state, will you approximate about how far you were standing from Mr. Greer, when you saw him in the doorway?
NORMAND: I wasn't standing. I was sitting, your honor, when Mr. Greer came in, and got up because he had a box in his hands for Mr. Dines. And then I left for the bedroom door to speak to Miss Purviance, and ask for her powder box.

THE COURT: What I want to fix is the distance between the point where Mr. Greer spoke, and when you went to the door to see Miss Purviance. The question is how far it would be from the point where Mr. Greer stopped, to where you were talking to Miss Purviance, at the door of the bedroom?

NORMAND: Here is your door [indicating on diagram], and about that man's shoes there [indicating], about that far is where Mr. Dines was.

THE COURT: Which man?

NORMAND: I don't know that man.

SHELLEY: Eight or nine feet?

HAHN: Eight or nine feet.

THE COURT: All right.

HEINECKE: What did you and Miss Purviance do immediately after you saw his condition?

CONLIN: Objected to as incompetent, irrelevant and immaterial, leading and suggestive, assuming a state of facts not in evidence.

HEINECKE: If anything.

CONLIN: No bearing on this defendant.

THE COURT: Overruled.

HAHN: If your honor please, Miss Purviance and Miss Normand's action what they did in the absence of the defendant are prejudicial to the defendant. I don't know what she may state. It has nothing to do with the issues in this case. The question is very broad. You might as well ask her what she did at midnight.

THE COURT: The question is what she immediately did. I don't think it is prejudicial at all. I shall not allow the witness to go into any detailed statement of what happened for any extended period afterwards, but what happened immediately, I think is material.

HAHN: Whether the defendant was there or not?

THE COURT: Yes, you may answer.

HEINECKE: What did you do immediately after?

NORMAND: Why, we rushed out of the room and saw Mr. Dines in this condition. We both, Miss Purviance and I, took his arms on each side, and took him into the bedroom and put him on the bed.

THE COURT: I think that answers it.

HAHN: Just a minute.

THE COURT: And put him on the bed?

NORMAND: On the bed.

HEINECKE: That is all.

Hahn, on re-cross examination, asked:

HAHN: You don't remember what you did immediately after the shooting, do you?

NORMAND: Yes, I do. I remember I turned around after I heard what I thought were firecrackers and saw Mr. Dines [illustrating] in this condition.

HAHN: Why, you said a few minutes ago it was probably four or five minutes?

NORMAND: Well, we were talking, and I didn't pay much attention to it, but as soon as we did see the condition that Mr. Dines was in, we both ran to him, and Miss Purviance took him on one side and I took him on the other side and we took him into the bedroom.

The Court: You heard no conversation between Dines and Greer either before or after the shooting?

Normand: No, your honor.

Hahn: You really don't remember whether it was four or five minutes or four or five seconds that you walked out of that bedroom with Miss Purviance, do you.

Normand: No, I don't.

Colin: This four or five minutes that you testified having elapsed, do you mean that it was four or five minutes between the time that Mr. Greer came into the apartment and was talking with Mr. Dines four or five minutes, or was it four or five minutes from the time the firecrackers went off and you turned around and saw Mr. Dines?

Shelley: We will object to that as immaterial.

Normand: I can't give you the absolute detailed time, except I got up from the couch and walked to the bedroom door, and stood and talked to Miss Purviance, and the next thing I heard was the shots; the exact time I don't know.

Conlin: That is all.

Chapter Notes

Introduction

1. Stephen Normand, "Mabel Normand: Her Grand-Nephew's Memoir," *Films in Review*, August-September 1974, 385. Print.
2. William Thomas Sherman, *Mabel Normand: A Sourcebook to Her Life and Films*, 6th edition (Seattle: Cinema Books, 2008), 422. Print.

Chapter 1

1. Stuart K. Oderman, *Roscoe "Fatty" Arbuckle: A Biography of the Silent Film Comedian, 1887–1933* (Jefferson, NC: McFarland, 1994), 44. Print.
2. Lawrence D. Schuffman, "The Liberty Loan Bond," *Financial History* (2007). Web. 8 January 2014.
3. William Thomas Sherman, *Mabel Normand: A Sourcebook to Her Life and Films*, 6th edition (Seattle: Cinema Books, 2008), 140. Print.
4. "Stake Uncle Sam to Play Your Hand," Imdb.com. Web. 8 January 2014.
5. Frederick James Smith, "Mabel in a Hurry," *Motion Picture Magazine*, November 1918. As cited in William Thomas Sherman, *Mabel Normand: A Sourcebook to Her Life and Films*, 6th edition (Seattle: Cinema Books, 2008), 139. Print.
6. *New York Morning Telegraph*, April 28, 1918. As cited in William Thomas Sherman, *Mabel Normand: A Sourcebook to Her Life and Films*, 6th edition (Seattle: Cinema Books, 2008), 129. Print.
7. Dollar Times (www.dollartimes.com). Web. February 2014.

Chapter 2

1. "Eventide," *Los Angeles Times*, February 25, 1930. As cited in William Thomas Sherman, *Mabel Normand: A Sourcebook to Her Life and Films*, 6th edition (Seattle: Cinema Books, 2008), 312. Print.
2. Jim Wigton, "The Pottenger Sanatorium" (monrovia.patch.com/articles/the-pottenger-sanitorium-monrovia), March 2012. Web.
3. Ibid.
4. Code of Cannon Law: Cannon 999. Catechism of the Roman Catholic Church. Print.
5. Marilyn Slater, "Julia Benson," Looking for Mabel Normand (http://looking-for-mabel.webs.com/juliabenson/), June 2012. Web.
6. Herbert Howe, "The Diaries of Mabel Normand," *Pantomime*, 12 October 1921. As cited in William Thomas Sherman, *Mabel Normand: A Sourcebook to Her Life and Films*, 6th edition (Seattle: Cinema Books, 2008), 173. Print.
7. Don Schneider and Stephen Normand, "Excerpts from a Series of Interviews with Minta Dufee Arbuckle." As cited in William Thomas Sherman, *Mabel Normand: A Sourcebook to Her Life and Films*, 6th edition (Seattle: Cinema Books, 2008) 405. Print.
8. Betty Fussell, *Mabel: Hollywood's First I-Don't-Care Girl* (New Haven: Ticknor & Fields, 1982), 232.
9. Ibid., 229.
10. Ibid.
11. "Mabel Normand Dies After Lengthy Illness," *Los Angeles Times*, February 24, 1930. As cited in William Thomas Sherman, *Mabel Normand: A Sourcebook to Her Life and Films*, 6th edition (Seattle: Cinema Books, 2008) 310. Print.

12. Fussell, 230.
13. Sidney Sutherland, "Madcap Mabel Normand: The Story of a Great Comedienne," *Liberty*, October 11, 1930. As cited in William Thomas Sherman, *Mabel Normand: A Sourcebook to Her Life and Films*, 6th edition (Seattle: Cinema Books, 2008), 381. Print.

Chapter 3

1. "Former Schoolmates Recall Island Star of Silent Films," *Staten Island Advance*, October 8, 1973. Print.
2. Sidney Sutherland, "Madcap Mabel Normand: The Story of a Great Comedienne," *Liberty*, October 11, 1930. As cited in William Thomas Sherman, *Mabel Normand: A Sourcebook to Her Life and Films*, 6th edition (Seattle: Cinema Books, 2008), 358. Print.
3. Ibid.
4. Dawn Crystal, "Mabel Normand's Life Story," YouTube, June 2010. Web.
5. Ibid.
6. "Cauls" (http://www.cafemon.com/journals/read/1627074), January 2014. Web.
7. Dawn Crystal, "Mabel Normand's Life Story," YouTube, June 2010. Web.
8. "Carmencita," *Library of Congress*, YouTube, January 2014. Web.
9. *Mack Sennett Collection, Folder 1546: Clippings*. The Margaret Herrick Library. March 2009.
10. *Staten Island Advance*.
11. William Thomas Sherman, *Mabel Normand: A Sourcebook to Her Life and Films*, 6th edition (Seattle: Cinema Books, 2008), 10. Print.
12. "Old Fall River Line" (http://www.americanheritage.com/content/old-fall-river-line), July 2013. Web.
13. William Thomas Sherman, *Mabel Normand: A Sourcebook to Her Life and Films*, 6th edition (Seattle: Cinema Books, 2008), 10. Print.
14. Ibid., 11.
15. Beverly Crane, "A Chummy Little Chat with Mabel Normand," *Movie Weekly*, April 5, 1921. As cited in William Thomas Sherman, *Mabel Normand: A Sourcebook to Her Life and Films*, 6th edition (Seattle: Cinema Books, 2008) 358. Print.

Chapter 4

1. Sidney Sutherland, "Madcap Mabel Normand," *Liberty*, September 6, 1930. As cited in William Thomas Sherman, *Mabel Normand: A Sourcebook to Her Life and Films*, 6th edition (Seattle: Cinema Books, 2008) 360. Print.
2. *Mack Sennett Collection, Folder 1546: Clippings*. The Margaret Herrick Library. March 2009.
3. Sutherland, 359.
4. Ibid., 360.
5. Ibid.
6. David Raymond, "The Tragic Side of Mabel Normand—Obtaining an Interview Under Difficulties," *Motion Picture*, June 1918. As cited in William Thomas Sherman, *Mabel Normand: A Sourcebook to Her Life and Films*, 6th edition (Seattle: Cinema Books, 2008) 132. Print.
7. Sutherland, 360.
8. Ibid.
9. Susan Meyer, "Charles Dana Gibson and the Gibson Girls," *Lively Roots* (http://www.livelyroots.com/gibsongirls.htm), January 2014. Web.
10. James Montgomery Flagg, "My Favorite Model," *American Weekly*, December 29, 1947 (http://looking-for-mabel.webs.com/flaggmodel.htm). October 2011.
11. Florence Lawrence, "My First Day in the Movies—Mabel Normand," *Los Angeles Examiner*, October 14, 1923. As cited in William Thomas Sherman, *Mabel Normand: A Sourcebook to Her Life and Films*, 6th edition (Seattle: Cinema Books, 2008), 240. Print.
12. Ibid.
13. Sutherland, 360.
14. Ibid., 358.
15. Ibid., 360.
16. *Mack Sennett Collection, Folder 1546: Clippings*. The Margaret Herrick Library. March 2009.

Chapter 5

1. William Thomas Sherman, *Mabel Normand: A Sourcebook to Her Life and Films*, 6th edition (Seattle: Cinema Books, 2008) 12. Print.
2. YouTube, "The Great Train Robbery." Online video clip, *Ella's Archives*, September 2012. Web.
3. "Thomas Alva Edison and the Edison Trust," *Silent Cinema in Quebec* (http://www.cinemamuetquebec.ca), November 2011. Web.
4. "William Kennedy-Laurie Dickson," *Who's Who of Victorian Cinema* (http://victorian-cinema.net/dickson.htm), November 2012. Web.
5. Ibid.
6. William Drew, "D. W. Griffith (1875–1948)" (http://gildasattic.com/dwgriffith.html), December 2013. Web.

7. "D.W. Griffith as an Actor," *Grapevine Video* (http://www.grapevinevideo.com/dw_griffith_actor.html), March 2014. Web.
8. Richard Schickel, *D. W. Griffith: An American Life* (New York: Limelight Editions, 1996), 126. Print.
9. Ibid.
10. Sherman, 10.
11. Sidney Sutherland, "Madcap Mabel Normand," *Liberty*, September 6, 1930, as cited in Sherman, 360. Print.
12. Sherman, 11.
13. Ibid.
14. Sutherland, 361.
15. "Mabel Normand's Own Life Story," *Liberty*, September 6, 1930, *Los Angeles Examiner*, as cited in Sherman, 342. Print.
16. "Mabel Normand Tells How She Entered Films," *New York Morning Telegraph*, November 24, 1918, as cited in Sherman, 337. Print.
17. Sutherland, 362.
18. Mack Sennett and Cameron Shipp, *King of Comedy* (San Jose: To Excel, 2000), 14. Print.
19. Sennett, 23.
20. *Mack Sennett Collection*. The Margaret Herrick Library. December 2014.
21. Sennett, 50.
22. Rob King, *The Fun Factory* (Berkeley: University of California Press), 57. Print.
23. Sennett, 51.
24. Sennett, 67.
25. Richard Schickel, *D. W. Griffith: An American Life* (New York: Limelight Editions), 166–167. Print.
26. *Movie Weekly*, May 14, 1921. As cited in William Thomas Sherman, *Mabel Normand: A Sourcebook to Her Life and Films*, 6th edition (Seattle: Cinema Books, 2008), 172. Print.
27. *Mary Pickford*, DVD. Directed by Sue Williams, 2005; PBS Home Video.
28. Schickel, 146.
29. Stuart Oderman, *The Keystone Krowd* (Albany, GA: BearManor Media, 2007), 149. Print.
30. Harry Carr, "The Tragic Life Story of Mabel Normand," *Screen Secrets*, October–November 1929. Print.
31. Ibid.
32. "Blanche Sweet," *Golden Silents* (http://www.goldensilents.com/stars/blanchesweet.html), July 2013. Web.
33. "Constance Talmadge," *Golden Silents* (http://www.goldensilents.com/stars/constancetalmadge.html), July 2013. Web.
34. Sherman, 20.
35. Sennett, 68.
36. Sennett, 69.
37. Norman Lusk, "Memories on My Own Screen," *Picture Play*, December 1922, as cited in Sherman, 230. Print.

Chapter 6

1. Mack Sennett and Cameron Shipp, *The King of Comedy* (San Jose: To Excel, 2000), 67. Print.
2. Sherman, 98.
3. "Mabel Normand Places," *Movieland Directory* (http://movielanddirectory.com), July 2013. Web.
4. Stuart Oderman, *Roscoe "Fatty" Arbuckle: A Biography of the Silent Film Comedian, 1887–1933* (Jefferson, NC: McFarland, 1994), 71. Print.
5. *New York Dramatic Mirror*, May 10, 1911.
6. "Before They Were Stars: Mabel Normand." *Dramatic Mirror*, March 20, 1920. As cited in William Thomas Sherman, *Mabel Normand: A Sourcebook to Her Life and Films*, 6th edition (Seattle: Cinema Books, 2008), 338. Print.
7. Sherman, 33.
8. *Los Angeles Times*, February 12, 1913. As cited in William Thomas Sherman, *Mabel Normand: A Sourcebook to Her Life and Films*, 6th edition (Seattle: Cinema Books, 2008), 74. Print.
9. Ibid.
10. "Philip Parmalee," *Air and Space Magazine* (http://www.airspace.mag.com).
11. "Horace Keany," *Early Aviators* (http://earlyaviators.com/ekeany.htm).
12. Gertrude Price, "'Mabel of the Movies' Calls Herself the Airman's Hoo Doo," *Fort Wayne Sentinel*, March 5, 1913.

Chapter 7

1. *Motography*, May 17, 1913. As cited in William Thomas Sherman, *Mabel Normand: A Sourcebook to Her Life and Films*, 6th edition (Seattle: Cinema Books, 2008), 75. Print.
2. Sherman, 98.
3. "Mack Sennett and Company: A Silverlake Legacy" (http://silverlake.org/about_silverlake/sennett_stuio.htm), October 2012. Web.
4. Sherman, 93.
5. Mack Sennett and Cameron Shipp, *The King of Comedy* (San Jose: To Excel, 2000) 110. Print.
6. Sidney Sutherland, "Madcap Mabel Normand," *Liberty*, September 6, 1930. As cited in William Thomas Sherman, *Mabel Normand: A Sourcebook to Her Life and Films*, 6th edition (Seattle: Cinema Books, 2008), 359. Print.
7. Sutherland, 363.
8. *Motion Picture News*, August 24, 1912. As cited in William Thomas Sherman, *Mabel Normand: A Sourcebook to Her Life and Films*,

6th edition (Seattle: Cinema Books, 2008), 71. Print.
  9. King Vidor, *A Tree Is a Tree* (Hollywood: Samuel French, 1953),191. Print.
  10. Sutherland, 363. Print.
  11. *Moving Picture World*, October 5, 1912. As cited in William Thomas Sherman, *Mabel Normand: A Sourcebook to Her Life and Films*, 6th edition (Seattle: Cinema Books, 2008), 72. Print.
  12. "Max Linder," *Movies by Farr* (http://www.bestmoviesbyfarr.com/movies/laugh-with-max-linder/1921/), November 2013. Web.
  13. Sherman, 121.
  14. Sennett, 80.

Chapter 8

  1. Gertrude Price, "'Mabel of the Movies' Calls Herself the Airman's Hoo Doo," *Fort Wayne Sentinel*, March 5, 1913.
  2. Adela Rogers St. Johns, *The Honeycomb* (New York: Doubleday, 1969), 103. Print.
  3. Ibid., 104.
  4. Ibid., 105.
  5. Ibid., 103.
  6. Ibid.
  7. Ibid.
  8. Ibid.
  9. Anita Loos, *A Girl Like I* (New York: Viking, 1966), 116.
  10. Rob King, *The Fun Factory* (Berkeley: University of California Press, 2009), 64. Print.
  11. Steven J. Ross, *Hollywood Left and Right: How Movie Stars Shaped American Politics* (New York: Oxford University Press, 2011).
  12. William Thomas Sherman, *Mabel Normand: A Sourcebook to Her Life and Films*, 6th edition (Seattle: Cinema Books, 2008), 72. Print.
  13. Ibid.
  14. "Mabel Normand, Movie Star, Simply Dotes on Boxers," *The Day Book*, March 22, 1919.
  15. Sherman, 38.
  16. *Photoplay*, December 1913, as cited in Sherman, 79. Print.
  17. "Actress Has Narrow Escape. Mabel Normand Is Nearly Pounded to Death by Surf on Rocks," *New York Dramatic Mirror*, November 23, 1912.
  18. *Mack Sennett Weekly*, January 28, 1917, as cited in Sherman, 119. Print.
  19. Sherman, 33.
  20. Stuart Oderman, *Roscoe "Fatty" Arbuckle: A Biography of the Silent Film Comedian* (Jefferson, NC: McFarland, 1994), 3–5. Print.
  21. Ibid., 19.
  22. Ibid., 43–44.
  23. *Photoplay*, June 1916, as cited in Sherman, 110. Print.

Chapter 9

  1. Sidney Sutherland, "Madcap Mabel Normand," *Liberty*, September 6, 1930. As cited in William Thomas Sherman, *Mabel Normand: A Sourcebook to Her Life and Films*, 6th edition (Seattle: Cinema Books, 2008), 367. Print.
  2. Charlie Chaplin, *My Autobiography* (New York: Penguin, 1964), 153.
  3. Ibid., 154.
  4. Mack Sennett and Cameron Ship, *The King of Comedy* (San Jose: To Excel, 2000), 160. Print.
  5. "Charlie Chaplin," *The History Channel*. (http://www.history.co.uk/biographies/charlie-chaplin.htm). Web.
  6. Sennett, 148–149.
  7. William Thomas Sherman, *Mabel Normand: A Sourcebook to Her Life and Films*, 6th edition (Seattle: Cinema Books, 2008), 33. Print.
  8. Ibid., 39.
  9. A. Scott Berg, *Goldwyn: A Biography* (New York: Alfred A. Knopf, 1989), 71. Print.
  10. Chaplin, 150.
  11. Stuart Oderman, *Roscoe "Fatty" Arbuckle: A Biography of the Silent Film Comedian, 1887–1933* (Jefferson, NC: McFarland, 1994), 58. Print.
  12. Chaplin, 163.
  13. Ibid., 141.

Chapter 10

  1. William Thomas Sherman, *Mabel Normand: A Sourcebook to Her Life and Films*, 6th edition (Seattle: Cinema Books, 2008), 81. Print.
  2. Victoria Sturtevant, *A Great Big Girl Like Me: The Films of Marie Dressler* (Urbana: University of Illinois Press, 2009).
  3. *Variety*, April 7, 1914, as cited in Sherman, 81. Print.
  4. "The Rivals," *Movie Pictorial*, June 13, 1914, as cited in Sherman, 81. Print.
  5. Ibid.
  6. Ibid.
  7. Simon Louvish, *Keystone: The Life and Clowns of Mack Sennett* (New York: Faber and Faber, 2003), 100. Print.

Chapter 11

  1. Stuart Oderman, *Roscoe "Fatty" Arbuckle: A Biography of the Silent Film Comedian, 1887–1933* (Jefferson, NC: McFarland, 1994), 47. Print.

2. A. Scott Berg, *Goldwyn: A Biography* (New York: Alfred A. Knopf, 1989), 71. Print.
3. "Playing Post Office," *Los Angeles Times*, May 19, 1915, as cited in Sherman, 92. Print.
4. "Fatty Arbuckle Shorts," Turner Classic Movies (http://www.tcm.com), January 2014. Web.
5. Oderman, 79–80.
6. Sherman, 408.
7. Grace Kingsley, *Los Angeles Times*, September 2, 1921, as cited in Sherman, 176. Print.
8. "Mabel Normand Breaks Heart of Prince Ibrahim of Egypt; Cleopatra's Throne No Lure," *San Francisco Chronicle*, July 29, 1922, as cited in Sherman, 224. Print.
9. *Photo-Play Review*, April 20, 1915, as cited in Sherman, 90. Print.
10. Berg, 71.
11. Anita Loos, *A Girl Like I* (New York: Viking, 1966), 117.
12. Sidney Sutherland, "Madcap Mabel Normand," *Liberty*, September 6, 1930, as cited in Sherman, 367. Print.
13. Oderman, 185.
14. Harry Carr, "The Tragic Life Story of Mabel Normand," *Screen Secrets*, October-November 1929.
15. *Variety*, August 28, 1914, as cited in Sherman, 84. Print.
16. *Photoplayers Weekly*, July 22, 1915, as cited in Sherman, 93. Print.
17. *Motion Picture News*, August 15, 1914, as cited in Sherman, 84. Print.
18. James R. Quirk, "Mabel Normand Says Good-Bye," *Photoplay*, May 1930, as cited in Sherman, 322. Print.
19. Richard Sucre, "The Great White Plague: The Culture of Death and the Tuberculosis Sanatorium" (http://www.faculty.virginia.edu/blueridgesanatorium.htm), February 2014. Web.
20. Herb Howe, "Hollywood's Hall of Fame: Mabel Normand," *New Movie Magazine*, April 1931. Print.
21. Ibid.
22. "The Causes of World War I," firstworldwar.com (http://www.firstworldwar.com/origins/causes.htm), May 2013. Web.
23. Ibid.
24. Sherman, 90.
25. Kalton C. Lahue, *Dreams For Sale: The Rise and Fall of The Triangle Films Corporation* (South Brunswick, NJ: A. S. Barnes, 1971), 48. Print.
26. Ibid.
27. Sherman, 33.
28. Sutherland, 368. Print.
29. Stuart Oderman, *The Keystone Krowd: Mack, Mabel, the Kips and the Girls, 1908–1915* (Albany, GA: BearManor Media, 2007), 115. Print.
30. Mack Sennett and Cameron Ship, *The King of Comedy* (San Jose: To Excel, 2000), 105. Print.

Chapter 12

1. Adela Rogers St. Johns, *Love, Laughter and Tears: My Hollywood Story* (New York: Doubleday, 1978), 57. Print.
2. Stuart Oderman, *The Keystone Krowd: Mack, Mabel, the Kips and the Girls, 1908–1915* (Albany, GA: BearManor Media, 2007), 177. Print.
3. Mack Sennett and Cameron Ship, *The King of Comedy* (San Jose: To Excel, 2000), 110. Print.
4. Oderman, 190.
5. Stephen Normand, "Mabel Normand: Her Grand-Nephew's Memoir," *Films in Review*, August-September 1974, 393. Print.
6. Ibid.
7. Ibid.
8. Brent Walker, *Mack Sennett's Fun Factory* (Jefferson, NC: McFarland, 2010), 54. Print.
9. Oderman, 177.
10. Ibid., 187.
11. "Mabel Normand Sites," *Movieland Directory* (http://movielanddirectory.com/star.cfm?star=60849), November 2014. Web.
12. Oderman, 75.
13. Ibid.
14. Ibid.
15. "Mabel Normand Fighting Death," *Los Angeles Herald*, September 20, 1915, as cited in Sherman, 98. Print.
16. "Film Star Hurt in Rough Comedy," *Santa Monica Outlook*, September 21, 1915, as cited in Sherman, 98. Print.
17. *New York Clipper*, October 9, 1915.
18. Stuart Oderman, *Roscoe "Fatty" Arbuckle: A Biography of the Silent Film Comedian, 1887–1933* (Jefferson, NC: McFarland, 1994), 75. Print.
19. Ibid., 76.

Chapter 13

1. Stuart Oderman, *Roscoe "Fatty" Arbuckle: A Biography of the Silent Film Comedian, 1887–1933* (Jefferson, NC: McFarland, 1994), 193. Print.
2. Mack Sennett and Cameron Ship, *The King of Comedy* (San Jose: To Excel, 2000), 198. Print.
3. Personal interview, Tiffany Harris, July 2011.

4. Simon Louvish, *Keystone: The Life and Clowns of Mack Sennett* (New York: Faber and Faber, 2003).
5. Adela Rogers St. Johns, *Love, Laughter and Tears: My Hollywood Story* (New York: Doubleday, 1978), 57. Print.
6. "Would You Ever Suspect It?" *Photoplay*, August 1918, as cited in Sherman, 134. Print.
7. Sennett, 203. Print.
8. Ibid., 199.
9. Ibid., 198.
10. "Interview with Anita Garvin," *Mabel Normand Home Page*, April 2012. Web.
11. Oderman, 94.

Chapter 14

1. Sidney Sutherland, "Madcap Mabel Normand," *Liberty*, September 6, 1930, as cited in Sherman, 368. Print.
2. Mack Sennett and Cameron Ship, *The King of Comedy* (San Jose: To Excel, 2000), 199. Print.
3. *Mack Sennett Collection, Folder 1546: Clippings*. The Margaret Herrick Library. March 2009.
4. *Photoplayers Weekly*, May 20, 1916, as cited in Sherman, 109. Print.
5. Sherman, 116.
6. Jeanine Basinger, *Silent Stars* (Knopf, 2012). Internet resource.
7. Ibid.
8. Ibid.
9. Herb Howe, "Movieland Hall of Fame: Mabel Normand," *New Movie Magazine*, April 1931. Print.
10. Ibid.
11. Simon Louvish, *Keystone: The Life and Clowns of Mack Sennett* (New York: Faber and Faber), 119. Print.
12. Harry Carr, "The Tragic Life Story of Mabel Normand," *Screen Secrets*, October-November 1929. Print.
13. Sennett, 199.
14. "Tuberculosis," missed.org. (http://www.missed.org/tb.html), August 2011. Web.
15. Randolph Bartlett, "Why Aren't We Killed?" *Photoplay*, March 24, 1916, as cited in Sherman, 104. Print.
16. "Harrison Narcotics Tax Act (1914)" (http://www.druglibrary.org/schaffer/library/studies/cu/cu8.html), July 2014. Web.
17. Sherman, 21.
18. Sennett, 200.
19. Basinger, 91.
20. Sherman, 22.
21. Sutherland, 305.
22. "Lew Cody," silenthollywood.com (http://silenthollywood.com/lewcody.htm/lewcody.html), December 2014. Web.
23. Sutherland.
24. "1915 San Diego-The Panama-California Exposition," Panaman-California Exposition March 1915–January 1917 (http:www.pinterst.com/flickrcjb/1915-san-diego-the-panama california-exposition.html).
25. "Mabel Normand Calls Peace Army," *Arizona Gazette*, November 17, 1916.
26. Ibid.
27. Sennett, 200.
28. *Anita Record*, Anita, Iowa, November 27, 1919.
29. Kalton C. Lahue, *Dreams For Sale: The Rise and Fall of the Triangle Film Corporation* (South Brunswick, NJ: A. S. Barnes, 1971), 151. Print.
30. Eileen Whitfield, *Mary Pickford: The Woman Who Made Hollywood* (Lexington: University Press of Kentucky), 151. Print.
31. Telegram, *Mack Sennett Collection, Folder 1546: Clippings*. The Margaret Herrick Library, March 2009.
32. Adela Rogers St. Johns, "The Butterfly Man and the Little Clown," *Photoplay*, June 1929, as cited in Sherman, 306. Print.

Chapter 15

1. A. Scott Berg, *Goldwyn: A Biography* (New York: Alfred A. Knopf, 1989), 71. Print.
2. "Mabel Normand's Own Life Story," *Los Angeles Examiner*, March 9, 1924, as cited in Sherman, 347. Print.
3. *Goldwyn: The Man and His Movies*, DVD. Directed by Peter Jones and Mark A. Catalena, 2001; Sony Home Entertainment.
4. *Goldwyn*, DVD.
5. Betty Harper Fussell, *Mabel: Hollywood's First I-Don't-Care Girl* (New Haven: Ticknor & Fields, 1982), 391. Print.
6. Berg, 77.
7. Ibid.
8. "Goldwyn Gets Normand," *New York Morning Telegraph*, July 29, 1917, as cited in Sherman, 120. Print.
9. Mack Sennett and Cameron Ship, *The King of Comedy* (San Jose: To Excel, 2000), 208. Print.
10. Berg, 77.
11. *Mack Sennett Collection, Folder 1546: Clippings*. The Margaret Herrick Library. March 2009.
12. Arthur Marx, *Goldwyn: A Biography of the Man Behind the Myth* (New York: W. W. Norton, 1976), 84. Print.
13. Berg, 77.

14. Sennett, 213.
15. Sidney Sutherland, "Madcap Mabel Normand," *Liberty*, September 6, 1930, as cited in Sherman, 368. Print.
16. Sutherland.
17. "Mabel Acquires an Outfit," *Morning Telegraph*, July 4, 1920.
18. Samuel Goldwyn, *Behind the Screen* (New York: George H. Doran, 1923), 115. Print.
19. Marx, 89.
20. *Hutchison (Kansas) Herald*, September 17, 1939.
21. Sutherland.
22. Marx, 84.
23. "President's Wife Meets Film Star," *New York Morning Telegraph*, June 9, 1918.
24. Norman Lusk, "Memories on My Own Screen," *Picture Play Magazine*, January 1923.
25. Stephen Normand, "Mabel Normand: Her Grand-Nephew's Memoir," *Films in Review*, August-September 1974, 391. Print.
26. Normand, 391.
27. Goldwyn, 119.
28. Ibid., 113.
29. Ibid.
30. Goldwyn 120.
31. Marx 84.
32. Harry Carr, "The Tragic Life Story of Mabel Normand," *Screen Secrets*, October-November 1929. As cited in William Thomas Sherman, *Mabel Normand: A Sourcebook to Her Life and Films*, 6th edition (Seattle: Cinema Books, 2008), 370. Print.
33. *Moving Picture World*, June 8, 1918. As cited in William Thomas Sherman, *Mabel Normand: A Sourcebook to Her Life and Films*, 6th edition (Seattle: Cinema Books, 2008), 132. Print.
34. Personal interview, Marilyn Slater, June, 2011.

Chapter 16

1. *The Journal and Republican*, July 24, 1919, as cited in Sherman, 151. Print.
2. Rob King, *The Fun Factory* (Berkeley: University of California Press, 2009), 232. Print.
3. "A New National Character," *The Tattler*, no date. As cited in William Thomas Sherman, *Mabel Normand: A Sourcebook to Her Life and Films*, 6th edition (Seattle: Cinema Books, 2008) 144. Print.
4. Gene Fowler, *Father Goose* (New York: Covici-Friede, 1934), 321. Print.
5. Kalton C. Lahue, *Dreams for Sale: The Rise and Fall of the Triangle Film Corporation* (South Brunswick, NJ: A. S. Barnes, 1971), 189. Print.

6. Robin Coons, "Mickey," *Hollywood Chatter*, June 30, 1939.
7. King, 232.
8. "The Ecclesiastical Review," *The Roman Catholic Church* 60, 558.
9. Mack Sennett and Cameron Ship, *The King of Comedy* (San Jose: To Excel, 2000), 210. Print.
10. Sennett, 211.
11. King, 232.
12. *Tattler*.
13. Simon Louvish, *Keystone: The Life and Clowns of Mack Sennett* (New York: Faber and Faber, 2003), 160. Print.
14. Sherman, 142.

Chapter 17

1. "The Girl on the Cover," *Picture Play*, February, 1918, as cited in William Thomas Sherman, *Mabel Normand: A Sourcebook to Her Life and Films*, 6th edition (Seattle: Cinema Books, 2008) 127. Print.
2. Arthur Marx, *Goldwyn: A Biography of the Man Behind the Myth* (New York: W. W. Norton, 1976), 88. Print.
3. "Compromising with Mabel," *New York Morning Telegraph*, February 11, 1919, as cited in Marx, 146. Print.
4. "Mabel Normand Says," *New York Morning Telegraph*, August 24, 1919, as cited in Marx, 152. Print.
5. "Mabelescent: Which Although Unclassified Typifies the Normand Naivete," *Photo Play World*, May 1920, as cited in Marx, 279. Print.
6. Eileen Whitfield, *Pickford: The Woman Who Made Hollywood* (Lexington: University of Press of Kentucky, 1997), 269. Print.
7. Anita Loos, *A Girl Like I* (New York: Viking, 1966), 117. Print.
8. Sidney D. Kirkpatrick, *A Cast of Killers* (Boston: G. K. Hall, 1987), 125. Print.
9. Brent E. Walker, *Mack Sennett's Fun Factory* (Jefferson, NC: McFarland, 2010), 74. Print.
10. Grace Kingsley, "Mabel Rescues Apron," *New York Morning Telegraph*, March 2, 1919, as cited in Sherman, 148. Print.
11. Personal interview, Marilyn Slater, July 2011.
12. David Raymond, "The Tragic Side of Mabel Normand," *Play World*, June 1918, as cited in Sherman, 131. Print.
13. Sherman, 424.
14. *New York Morning Telegraph*, September 14, 1918, as cited in Sherman, 137. Print.
15. *Taylorology*, 58.
16. Sidney Sutherland, "Madcap Mabel Nor-

mand," *Liberty*, September 6, 1930, as cited in Sherman.
17. Samuel Goldwyn, *Behind the Screen* (New York: George H. Doran, 1923), 120. Print.
18. Marx, 88.
19. "The Jinx," December 19, 1919, as cited in Sherman, 157. Print.
20. *New York Morning Telegraph*, June 13, 1920, as cited in Sherman, 157. Print.
21. Sutherland, 370. Print.
22. Personal interview, Marilyn Slater, August 2015.
23. A. Scott Berg, *Goldwyn: A Biography* (New York: Alfred A. Knopf, 1989), 79. Print.
24. Goldwyn, 118.
25. Sherman, 387.

Chapter 18

1. Mack Sennett and Cameron Ship, *The King of Comedy* (San Jose: To Excel, 2000), 212. Print.
2. "Molly O'" (http://irishmusicdaily.com/my-irish-molly-o'/"myirishmollyo'-american irishsong.htm), June 2013. Web.
3. Eileen Whitfield, *Pickford: The Woman Who Made Hollywood* (Lexington: University Press of Kentucky, 1997), 112. Print.
4. Sherman, 384.
5. Sennett, 213.
6. Ibid., 212.
7. *Los Angeles Record*, November 12, 1921.
8. *New York Times*, as cited in Sherman, 181. Print.
9. James W. Dean, "Molly O,'" *Albany New York Times Union*, November 25, 1921.
10. Sherman, 24.

Chapter 19

1. Robert Giroux, *A Deed of Death: The Story Behind the Unsolved Murder of William Desmond Taylor* (New York: Knopf, 1990), 32. Print.
2. "Give Mabel Normand a Chance," *Movie Weekly*, February 2, 1924, as cited in William Thomas Sherman, *Mabel Normand: A Sourcebook to Her Life and Films*, 6th edition (Seattle: Cinema Books, 2008), 267. Print.
3. *The Mabel Normand Estate*.
4. Michelle Vogel, *Olive Thomas: The Life and Death of a Silent Film Beauty* (Jefferson, NC: McFarland, 2007), 35. Print.
5. Ibid., 36.
6. Ibid., 77.
7. Sherman, 387.

8. Stuart Oderman, *Roscoe "Fatty" Arbuckle: A Biography of the Silent Film Star* (Jefferson, NC: McFarland, 2007), 152–156. Print.
9. Ibid., 153–154.
10. Ibid., 193.
11. Ibid., 157.
12. Ibid., 186.
13. Ibid., 189.
14. Ibid., 192.
15. "The Fatty Arbuckle Case," *Tru-TV* (http://trutv.com/notorious_murders/classics/fatty_arbuckle/2.html), June 2013. Web.
16. "Hollywood Joyous; Predicts Fatty Will Come Back,"*Oakland Post Inquisitor*, April 14, 1922.
17. Bruce Long, *William Desmond Taylor: A Dossier* (Metuchen, NJ: Scarecrow Press, 1991), 367. Print.
18. "Screen Star Comes Out of Seclusion," *San Francisco Examiner*, February 9, 1923.
19. Long, 184.
20. *New York Daily Mirror*, October 7, 1916.
21. Ibid.

Chapter 20

1. Robert Giroux, *A Deed of Death: The Story Behind the Unsolved Murder of William Desmond Taylor* (New York: Knopf, 1990), 22. Print.
2. Charles Higham, *Murder in Hollywood: Solving a Silent Screen Murder* (Madison: University of Wisconsin Press, 2004). 26. Print.
3. Ibid., 28.
4. Ibid., 29.
5. Ibid., 33.
6. Sidney D. Kirkpatrick, *A Cast of Killers* (Boston: G. K. Hall, 1987), 20. Print.
7. "The Colorful and Romantic Story of William D. Taylor's Remarkable Life," *Taylorology* 23 (http://www.taylorology.com/issues/taylor23.txt), July 2012. Web.
8. Giroux, 72.
9. Kirkpatrick, 22.
10. Bruce Long, *William Desmond Taylor: A Dossier* (Metuchen, NJ: Scarecrow Press, 1991), 226. Print.
11. Giroux, 87.
12. Long, 226.
13. "Mabel Normand's Own Life Story," *Los Angeles Examiner* March 16, 1924, as cited in William Thomas Sherman, *Mabel Normand: A Sourcebook to Her Life and Films*, 6th edition (Seattle: Cinema Books, 2008), 347. Print.
14. Sidney Sutherland,"Madcap Mabel Normand," *Liberty*, September 6, 1930, as cited in Sherman, 372. Print.
15. "The Jinx on Mabel," *Taylorology* 74 (http:

//www.taylorology.com/issues/taylor74.txt), June 2012. Web.

Chapter 21

1. Wallace Smith, *Chicago American*, February 11, 1922.
2. Sidney Sutherland, "Madcap Mabel Normand," *Liberty*, September 6, 1930, as cited in Sherman, 372. Print.
3. "Climate of the Los Angeles Basin" (http://www.wrcc.dri.edu/cgi-bin/cimain.pl?ca5082).
4. Bruce Long, *William Desmond Taylor: A Dossier* (Metuchen, NJ: Scarecrow Press, 1991), 263. Print.
5. Ibid., 263.
6. Ibid., 266.
7. Ibid., 264.
8. Ibid., 265.
9. Ibid., 217.
10. Ibid., 266.
11. Ibid.
12. *Mack Sennett Collection, Folder 851:* "The Little Minister."
13. Long, 252.
14. "First Detailed Story by Mabel Normand," *Los Angeles Examiner*, February 11, 1922.
15. Long, 296.

Chapter 22

1. Adela Rogers St. Johns, *Boston Advertiser*, February 20, 1922, as cited in William Thomas Sherman, *Mabel Normand: A Sourcebook to Her Life and Films*, 6th edition (Seattle: Cinema Books, 2008), 210. Print.
2. Robert Giroux, *A Deed of Death* (New York: Knopf, 1990), 7. Print.
3. Ibid.
4. Ibid., 10.
5. Ibid.
6. Ibid., 9.
7. "William Desmond Taylor," *L. A. Mourgue Files* (http://lamorguefiles.blogspot.com/2011/02/director-william-desmond-taylor-found.html).
8. Giroux, 10.
9. Sidney D. Kirkpatrick, *A Cast of Killers* (Boston: G. K. Hall, 1987), 5. Print.
10. Ibid., 6.
11. Ibid., 4.
12. Ibid., 139.
13. "Do Not Worry Is Advice Wired by Mabel Normand to Staten Island Parents," *New York Globe*, February 13, 1922, as cited in Sherman, 210. Print.

14. Ibid.
15. Ibid., 223.
16. Ibid., 224.
17. Giroux, 163.
18. Ibid.
19. Ibid., 177.
20. Ibid., 236.
21. Ibid., 238.
22. Ibid., 203.
23. Bruce Long, *William Desmond Taylor: A Dossier* (Metuchen, NJ: Scarecrow Press, 1991), 400. Print.
24. Giroux, 131.
25. Ibid., 179.
26. Kirkpatrick, 127–128.

Chapter 23

1. Charles Higham, *Murder in Hollywood: Solving a Silent Screen Mystery* (Madison: University of Wisconsin Press, 2004), 143. Print.
2. Ibid., 149.
3. *Chicago Tribune*, February 5, 1922, as cited in Sherman, 195. Print.
4. Sidney D. Kirkpatrick, *A Cast of Killers*. (Boston: G. K. Hall, 1987), 118. Print.
5. Matthew Bernstein, ed., *Controlling Hollywood: Censorship and Regulation in the Studio Era* (New Brunswick: Rutgers University Press, 1999),5. Print.
6. Stuart Oderman, *Roscoe "Fatty" Arbuckle: A Biography of the Silent Film Star* (Jefferson, NC: McFarland, 2007)190. Print.
7. Ibid., 196.
8. Sherman, 437.
9. *Chicago Daily News*, April 11, 1923, as cited in Sherman, 237. Print.

Chapter 24

1. *San Francisco Chronicle*, July 6, 1922, as cited in Sherman, 224. Print.
2. *New York Morning Telegraph*, June 19, 1922, as cited in Sherman, 219. Print.
3. Ibid.
4. Ibid.
5. *San Francisco Chronicle*, July 6, 1922, as cited in Sherman, 224. Print.
6. Private letter.
7. Elsie Codd, "Seeing Limehouse with Mabel," *Picture and Picturegoers*, September, 1922, as cited in Sherman, 226. Print.
8. Ibid.
9. Adela Rogers St. Johns, *Love, Laughter and Tears: My Hollywood Story* (New York: Doubleday, 1978), 56. Print.

10. "Limehouse Nights," *San Francisco Chronicle* July 6, 1922, as cited in Sherman, 224. Print.
11. Elsie Codd, *Picture and Picturegoers*, September, 1922.
12. Ibid.
13. "The Chinese Limehouse" (http://utoldlondon.org.uk/blog/read/the-chinese-limehouse.htm), May 2013. Web.
14. *New York Morning Telegraph*, September 8, 1922, as cited in Sherman, 226. Print.
15. "Henry Wilson" (http://www.firstworldwar.com/bio/wilson_henry.html), November 2014. Web.
16. *Los Angeles Times*, September 13, 1922, as cited in Sherman, 226. Print.
17. Personal interview, Marilyn Slater, August, 2015.
18. *Los Angeles Times*, September 13, 1922, as cited in Sherman, 226. Print.
19. *Los Angeles Times*, September 16, 1922, as cited in Sherman, 227. Print.
20. Sherman, 25.
21. Ibid.
22. "Scout Old World for Scenes," *Los Angeles Times*, September 13, 1922, as cited in Sherman, 226. Print.

Chapter 25

1. William Thomas Sherman, *Mabel Normand: A Sourcebook to Her Life and Films*, 6th edition (Seattle: Cinema Books, 2008), 321. Print.
2. Mack Sennett and Cameron Ship, *The King of Comedy* (San Jose: To Excel, 2000), 269. Print.
3. Sherman, 27.
4. "Miss Normand Asks Public for Fair Play," *New York Times*, January 6, 1924.
5. Ibid.
6. Sidney Sutherland, "Madcap Mabel Normand," *Liberty*, September 6, 1930, as cited in Sherman, 378. Print.
7. "Mabel Normand and Edna Purviance Witness Shooting of Courtland S. Dines in Los Angeles," *The Landmark*, Statesville, NC, January 8, 1924.
8. "Miss Normand Asks Public for Fair Play," *New York Times*, January 6, 1924.
9. Sennett, 271.
10. Sutherland.
11. *Mack Sennett Collection: Folder 866, Preliminary Synopsis of "Mary Anne,"* October 25, 1922. The Margaret Herrick Library. December 2014.
12. *Memphis Commercial Appeal*, August 17, 1924.
13. *Morning Telegraph*, March 21, 1924.
14. "Call Mabel Normand to the Greer Trial," *New York Times*, April 17, 1924.
15. Sherman, 26.
16. *Los Angeles Herald*, June 17, 1924.
17. Ibid.
18. Ibid.
19. Ibid.
20. "Greer Arrested on Acquittal of Dines Shooting," *Arizona Republican*, June 20, 1964.
21. "The Egg," *Wisconsin State Journal*, January 20, 1924.
22. Sherman, 27.
23. *Mack Sennett Collection: Folder 1076, Clippings*. December 2014.
24. "Statement About Suit by Actress," *Los Angeles Times*, October 12, 1924.
25. *Mack Sennett Collection: Folder 1076, Clippings*. December 2014.
26. "Mabel Loses Libel Tilt," *Los Angeles Daily Times*, November 20, 1924.
27. Sidney Sutherland, "Madcap Mabel Normand," *Liberty*, September 6, 1930, as cited in Sherman, 379. Print.
28. Ibid.
29. Ibid.
30. Ibid.
31. Ibid.
32. "Mabel Normand Now Wife of Lew Cody," *New York Times*, September 18, 1926.
33. "Tragic Dines Affair," *Los Angeles Examiner*, March 23, 1924.

Chapter 26

1. William Thomas Sherman, *Mabel Normand: A Sourcebook to Her Life and Films*, 6th edition (Seattle: Cinema Books, 2008), 61. Print.
2. "Welcome to the World of Laughter," Hal Roach (http://www.hal-roach.com), February 9, 2015. Web.
3. *The Hal Roach Papers*, University of Southern California Special Collections, June 2014.
4. "Madcap Mabel Normand, the True Story of a Great Comedienne," *Liberty Magazine*, October 11, 1930.
5. "In Hollywood," *Kokomo Tribune*, March 22, 1926, 10.
6. Ted Oduka and James L. Neibaur, *Stan Without Oliver: The Stan Laurel Solo Films, 1917–1927* (Jefferson, NC: McFarland), 172.
7. "Mabel Normand to Return to Movies," *Nevada State Journal*, February 23, 1926. 1.
8. "Raggedy Rose," *Silent Era* (www.silentera.com/psfl/data/r/raggedyrose1926.html), February 9, 2015. Web.
9. "Asa Keyes 1923–1928," *Los Angeles County District Attorney's Office* (http://www.da.co.la.ca.us), February 9, 2015. Web.

10. "Taylor Case Is Shorn of Its Mystery," *Oakland Tribune*, March 28, 1926. 17.
11. Ibid.
12. Ibid.
13. "Mabel Normand Now Absolved," *Ogden Standard Examiner*, March 28, 1926.
14. "Interview with Anita Garvin," *Mabel Normand Home Page* (www.mn-h.com/anita1.htm), February 9, 2015. Web.
15. "New Contract Brings Popular Mabel Normand Back to Screen to Stay," *Cedar Rapids Tribune*, July 9, 1926. 2.
16. "Oliver Hardy 1892–1958," *The Crazy World of Laurel and Hardy* (http://www.stanlaurelandoliverhardy.com/olly.htm), February 9, 2015. Web.
17. University of Southern California Special Collections.
18. "Moviana," *Kokomo Tribune*, August 7, 1926. 13.
19. "Movieland by Jack Wooldridge," *Oakland Tribune*, July 11, 1936. 59.
20. "Lew Cody and Mabel Normand Wed," *Oelwein Daily Register*, September 17, 1926. 7.
21. Sidney Sutherland, "Madcap Mabel Normand," *Liberty Magazine*, September 6, 1930.
22. Mack Sennett and Cameron Shipp, *King of Comedy* (San Jose: To Excel, 2000), 272.
23. William Thomas Sherman, *Mabel Normand: A Sourcebook to Her Life and Films*, 6th edition (Seattle: Cinema Books, 2008) 28. Print.
24. "Actress's Condition Grave," *Los Angeles Times* March 20, 1929, as cited in Sherman, 304. Print.
25. Gene Fowler. *Father Goose* (New York: Covici-Friede, 1934), 393.
26. Ibid.
27. Ibid.

Chapter 27

1. Will Rogers syndicated column, as cited in William Thomas Sherman, *Mabel Normand: A Sourcebook to Her Life and Films*, 6th edition (Seattle: Cinema Books, 2008), 311. Print.
2. Mabel Normand-Cody Probate Records, County of Los Angeles.
3. Personal interview, Marilyn Slater, July 2011.
4. "Normand Funeral Friday," *Los Angeles Times* February 25, 1930, as cited in Sherman, 312. Print.
5. Mabel Normand-Cody Probate Records, County of Los Angeles.
6. "Mabel Normand Dies After Lengthy Illness," *Los Angeles Times*, February 24, 1930, as cited in Sherman, 310. Print.
7. "Normand Funeral Friday," *Los Angeles Times* February 24, 1930, as cited in Sherman, 312. Print.
8. "Mack Sennett Grieved Over Star's Death," *Los Angeles Times* February 24, 1930, as cited in Sherman, 310. Print.
9. Mabel Normand-Cody Probate Records, County of Los Angeles.
10. "Mabel Normand Funeral," *Los Angeles Record*, February 28, 1930, as cited in Sherman, 316. Print.
11. *The Lewiston Daily Sun*, March 1, 1930.
12. "Mabel Normand Funeral," *Los Angeles Record*, February 28, 1930, as cited in Sherman, 316. Print.
13. "Mabel Normand at Rest," *Los Angeles Times*, March 1, 1930, as cited in Sherman, 317. Print.
14. King Vidor, *A Tree Is a Tree* (Hollywood: Samuel French, 1953), 190. Print.
15. "Normand Rites Set for Today," *Los Angeles Times*, February 28, 1930, as cited in Sherman, 316. Print.
16. *Baltimore Evening Sun*, March 1, 1930.
17. Mabel Normand-Cody Probate Records, County of Los Angeles.
18. Ibid.

Epilogue

1. *Los Angeles Examiner*, March 23, 1924. "Mabel Normand's Own Life Story, Chapter 6. Comedienne Says Taylor Slayer will be Captured," as cited in William Thomas Sherman, *Mabel Normand: A Sourcebook to Her Life and Films*, 6th edition (Seattle: Cinema Books, 2008) p. 349. Print.
2. Mack Sennett and Cameron Shipp, *The King of Comedy* (San Jose: To Excel, 2000), 45. Print.

Bibliography

Alleman, Richard. *New York: The Movie Lover's Guide*. New York: Broadway Books, 1988. Print.
Anderson, Mark Lynn. *Twilight of the Gods: Hollywood and the Human Sciences in 1920's America*. Berkeley: University of California Press, 2011. Print.
Balio, Tino. *United Artists Volume 1, 1919–1950*. Madison: University of Wisconsin Press, 2009. Print.
Bausum, Ann. *With Courage and Cloth: Winning the Fight for a Woman's Right to Vote*. Washington, D.C.: National Geographic, 2004. Print.
Behr, Edward. *Prohibition: Thirteen Years That Changed America*. New York: Arcade, 1996, 2011. Print.
Bengston, John. *Silent Traces: Discovering Early Hollywood Through the Film of Charlie Chaplin*. Santa Monica, CA: Santa Monica Press, 2006. Print.
Berg, A. Scott. *Goldwyn: A Biography*. New York: Riverhead Books, 1989. Print.
Bernstein, Matthew. *Controlling Hollywood: Censorship and Regulation in the Studio Era*. New Brunswick: Rutgers University Press, 1999.
Brownlow, Kevin. *The Parade's Gone By*. Berkeley: University of California Press, 1968. Print.
Chaplin, Charles. *My Autobiography*. New York: Plume, 1964, 1992. Print.
Davis, Lon. *Silent Lives: 100 Biographies of the Silent Era*. Albany, GA: BearManor Media, 2008. Print.
DeBauch, Leslie Midkiff. *Reel Patriotism: The Movies and World War I*. Madison: University of Wisconsin Press, 1997. Print.
Donnelley, Paul. *Fade to Black: A Book of Movie Obituaries*. London: Omnibus, 2005. Print.
Everson, William K. *American Silent Film*. New York: Da Capo, 1998.
Fleming, E. J. *Paul Bern: The Life and Famous Death of the MGM Director and Husband of Harlow*. Jefferson, NC: McFarland, 2009. Print.
Fort Lee Film Commission. *Fort Lee: Birthplace of the Motion Picture Industry*. Charleston, SC: Arcadia Publishing, 2006. Print.
Fowler, Gene. *Father Goose: The Story of Mack Sennett*. New York: Covici-Friede, 1934. Print.
Fussell, Betty Harper. *Mabel: Hollywood's First I-Don't-Care Girl*. New Haven: Ticknor & Fields, 1982. Print.
Geary, Rick. *Famous Player: The Mysterious Death of William Desmond Taylor*. New York: NBM Comics Lit, 2009. Print.
Giroux, Robert. *A Deed of Death, the Story Behind the Murder of Hollywood Director William Desmond Taylor*. New York: Alfred A. Knopf, 1990. Print.
Goldwyn, Samuel. *Behind the Screen*. New York: George H. Doran, 1923. Print.

Herndon, Booton. *Mary Pickford and Douglas Fairbanks: The Most Popular Couple the World Has Known.* New York: W. W. Norton, 1977. Print.
Higham, Charles. *Murder in Hollywood: Solving a Silent Screen Mystery.* Madison: University of Wisconsin Press, 2004. Print.
King, Rob. *The Fun Factory.* Berkeley: University of California Press, 2009. Print.
Kirkpatrick, Sidney D. *A Cast of Killers.* New York: E. P. Dutton, 2007. Print.
Koszarski, Richard. *Fort Lee: The Film Town.* Rome: John Libbey, 2004.
Lahue, Kalton C. *Dreams for Sale: The Rise and Fall of the Triangle Film Corporation.* South Brunswick, NJ: A. S. Barnes, 1971. Print.
_____. *Mack Sennett's Keystone: The Man, the Myth and the Comedies.* South Brunswick, NJ: A. S. Barnes, 1971. Print.
Leider, Emily W. *Dark Lover.* New York: Farrar, Straus and Giroux, 2003. Print.
Long, Bruce. *William Desmond Taylor: A Dossier.* Metuchen, NJ: Scarecrow, 1991.
Loos, Anita. *A Girl Like I.* New York: Viking, 1966. Print.
_____. *The Talmadge Girls.* New York: Viking, 1978. Print.
Louvish, Simon. *Keystone: The Life and Clowns of Mack Sennett.* New York: Faber and Faber, 2003. Print.
Marx, Arthur. *Goldwyn: A Biography of the Man Behind the Myth.* New York: W. W. Norton, 1976. Print.
Merritt, Greg. *Room 1219, the Life of Fatty Arbuckle, the Mysterious Death of Virginia Rappe, and the Scandal That Changed Hollywood.* Chicago: Chicago Review Press, 2013. Print.
Moore, Colleen. *Silent Star.* Garden City, NY: Doubleday, 1968. Print.
Oderman, Stuart. *The Keystone Krowd, Mack, Mabel, the Kops and the Girls (1908–1915).* Albany, GA: BearManor Media, 2007. Print.
_____. *Roscoe "Fatty" Arbuckle: A Biography of the Silent Film Comedian, 1887–1933.* Jefferson, NC: McFarland, 1994. Print.
Richards, Marlee. *America in the 1910's.* Minneapolis: Twenty-First Century Books, 2010. Print.
St. Johns, Adela Rogers. *The Honeycomb.* Garden City, NY: Doubleday, 1969. Print.
_____. *Love Laughter and Tears: My Hollywood Story.* Garden City, NY: Doubleday, 1978. Print.
Sann, Paul. *The Lawless Decade: Bullets, Broads, and Bathtub Gin.* New York: Crown, 2010. Print.
Schickel, Richard. *D. W. Griffith: An American Life.* New York: Limelight Editions, 1984. Print.
Sennett, Mack, and Cameron Shipp. *King of Comedy.* San Jose: To Excel, 2000. Print.
Sherman, William Thomas. *Mabel Normand: A Sourcebook to Her Life and Films,* 6th edition. Seattle: Cinema Books, 2008.
Slide, Anthony. *The Big V: A History of the Vitagraph Company. New and Revised Edition.* Metuchen, NJ: Scarecrow, 1987. Print.
Stenn, David. *Clara Bow: Runnin' Wild.* New York: Cooper Square Press, 2000. Print.
Streatfeild, Dominic. *Cocaine: An Unauthorized Biography.* New York: Picador, 2001. Print.
Swanson, Gloria. *Swanson on Swanson.* New York: Pocket Books, 1980. Print.
Vance, Jeffrey. *Douglas Fairbanks.* Berkeley: University of California Press, 2008. Print.
Vogel, Michelle. *Olive Thomas: The Life and Death of a Silent Film Beauty.* Jefferson, NC: McFarland, 2007. Print.
Wagner, Walter. *You Must Remember This.* New York: G. P. Putnam's Sons, 1975. Print.
Walker, Brent E. *Mack Sennett's Fun Factory: A History and Filmography of His Studio and His Keystone and Mack Sennett Comedies, with Biographies of Players and Personnel.* Jefferson, NC: McFarland, 2010. Print.
Whitfield, Eileen, *Pickford: The Woman Who Made Hollywood.* Lexington: University Press of Kentucky, 1997. Print.

Index

Acquitania 150
Adams, David 136
The Adventures of Dollie 22
Affiliated Picture Interests of California 125
Al Ringling Theatre 15
The Alarm 195
All Star Feature Film Corporation 9
Allen, Phyllis 197
The Ambitious Butler 185
American Hospital 121
American Mutoscope 21, 22
American Pathe 21
American Star 21
The Answering Voice: One Hundred Love Lyrics by Women 12
Anything Once 169, 203
Arbuckle, Mollie 50
Arbuckle, Roscoe 48, 50, 63, 71, 74, 75, 76, 78, 121, 122, 123, 124, 138, 142, 143, 175, 191, 192, 193, 195, 196, 197, 198, 199
Arbuckle, William 50
Art Students League of New York 16
Arvidson, Linda 21, 26
Ashton, Saylia 183, 184
At Coney Island 185
At It Again 186
At the French Ball 22
Aubert, Shirley 199
August, Edwin 181, 182
Avery, Charles 190, 191
Ayers, Agnes 127

Baby Day 192
Back to the Woods 97, 199
Baker, Corrine 200
Bangville Police 190
The Baron 180
Barry, Leon 202
Barrymore, John 93, 171
The Battle of Who Run 188
Baumann, Charles O. 36, 40

The Beating He Needed 185
Beery, Wallace 127
Belasco, David 26
Belmore, Lionel 202
Bender, Louella 106
Bennett, Charles 196
Benson, Julia 2, 12, 106, 140, 171, 173, 175
Bern, Paul 112, 175
Besserer, Eugenie 201
Betty Becomes a Maid 28, 179
Biograph Company 21, 22, 27, 28, 32
Biograph Studios 24
Birth of a Nation 36, 98
Bison Studio 36
Blinn, Holbrook 163
The Blue Mouse 162
Boehm, Clarice 10
Bolder, Robert 201
The Bond 9
Bonner, Priscilla 155
Booth, Charles Gorman 184
Boquel, Joe 34
Bordeaux, Joe 75, 198, 200
Boulden, Edward 199
Bow, Clara 13
Bowers, John 200
The Bowling Match 192
Bradbury, James, Jr. 102
The Brave Hunter 182
The Breakfast Club 166
Brent, Evelyn 155
The Bright Lights 199
Brock and Feagens Jewelry Store 131
Broken Blossoms 152
Bronco Film Company 38
Brookin, Walter 65
Brown's Séance 186
Bruce, Kate 180, 181, 183, 184
Bryson, Winifred 202
Buckingham Palace 152
Bunny, John 27, 180

242　Index

Burke, Thomas 151
Burns, Edith 156
Burton, John 201
Busch, Mae 39, 71
Butler, Kathleen 184
Butler, William J. 180, 183
Butterick Company 17

Calvary Cemetery 1, 175
Calvin, William 200
Cannon, Pomeroy 201
Carewe, Edwin 76
Carmecita 15
Carpenter, Florence 201
Carr, Harry 82
Case, John 10
Catalina Island 65
Catholic Church 11, 16, 100
Caught by Wireless 22
Caught in a Cabaret 49, 55, 56, 194
Cavender, Glen 197
The Champion 193
The Changing of Silas Warner 180
Chaplin, Charlie 9, 53, 55, 56, 57, 58, 60, 61, 62, 174, 175, 178, 194, 195, 196, 197
Chaplin, Syd 196
Chapman, Edythe 201
Chiappa, Fr. 67
The Chicago Daily News 143
Church, Dorothea 161
The Church of the Good Shepherd 65
Clarges, Verner 180
Clifton College 126
Cloud, Dark 181
Cody, Lew 83, 84, 117, 166, 167, 168, 169, 170, 171, 172, 173, 175, 176, 200
Cogley, Nick 185, 188, 189, 190, 191, 193, 200
Cohen, Milton 160
Cohen Collects a Debt 38, 184
Cohen Saves the Flag 193
Comique Film Corporation 78
Conkling, Chester 194, 195, 199
Cooley, Hallam 201
Coolidge, Calvin 24
Cooper, Earl 192
Costello, Maurice 179
Courtial, Juliet 150
Crail, Charles 160
Crane, Ogden 201
Crisp, Donald 180
Crossly, Syd 203
Crowley, Aleister 120
Cummings, Richard 201
Cunard Ship Line 150

Dahl, Helen 199
Dalton, "Sunny Jim" 60, 61
A Dash Through The Clouds 35, 184

Davenport, Alice 185, 186, 187, 188, 190, 191, 194, 197, 198, 202
Davenport, Blanche 200
Davidson, Max 165, 170, 203
Davis, William 131, 132, 133, 134
The Deacon Outwitted 188
The Deacon's Daughter 22
The Deacon's Troubles 186
A Dead Man's Honor 180
Deane-Tanner, Ethel Cunningham 126, 147, 148
Deane-Tanner, Ethel "Daisy" 129, 147
Deeley, Ben 202
De Grasse, Sam 200
Dell, Edith M. 132
Dent, Vernon 202
Desmond, William 202
A Desperate Lover 186
Devereaux, Minnie 200, 202
Diana of the Movies 162
Dileneator 17
Dillon, Eddie 32, 180, 182, 183, 183
Dimmick, Malvern 168
The Diving Girl 28, 32, 180
Dodging a Million 94, 199
Double Speed 124
Dressler, Marie 58, 59, 60, 154, 175, 196
The Duel 187
Dunn, Bobby 198
Durfee, Minta 50, 63, 68, 71, 72, 73, 74, 75, 76, 83, 105, 172, 193, 197, 200

Edison, Thomas 21
Edison Trust 21
Edward, Prince of Wales 63, 64
Elkas, Edward 199
Elliott, Robert 200
Elmer, Billy 201
Elmore, Pearl 200
Empire Film Exchange 36
The Engagement Ring 32, 182
Essany Film Company 71
Essany Film Manufacturing Company 62, 63
The Eternal Mother 181
Evans, Frank 182, 183, 184
The Extra Girl 155, 156, 158, 159, 202
Eyton, Charles 135, 139

Factor, Max 169
Fairbanks, Douglas 115, 175, 176
Faire, Virginia Brown 155
Fall River Line 16
A Family Mix Up 187
Famous Players-Lasky 89, 135
Farley, Dot 190, 193
Farrar, Geraldine 198, 109, 110
The Fatal Chocolate 182
The Fatal Mallet 55, 56, 195
The Fatal Taxicab 192

Index

Fatty and Mabel Adrift 76, 77, 198
Fatty and Mabel at the San Diego Exposition 197
Fatty and Mabel's Married Life 51, 197
Fatty and Mabel's Simple Life 52, 197
Fatty's Flirtation 193
Fatty's Wine Party 196
Fazenda, Louise 175
The Fickle Spaniard 183
Fields, W.C. 23
Finch, Flora 180
Finlayson, Jimmy 168, 170, 200
Fischbach, Fred 121
The Five O'Clock Man 162
Flagg, James Montgomery 18, 19
The Flirting Husband 185
The Floor Below 94, 199
Florey, Robert 49
Foiling Fickle Father 188
For Lizzie's Sake 187
For the Love of Mabel 191
Ford, Eugenie 200
Forde, Victoria 185
The Foreman of the Jury 190
Foxe, Earle 200
Francis, Alice B. 179, 200
Franciscan Poor Claire Nuns 12
Francisco, Betty 155
Franklin, Chester 187
Franz Ferdinand of Austria 67
Frederick, Pauline 94, 108, 110, 200
French, Charles K. 202
Freud, Sigmund 12, 62
The Furs 183

A Game of Poker 189
Garvin, Anita 165, 203
Gasfilmofund 119
Gaumont Graphic Newsreel #39 199
Geldart, Clarence 203
A Gentleman of Nerve 55, 196
Gerber, Neva 128
Gerrard, Charles 200
Getting Acquainted 197
Gibson, Charles Dana 18, 19, 20
Gibson, Margaret 148
A Glimpse of Los Angeles 194
Goebel, Art 175, 176
Goldwyn, Samuel 79, 88, 89, 90, 91, 92, 95, 96, 97, 103, 113, 175, 176
Goldwyn Pictures 91
Goldwyn Studios 100, 105
Good Samaritan Hospital 156, 158, 161
Gordon, Eleanor 127
Gordon, James 201
Gordon, Julia Swayne 180
Graham, Arthur 98
Grauman, Sid 175
Graves, Ralph 202

Graybill, Joseph 180
The Great Train Robbery 21
Greer, Horace 157, 159
Gribbon, Eddie 202
Gribbon, Harry 197
Griffith, Beverly 188
Griffith, D.W. 21, 22, 23, 24, 25, 26, 27, 28, 29, 31, 32, 34, 49
Grisel, Edward Bernard 200
The Growth of the Soil 12
The Gusher 193
The Gypsy Queen 192

Hackett, Albert Hatton 202
Hal Roach Studio 165
Hale, Creighton 170, 175, 203, 204
Hamilton, Effe 126
Hamsun, Knut 12
The Hansom Driver 191
Harding, Warren G. 143
Hardy, Oliver 166, 160, 170, 171, 204
Harlem Grand Theatre 9
Harlow, Jean 113
Harrison Narcotics Act 83
Harron, Robert 180, 181
Hartman, Ferris 75
Hatch, Riley 200
Hatton, Raymond 190
Haver, Phyllis 155
Hayden, Nora 203
Hayes, Frank 198
Hays, Will 143
He Did and He Didn't 77, 199
He Must Have a Wife 184
Head Over Heels 112, 201
Heirs, Walter 201
Helen's Marriage 33, 183
Hellman's Bank 131
Hello Mabel 6, 196
Help! Help! 182
Henderson, Dell 23, 32, 180, 183, 184
Henderson, Grace 32, 180, 184
Her Awakening 27, 181
Her First Adventure 22
Her Friend the Bandit 49, 55, 195
Her New Beau 187
Herbert, Frank J. 199
Herbert, J.W. 200
Hernandez, Ana 202
Hersholt, Jean 175
Hickman, Alfred 199
Hide and Seek 189
His Chum the Baron 190
His Mother 180
His Trysting Place 55, 196
Hitchcock, Raymond 198
Holmes, Helen 189, 190
Holmquist, Sigrid 155
Hot Stuff 32, 182

Houseman, Arthur 200
How Betty Won the School 28, 182
Howe, Herb 81, 82
Hubby's Job 190
Humphrey, William 180
Hunn, Bert 191
Hunt, Leslie 200
Hutt, Henry 18
Hyde, A.G., III 111
Hyde, Harry 181

Ibrahim of Egypt, Prince 63, 153
In Old California 28
Ince, Thomas 36, 67, 171, 180
The Indiscretions of Betty 28, 179
Interpretation of Dreams 5, 12, 134
Islee, Charlie 124, 191, 192, 193

James, William P. 175
Jaumier, Georges 128
Jefferson, Thomas 200
Jefferson, William 199
Jeske, George 193
Jinx 110, 111, 201
Joan of Plattsburg 94, 199
Jobson, Edward 201
Johnstone, Betty 72
Jones, Bill 42
Jones, F. Richard 83, 86, 115, 118, 164, 188
Joy, Leatrice 175
Joyce, Alice 22, 23
Judith of Bethulia 29
Just Brown's Luck 188
Justice, O.M. 72

Kaarboe, Olay 122
Kalem Film Company 21
Karloff, Boris 168
Katchem Kate 183
Kay-Bee Company 21
Kearny, Horace 35
Kelly, Joe *see* Greer, Horace
Kelly, T. Howard 1
Kennedy, Edgar 193, 198, 200
Kennedy, Edward 191
Kennedy, Madge 108, 109
Kennedy, Tom 105, 200
Kerry, Norman 175
Kessel, Adam 36, 40, 58, 67, 97
Keyes, Asa 159, 165
Keystone Studio 36, 38, 40, 41, 53, 63, 74, 80
King, Hamilton 17
Kirtley, Virginia 192
A Kiss in the Taxi 162
Kleinschmidt, Carl 17
Kunkel, George 201

Laffey, James 200
La Marr, Barbara 175

Lamming, Frank 33, 127
Landis, Cullen 201
Lanoe, J. Liquel 182, 183
La Roque, Rod 199, 200
Laurel, Stan 165, 166, 168, 170, 171
La Verne, Laura 200
Lehr, Abe 93, 94, 115
Lehrman, Henry 123, 186, 193
Lester, Kate 201
Levey, Burt 64
Lewis, Elbert 149
Lewis, Pat *see* Gibson, Margaret
Liberty Bonds 9
Liberty Loan Drive 9, 87
Library of Congress 42
Limehouse Nights 151
Linder, Max 40, 154
A Little Hero 190
The Little Minister 133
The Little Mouse 162
Lloyd, Harold 131, 165, 171, 176
Logan, Jacqueline 201
Long, Raphael 148, 149
Loos, Anita 105
Lorraine, Harry 201
Lorraine, Leota 200
Los Angeles Athletic Club 31, 91
Los Angeles Times 11, 63, 128
Louderback, Judge 124
Love and Courage 194
Love and Sickness at Sea 193
Lucas, Wilfred 183

Mabel and Fatty Viewing the World's Fair at San Francisco 49, 198
Mabel and Fatty's Wash Day 197
Mabel at the Wheel 49, 55, 194
Mabel, Fatty and the Law 197
Mabel, Lost and Won 198
Mabel's Adventures 187
Mabel's Awful Mistake 190
Mabel's Bear Escape 194
Mabel's Blunder 49, 196
Mabel's Busy Day 49, 55, 195
Mabel's Dramatic Career 48, 192
Mabel's Heroes 188
Mabel's Latest Prank 196
Mabel's Lovers 6, 186
Mabel's Married Life 195
Mabel's Nerve 194
Mabel's New Hero 192
Mabel's New Job 195
Mabel's Stormy Love Affair 194
Mabel's Strange Predicament 194
Mabel's Stratagem 187
Mabel's Willful Way 198
Mace, Fred 31, 32, 36, 40, 75, 181, 183, 184, 185, 186, 187, 188, 189, 190
Mack, Willard 163

Index

Mack at It Again 194
Mack Sennett Comedies 97
The Mack Sennett Weekly 97
Madam Frances 95
The Making of a Man 27, 181
Mann, Hank 192, 193
Mark Strand Theatre 15
Marsh, Mae 94, 175
Marsh, Marguerite 182, 200
Marshall, Tully 201
Mary Anne 155, 157
The Masquerader 55, 198
Mayne, Eric 202
McAdoo, William Gibbs 9
McCoy, Harry 194, 196, 197
McCutcheon, Wallace 22
McCutcheon, William, Jr. 199
McDonald, J. Ferrell 83
McDonald, William 136
McDowell, Claire 179, 183
McGrail, Walter 202
McLean Douglas 136
The Mender of Nets 32, 185
Menjou, Adolphe 112, 201, 202
Mickey 83, 84, 85, 86, 87, 88, 97, 98, 99, 100, 101, 102, 104, 105, 164, 200
A Midnight Elopement 187
Miller, Carl 203
Miller, Rube 190
Mineay, Charlotte 203
Minter, Mary Miles 128, 137, 145
A Misplaced Foot 193
The Mistaken Masher 187
Mr. Fix It 186
Mitchell, Rhea "Ginga" 127
Molly O' 114, 115, 116, 117, 118, 201
Moore, Owen 198, 200
Moore, Tom 94
Morrison, James 180
Motion Picture Patents Company 21
Motion Picture Producers of America 143
Moving Pictue World 40, 166
A Muddy Romance 49, 193
Mulhall, Jack 68, 117, 175, 202
Mullins, Fr. Michael 175, 176
Murray, Charlie 75, 195
Murray, T. Henderson 200
Mutual Film Corporation v. Industrial Commission 143
My Valet 198

Nance, Frank A. 138, 206, 207, 208, 209, 210
National Film Registry 49
Neason, Hazel 180
Neighbors 183
Neilan, Marshall 175
Nelson, Eva 195
The New Conductor 190

The New Neighbor 185
The New York Girl 195
New York Motion Picture Company 36
Nichols, George 83, 200, 201, 202
The Nickle Hopper 168, 203
Nietzche, Frederic 12
A Night in an English Music Hall 54
Nogel, Frankie 44
A Noise from the Deep 191
Normand, Claude 137
Normand, Claude, Jr. 9, 14, 87, 103, 137, 174, 175
Normand, Gladys 13, 174
Normand, Mary 14, 124, 174, 175
Normand, Ralph 14

Oakley, Laura 186, 189
Oakman, Wheeler 83, 200
Oh Diana! 162
Oh Mabel Behave 67, 202
Oh Those Eyes! 182
Ojeda, Manuel R. 201
Oldfield, Barney 48, 190, 192
One Hour Married 166, 203
Opperman, Frank 183, 195, 185, 198
O'Sullivan, Tony 183
Ott, Fred 21
Overholtzer Undertaking Parlor 138, 139
Ovey, George 202
Owens, Mamie 106, 131, 132, 140

Paget, Alfred 32, 181
Pallette, Eugene 127, 175, 204
Palmer, Patricia 140; *see also* Gibson, Margaret
Panama-California Exposition 84
Paramount Pictures 186
Parmalee, Philip 35, 184
Parrot, Charles 195, 196
Pat's Day Off 186
Pawn, Doris 201
Peavey, Henry 132, 135, 136, 138, 140, 141, 207, 208, 209
Peck's Bad Girl 107, 108, 200
Pedro's Dilemma 185
Perry, Charles 153
The Pest 108, 200
Phillips, Carmen 190
Phillips, Elvin R. 180
Photoplay Magazine 42, 47, 101
Picciola 180
Pickford, Charlotte 26
Pickford, Jack 26, 93, 121, 127, 184
Pickford, Lottie 26
Pickford, Mary 26, 27, 31, 32, 87, 114, 127, 128, 166, 174, 175, 182, 183
Pike, Alexander 112
Pinto 110, 111, 201
Pitts, Zasu 127

Pixley, Gus 184, 185
Plumer, Lincoln 199
The Police Gazette 44, 132, 134
Porter, Edwin S. 21
Pottenger, Dr. Francis M., Jr. 11
Pottenger Sanatorium 11, 12, 171, 172
Powell, Russ 201, 202
Prescott, Vivian 183
Price, Gertrude 42
Princip, Gavrilo 67
Professor Bean's Removal 191
Prohibition 121
Public School No. 17 15
Purviance, Edna 135, 138, 156, 160

Quick, Evelyn 190
Quick, James R. 163

Raggedy Rose 165, 166, 203
Rappe, Virginia 122
Rawlings, Herbert 199
Record of a Sneeze 15
A Red Hot Romance 188
Regent Theatre 15
Reid, Wallace 73, 105, 124, 140, 175
Rescued from the Eagles Nest 22
Ridgeway, Fritzi 201
Riley and Schultz 185
The Riot 191
Roach, Hal 164, 171
Robinson, W.C. 183
Rogers, Dora 198
Roland, Ruth 175
Rolph, James, Jr. 198
Romer, Leila 200
The Rube and the Baron 187
Rubens, Alma 105

Sailing Through 150
Sailors Snug Harbor Home 14
St. Francis Hotel 121
St. John, Al 75, 76, 191, 195, 198, 202
St. Johns, Adela Rogers 9, 42, 43, 44, 73, 82, 88, 135
St. Mary's Convent School 15
St. Paul's Pro-Cathedral 140
St. Vincent's Hospital 12
Sam Goldwyn Studios 76
Sands, Edward 128, 133, 148
Saved from Himself 181
Saving Mabel's Dad 187
Schertzinger, Victor 111, 112
The Sea Nymphs 197
Selby, Charlotte 128, 146, 147
Selig Film Company 21
Selig Polyscope 50
Selwin, Archibad 90
Sennett, Mack 12, 13, 14, 23, 24, 25, 27, 29, 31, 32, 33, 34, 35, 36, 37, 38, 40, 52, 53, 58, 60, 62, 65, 67, 68, 69, 70, 71, 72, 73, 75, 78, 79, 81, 87, 88, 91, 92, 97, 100, 102, 114, 115, 116, 117, 118, 178, 182, 183, 184, 185, 189, 190, 191, 193, 197, 198, 202
Shaw, George Bernard 154
Shea, William 180
Sheehan, Winifred 46
Sherman, Lowell 202
Shipp, Cameron 178
Should Men Walk Home? 170, 204
Sinnott, Catherine 24, 28, 30, 41, 69, 70
Sinnott, James 158
Sinnott, John 28
Sis Hopkins 108, 173, 206
Slater, Marilyn 2,
The Sleuths at the Floral Parade 188
The Slim Princess 111, 201
Smiley, Joseph 199
Socialist Propaganda Campaign 44
A Spanish Dilemma 32, 33, 182
Spanish-American War 9
The Speed Kings 48, 192
The Speed Queen 191
The Squaw's Love 25, 181
Stake Uncle Sam to Play Your Hand 9, 200
Stanslaw, Perhyn 18
Staten Island Ferry 17
Sterling, Ford 31, 36, 40, 47, 48, 52, 54, 67, 75, 175, 184, 185, 187, 188, 189, 190, 191, 192, 193, 197, 199, 202
Stevens, Edwin 201
Stockdale, Carl 202
Stolen Magic 198
A Strong Revenge 188
Studebaker, Hale 189, 190
Summerville, George "Slim" 195, 197
Sunset Boulevard 178
Sutherland, Eddie 105
Swain, Mack 195, 196
Swanson, Gloria 39, 68, 140, 177
Sweet, Blanche 28, 29, 31, 83, 89, 171, 181
Sylvester, Lillian 201

Tally's Electric Theatre 15
Talmadge, Constance 28, 29, 127, 175
A Tangled Affair 188
Tashman, Lilyan 202
Tavares, Arthur 187, 188
Taylor, Laurette 163
Taylor, William Desmond 124, 125, 126, 127, 128, 130, 132, 133, 134, 135, 136, 138, 139, 141, 145, 146, 147, 148, 149
Tellegen, Lou 64, 94
The Telltale Light 191
Telzlaff, Teddy 192
A Temperamental Husband 186
Terrell, Herb 93
That Little Band of Gold 57, 197
Thomas Ince Film Company 149

Thomas, Olive 121
Thompson, Hugh 112, 201
Those Country Kids 195
Those Good Old Days 189
Three Soldiers 133
Thus Spake Zarathustra 12
Tillie's Nightmare 58
Tillie's Punctured Romance 55, 58, 196
Titanic 150
Tomboy Bessie 33, 183
Toncray, Kate 183, 184
Too Much Speed 124
The Tourists 33, 183
The Tragedy of a Dress Suit 191
Triangle Film Corporation 67, 74, 87, 97, 100
Troublesome Secretaries 179
Trow, Buster 201
Tucker, Sophie 154
Turner, Florence 179
Turpin, Ben 171, 175
Twelve O'Clock 189
Two Overcoats 180

UCLA 119
The Unveiling 181
Upstairs 110, 201

Valentino, Rudolph 140, 173
Valley of the Giants 124
Variety 110
The Venus Model 199
Vernon Country Club 42
Vidor, King 39, 175
Volsted Act 120
Von Eltz, Theodore 203

The Waiter's Picnic 50, 191
Walker, Lillian 26
Wallace, Ramsey 202

Wallace, Richard 165
Walthall, Henry B. 21, 179
The Water Nymph 38, 185
Wells, H.G. 154
Wells, Linton 143
Wells, May 198
West, Charles 32, 182
West, Dorothy 181
What Father Saw 192
What Happened to Rosa? 112, 201
What the Doctor Ordered 33, 184
When a Man Is Married His Trouble Begins 180
When Doctors Disagree 108, 201
When Dreams Come True 192
When Kings Were the Law 183
Whispering Windows 154
White, Leo 203
Why He Gave Up 181
Wilheim II, Kaiser 9
Willful Peggy 179
Wilson, Edith 94
Wilson, Sir Thomas 152
Wilson, Woodrow 87, 102
Windham, Charles 50
Windsor, Claire 105
The Wisconsin State Journal 160
Wished on Mabel 51, 198
Women's Suffrage 44
Won in a Closet (Won in a Cupboard) 49
Woods, Al 159, 162
Woolwine, Thomas 142, 165

Young, James 83
Young, Noah 203

Zabelle, Flora 200
Ziegler, Thomas 135, 136, 209, 210